second edition

influencing attitudes and changing behavior

*an introduction to
method, theory, and applications
of social control
and personal power*

second edition

influencing attitudes and changing behavior

PHILIP G. ZIMBARDO

Stanford University

EBBE B. EBBESEN

University of California, San Diego

CHRISTINA MASLACH

University of California, Berkeley

ADDISON-WESLEY PUBLISHING COMPANY

*Reading, Massachusetts
Menlo Park, California
London • Amsterdam • Don Mills, Ontario • Sydney*

TOPICS IN SOCIAL PSYCHOLOGY

Charles A. Kiesler
Series Editor

ISBN 0-201-08796-0
DEFGHIJ-AL-79

Dedicated to our children
Adam, Nova, Pace, and Zara

The series *Topics in Social Psychology* is directed toward the student with no prior background in social psychology. Taken as a whole, the series covers the ever-expanding field of social psychology rea-

foreword

sonably well, but a major advantage of the series is that each individual book was written by well-known scholars in the area. The instructor can select a subset of the books to make up the course in social psychology, the particular subset depending on the instructor's own definition of our field. The original purpose of this series was to provide such freedom for the instructor while maintaining a thoughtful and expert treatment of each topic. In addition, the first editions of the series have been widely used in a variety of other ways: as supplementary reading in nonpsychology courses; to introduce more advanced courses in psychology; or for the sheer fun of peeking at recent developments in social psychology.

We have developed second editions that serve much the same purpose. Each book is somewhat longer and more open in design, uses updated materials, and in general takes advantage of constructive feedback from colleagues and students across the country. So many people found the first editions of the individual books useful that we have tried to make the second editions even more thorough and complete and therefore more easily separated from the rest of the series.

This volume covers the field of attitude change, which to my mind forms the core of modern social psychology. Zimbardo, Ebbesen, and Maslach have provided us with a thorough revision of their book while maintaining the fresh, innovative style of their highly regarded first edition.

Charles A. Kiesler

In 1969 when we were writing the first edition of *Influencing Attitudes and Changing Behavior*, students were demanding change in both their government's policy of intervention in Indochina and the intervention of college administrators

preface

in their personal lives. Antiwar protests escalated from rational teach-ins, with both sides represented, to sit-ins, violent encounters, and trashing. "Hands off Vietnam" and "No dormitory curfews" were issues of significance. Universities came under attack for their alleged ties to the military-industrial complex. They were equally criticized because of their irrelevant curricula, nonrepresentation of student opinion, and paternalistic regimentation of the nonacademic aspects of student life. Student beliefs were backed by action—strikes, graffiti, vandalism, bombings of ROTC buildings, and mounting of the barricades. Institutional beliefs were backed by strong measures of counter-reaction—shutting down the system in some places, expelling individuals in others, police action, and finally the use of military force to quell riots — with murderous consequences.

That chaos is clearly of another generation. Those demands for change seem remote and perhaps irrelevant to the pre-med, pre-law, pre-engineering, pre-career oriented student of today. But a good case can be made for the effectiveness of the social action of the classes of 1968 to 1971. Expanded student freedoms and shared participation in academic decision making are part of that legacy. Likewise, an unexpected consequence of the tireless efforts of antiwar protesters was the development of a White House paranoia that spawned Watergate. The revelations of the publicly aired congressional hearings about the Watergate break-in toppled a President and administration discovered to be employing illegal means to suppress dissension and control public opinion—among their other illegal and immoral activities.

ix

The quest for change is not dead, merely refocused. The question is no longer "What can I do for my country?" but "What can I do for myself?" Self-growth, self-actualization, and improved relations with one's mate have replaced (for many people) grander concerns for political-social-economic changes at the level of institutions and societies. "Getting one's stuff together" is where it's at.

This is not to ignore the force and validity of the women's liberation movement, nor the articulate pressures from all races and ethnic minorities for educational and vocational opportunities. Nevertheless, the tenor of the times finds more students in libraries, encounter groups, drop-in counseling centers, and meditation than advocating change in the more remote systems of external control.

The present edition of our text reflects an appreciation of a broader context that encompasses both concerns—those for social as well as for personal change in attitudes and behavior. Power and control assume greater importance in our thinking than they did previously. The narrow conception of attitude change that was central to our earlier work has widened considerably to encompass many forms of interpersonal and self-originating sources of influence upon how we feel, think, and act. It is not only the impact of formal communicators presenting speeches to captive audiences that interests us, but the sources of the persuasive power of friends, parents, therapists, media, and other agents and agencies of social control. Where before we advanced the methodology of the laboratory experiment as the yellow brick road to the kingdom of Oz, now it is but one path to wisdom.

The greater scope of this edition also emerges out of the loss of our naiveté about the nature of control processes in the "real world" beyond the laboratory. We have since served as consultants to citizens' groups and to social welfare, health, and legal professionals. Recent experiences as expert witnesses in prisoner litigation have been augmented by our field research in a variety of institutions on problems of decision making, staff morale and burn-out, and power maintenance.

Part of the joy for us in bringing these ideas to you comes from the fun and knowledge gained from working together. Christina Maslach, a collaborator in the first edition, moves up to the first team. We have each been influenced by the others, and in turn done our thing on them, so that "mine" and "yours" are blended into a most comfortable "ours."

We have dedicated this book to our children, who daily expose how little we really know about influencing their attitudes and changing their behavior—or so they think. However, we have written this book for the curious student, who is not yet a sophisticated social scientist but is a person being educated to understand *how* to think about problems of personal relevance and social significance so that he or she can recognize when the message is really *what* to think. We hope that you will come to feel that this book was conceived with *you* as the reader.

Palo Alto   P.Z.
January 1977   E.E.
                                                            C.M.

contents

4

reviewing
representative
research   85

5

critically analyzing
selected attitude
change research   123

translating principles
into practice:
the tactics and
strategies of change   153

postscript A
the experiment as
a source of information   197

postscript B
techniques of
attitude measurement   213

postscript C
on becoming a
social change agent   221

postscript D
student projects   235

posing problems of personal influence and social change

How effective are *you* in asserting yourself in order to satisfy your goals? How often are you successful in persuading others to see it your way? How often do you give in and do it their way? How certain are you that there are absolute limits to what anyone could make you do? There is no way *you* are going to be influenced to violate moral sanctions against maiming or killing others. No way you could be persuaded to betray your parents or be brainwashed to sell out your country. And, of course, nobody could get you to harm or injure yourself or destroy your health. Not without a gun at your head! Obviously so.

Wrong! Indeed, it is impossible to overestimate the extent to which you are influenced daily to be the kind of person other people want you to be. "Tastes" in food, dress, art, music, friends, hobbies, and other things are acquired through subtle interpersonal influence processes. You do not shout out your disagreement with your professor, because you are too polite for that. You tend to speak when you are spoken to, to not monopolize conversations, to respect the rights of others, and to expect fair play in return. The language you speak, your dialect, pronunciation, hand gestures, body semantics, and displays of affection or temper are all the products of how people communicated in your family, neighborhood, and cultural subgroup.

Attitudes, values, and behavioral tendencies are acquired gradually; we do not *change*, we *grow*. We are not succumbing and being persuaded, influenced, coerced, or induced to be other than we are. Rather, we perceive

1

that we have chosen freely to become our own person. It is the recognition of a change that seems more sudden, abrupt, and discontinuous than normal that raises the possibility of external, special forces at work. An action that violates what seems appropriate, or that does not fit our expectations, is more likely to be thought of as "coercion." These anomalous events that appear to have no precedent demand special explanations to fit them into a rational scheme. Such explanations confer upon them sense, order, and causality. The more extreme the change observed, the more "exotic" the causes invoked to account for it. Magic, witchcraft, gods, and demons are often implicated as the nonhuman intervenors into human affairs. As educational levels increase, the classes of suitable causes become more substantive, such as drugs, hypnosis, sexual advantage, economic pressures, and brainwashing. As we shudder to witness the Vietnamese being "indoctrinated" to accept Communism, we take pride in those who have immigrated to the United States as they are "educated" to become patriotic Americans.

The ways in which people go about explaining *changes* they observe in themselves and others reveal much about their basic conception of human nature. We learn from these explanations whether people in a given culture or historical time period believe that the powerful impulses that drive us are induced by demon possession, hormones, repressed sexuality, or motives of limitless achievement, or whether they conceive of humans as rational information processors guided by free will. Whatever the notions, they form the bases not only of our philosophies and religions but also of our personal theories about how to rear children, educate students, and treat deviant people judged "bad" or "mad."

DOONESBURY   **by Garry Trudeau**

Inherent in such models of the human condition are also assumptions about the fragility, resilience, stability, and modifiability of mind and behavior patterns. "You can't get blood from a turnip," but can you get people to donate theirs to a blood bank? "You can't teach an old dog new tricks," but how does a new dog learn old tricks? Do some people really die of "broken hearts," while others disprove expert diagnosis of terminal illness because of their "will to live"?

It soon becomes obvious that one's explanations about why people change in sudden or extreme ways derive from the general conception one holds about what makes people think, feel, and act as they do. It should also be noted that these conceptions or intuitive theories (as contrasted with formal theories) bias the way in which the problem is posed, the evidence sought, and thus the nature of the solution "found."

Your own conception of human nature has been shaped by a great many things in your life—your parents' religion, your educational experiences, your cultural values, your social class, your prevailing level of knowledge, and much more. You carry with you, for instance, beliefs about your own level of intellectual and athletic ability. You also have beliefs about how suggestible and vulnerable or tough-minded and strong you are. These beliefs about your own persuasibility come in part from personal experiences and comparisons with other people. But they are also a function of the way in which you would prefer to think of yourself.

The Illusion of Personal Invulnerability

Paradoxically, one barrier to more effective personal control over our own attitudes and actions is the "not me" syndrome.

"Others can be made to carry out evil deeds, but not me."
"You blindly obey authority figures, but not me."
"They are swayed by speeches and rhetoric, but not me."
"He is easily converted to that cause, but not me."
"She yields to group pressure, but not me."

Such an orientation is dangerous because it alienates us from the human condition. By setting ourselves apart from others, we do not learn the important message from their experience—namely, that the source of their suffering, loss of face, or fall from grace may lie not in their personal weaknesses nor in the stars, but in *the power of the situation*.

Not only do we preserve a favorable self-image by means of the "not me" illusion, but several other consequences also flow from this fallacy in explanation. Identification and sympathy with the "other" are prevented by virtue of the assumed difference between *their* character and *ours*. Further, if causes are assumed to be found within people, we need feel no responsibility for social, economic, or political conditions that could have caused the behavior. Thus we need not feel guilt for the victim's plight nor an urgency to remedy the situation. Solutions then center on ways to modify the *individuals* involved rather than ways to alter the existing *circumstances*. Finally, we become most vulnerable to influence attempts when our false pride in our ability to resist them reduces vigilance toward external forces. It is, of course, important to think positively about oneself, but not at the expense of a realistic appraisal of the power possessed by other individuals, groups, and settings to affect us. It may be important to perceive ourselves as unique and distinctive, but not at the cost of disregarding information about how the typical person reacts in a given situation.

Be forewarned that in this text we are actively attempting to reshape your thinking about this sense of invulnerability. We believe you can be more often master of your own destiny if you learn to identify potential or existing sources of influence. We know we have set a difficult task for ourselves, because research tells us that you are likely to ignore information about how the majority of people in a given situation react, and to favor information about the isolated cases that fit your preconceptions or personal preferences. We shall present data that show how powerful situations influence the attitudes and behavior of the majority of people exposed to them.

It is our hope that when asked whether you would have behaved like Eichmann in Germany or Ehrlichman in Washington, the National Guard at Kent State, the members of Charlie Company at My Lai, Patty Hearst, or a convert to a new social movement, your considered opinion will be: "I'm not sure," or "I probably would have behaved similarly if the situation were the same.'

The Case of Patty Hearst: Captive, Collaborator, Comrade?

On February 3, 1974, Patricia Campbell Hearst was just another sophomore at the University of California, Berkeley. In most ways she was indistinguishable from the average nineteen-year-old college student. Typical in appearance, general attitudes, and lifestyle, she might have lived her life with little more notoriety than an occasional society column mention of her presence at a family outing. The one way in which she was clearly different from her peers was in her family connection—she was a Hearst. The wealth and position of the Hearst family had not gone unnoticed by the members of a small band of young revolutionaries living together in Berkeley—the Symbionese Liberation Army.

The events of the next day began a scenario that catapulted Patty and the SLA from obscurity into international prominence. "HEARST DAUGHTER ABDUCTED BY ARMED 'COMMANDOS'" was the banner headline in the *San Francisco Chronicle*. The young kidnappers, described as "acting like commandos," carried Patty Hearst blindfolded and screaming from the apartment of her fiancé, who had been beaten almost to unconsciousness.

So little was known of the kidnap victim at that time that her identity in early newspaper articles was established through her connections with her family ("the granddaughter of the late William Randolph Hearst, a colorful figure in the history of American journalism"), a routine physical description ("5 feet 3 inches tall, 110 pounds, brown shoulder-length hair and brown eyes"), and little more. All that would change within a few short months, when everyone else would be defined through their relationship to Patty.

"I'M OK"

After eight days of silence, the SLA made contact. Patty's thin, halting voice on a tape recording sighed, "Mom, Dad, I'm OK. I'm not being beaten or starved or unnecessarily frightened." Then came the ransom terms from "Field Marshal" Cinque of the SLA. The Hearsts must provide food for all of California's people in need or their daughter would be executed. Several million dollars worth of food was given away to the needy in the next weeks, and the Hearst Foundation placed $4 million more in escrow to be used for further food giveaways providing that the victim be returned unharmed. The abduction of Patty Hearst was thus the first political kidnapping in the United States. The captors asked for money not for themselves but for "all people oppressed by capitalism." The entire nation was caught up in this prisoner-of-war drama being played out publicly with fullest media coverage.

Wide World Photos.

Wide World Photos.

Patty Hearst before her kidnapping.   *Patty Hearst as Tania.*

TANIA ISN'T PATTY ANY MORE

Scheduled to be released to return home to her parents, Patty startled everyone with the announcement on April 3 that she had decided to join the SLA, and had renounced her former lifestyle, denounced her parents, and taken the name Tania (after a revolutionary who fought beside Ché Guevara). She abandoned her fiancé with the hope that he too "could be a comrade," but she didn't really expect it. "All I expect," she said, "is that you try to understand the changes I've gone through."

What were those changes? How could a captive become a comrade, and change so dramatically in so short a time? Said Mrs. Hearst: "I know my daughter very well. I know she'd never join any organization like that without being coerced." Said Mr. Hearst: "We've had her twenty years and they've had her only sixty days and I don't believe she's going to change her philosophy that quickly in that time."

Speculations as to the type of coercive control exercised over gentle, fragile Patty to convert her into tough-minded Tania ran the gamut from drugs and hypnosis to torture, sexual abuse, and brainwashing. These explanations had in common the notion that Patty Hearst was a passive victim, brutalized and made vulnerable to exotic mind-control tactics that overwhelmed her reason and resistance.

The reasonableness of such justifications became somewhat strained when on April 15 she participated with the SLA in an armed robbery of a bank—in full view of TV monitors. Still harder to account for were her actions a month later when she saved two of her captors, William and Emily Harris, by covering their escape from arrest with a spray of bullets from her automatic rifle. But the strangest episodes were yet to come. On May 17, the day after this incident at a Los Angeles sporting good store, the SLA hideout (by then in Los Angeles) was discovered and destroyed by the police. All but three SLA members were killed in the shootout. The Harrises and Tania were not among the charred remains of the SLA.

Would Patty now return home or contact her parents to arrange negotiations with the authorities? That hope proved vain as she eluded an intensive FBI search for twenty months, a search estimated to have cost in excess of $3.5 million. On September 18, 1975, the surviving members of the SLA were captured. Here, at last, was the kidnapped victim for all the world to see in the flesh. Smiling for the press, fist clenched in the radical salute, she proclaimed herself to be Tania, the "urban guerrilla."

THE DEPROGRAMMING OF TANIA

Radicals now hoped that Tania would use the spotlight that was on her to champion revolutionary causes. It was not to be. Proud, fearless, hard-talking, gun-toting Tania had by degrees become contrite and confused, and told a story of being forced to collaborate in the bank robbery. Daily four-to-seven-hour sessions with a team of defense lawyers and psychiatric expert witnesses had created some "mental fatigue." As parents and friends also began regularly visiting her in jail, press releases described their conversations as "homey." Patty was "becoming her old self again." Some might say she was "returning to her senses," while cynics maintained instead that a sympathetic pre-trial image was being manufactured. Gradually, a retransformation was occurring in her speech and manner. Under the skillful direction of famous trial lawyer F. Lee Bailey, her explanations of the "whys" of her SLA actions emphasized the expected denial of freedom of choice, coercive control over her every action, and ultimately her constant fear for her very life. All of Bailey's forces and all of Bailey's men were putting Patty back together again.

MIND CONTROL ON TRIAL

There was no question that Patricia Hearst collaborated with the SLA in the Hibernia Bank robbery. At issue was her state of mind.

Wide World Photos.

Patty Hearst on her way to court.

The Court (Judge Carter) commented: "Now one of the issues to determine the guilt or innocence of the defendant is going to be whether or not the defendant was coerced at the time the alleged offense was committed, and to what extent that may go to the question of guilt or innocence." (*U.S.A.* vs. *Patricia Campbell Hearst*, 3/8/76, p. 3284)

Bailey's defense of his famous client rested on a theory of an innocent kidnapping victim who was physically and mentally tormented by her captors during her prolonged, blindfolded confinement in a closet, and finally forced at gunpoint to unwillingly join in the bank robbery. The standard legal defense of involuntary action taken under extreme duress was buttressed by the unprecedented defense of innocence as a consequence of being "brainwashed." Patty was compared to a prisoner of war whose mind was bent by persuasive tactics that amounted to that most extreme form of coercion known as "brainwashing."

Brainwashing with holy water   Defense psychiatrist Louis West of the University of California at Los Angeles attributed the impaired state of Patty's mind ("traumatic neurosis") to her ordeal as an SLA captive. He found in her symptoms of "coercive persuasion," a phenomenon Dr. West had personally observed in returned POWs who had been interrogated by Chinese captors during the Korean War. Yale psychiatrist Robert Lifton agreed that Patty's sense of self-identity had been broken by techniques of "thought reform," apparently based on Chinese models. The Tania tape recordings were in his expert opinion typical of confessions of civilian and military prisoners of the Chinese Communists, who proclaimed guilt over misdeeds and betrayed family, friends, and country. Lifton is credited with the first reliable reports of thought reform; these reports were based on interviews he conducted in the mid-1950s in Hong Kong with expelled Westerners and Chinese defectors.

The term *brainwashing* was the invention of journalist Edward Hunter, whose book *Brainwashing in Red China* (1951) documented the systematic attempts by Mao Tse-tung's Communist cadres to change the ideology of the Nationalist Chinese. The secret weapon? The victims were sent to "revolutionary universities" where they were exposed to intensive study and public self-examination sessions.

Following evidence of extensive collaboration between American POWs and their captors (and especially after propaganda broadcasts of germ warfare by captured United States military officers), a decision was made to give all repatriated POWs detailed psychological tests and interviews. While psychiatrists investigated the minds of the men, Edgar Schein (of Massachusetts Institute of Technology) and other researchers focused attention on the conditions that existed in the Chinese prison camps. Schein's text, *Coercive Persuasion* (1961), demystifies brainwashing by revealing that it is neither novel nor unique in the methods employed. What differentiates it from other forms of persuasion is the commitment of energy,

"*How will we be able to tell we haven't been brainwashed into finding that Patricia Hearst was brainwashed?*"

experience, and interpersonal sensitivity on the part of the Chinese interrogators. What mattered is not what they did, but how much they put into it.

Other important conclusions are drawn from the research of Schein and his colleagues:

1 It is difficult to assess the effectiveness of these brainwashing attempts because of the unevenness in which they were applied, the unknown variation in initial beliefs of target individuals, and the inadequate evidence of demonstrable post-brainwashing changes in overt behavior.

2 It is not possible to predict in an individual case whether a given person will be successfully influenced. This is because of the many variables that determine resistance to influence.

3 No personality or background factors were shown to be reliable predictors of who would collaborate and who would resist.

4 Coercive persuasion is an influence process that involves a complex series of events occurring over a period of time. For influence to occur, three elements are necessary: ". . . there must be induced a motive to change, there must be available some model or other information source which provides a direction of change, and there must be reward for and support of whatever change occurs." (Schein 1961, p. 284).

The most far-reaching conclusion advanced in Schein's analysis is the comparability between the process of coercive persuasion as observed in Chinese Communist prisons and that which takes place in many institutions in our own society. We are cautioned not to overlook *process* similarities because of *content* differences. "There is a world of difference in the content of what is transmitted in religious orders, prisons, educational institutions, mental hospitals, and thought reform centers. But there are striking similarities in the manner in which influence occurs. . . ." (Schein 1961, p. 285).

Radical psychiatrist Thomas Szasz attacks the concept of "brainwashing" as an overly dramatic metaphor. The metaphor simply stands for the universal human experience of one person influencing another. "Brainwashing" is used when we disapprove of that influence, just as "perversions" are sex acts *we* do not practice. He challenges the use of expert psychiatric testimony as the basis for ascertaining whether Patty Hearst has been brainwashed with the analogy of "trying to ascertain whether holy water is holy by having it examined by priests." Both attributes are conferred by "experts" on the substance (holy water or brains). Therefore, we must look to priests and not into the composition of the water to understand what holy water is. The same holds for brainwashing and psychiatrists (Szasz 1976).

Hypnotic control   If brainwashing is not a reasonable explanation for the obvious changes in Patty Hearst's attitudes and behavior, what about hypnosis? Why couldn't she have been hypnotized, instructed to change her beliefs, and given post-hypnotic amnesia for this manipulation? Can people be made to do things against their will under the influence of hypnosis? This fascinating question was put to experimental test by Martin Orne and Frederick Evans (1965), and the answer was almost "yes"—almost.

Hypnotized subjects were told by the experimenter to engage in a series of acts that were dangerous and harmful. First, each subject was

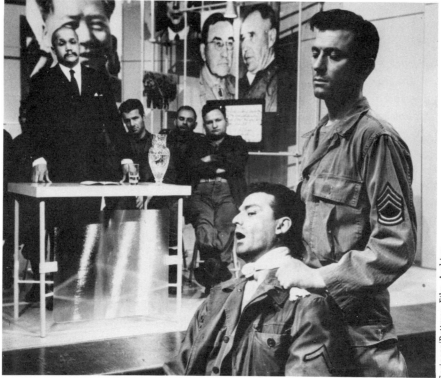

Laurence Harvey, under hypnosis, strangles comrade. Movie still from "The Manchurian Candidate."

Springer/Bettman Film Archive.

told to thrust his hand into a glass cage containing a poisonous snake. Next, the subject saw the hypnotist take a beaker of fuming nitric acid and drop a penny into it, which began to dissolve. The hypnotist asked the subject to remove the coin from the acid as quickly as possible with his bare hand and to then plunge both hand and coin into a basin of water. Finally, subjects were instructed to throw the beaker of acid into the face of one of the people in the laboratory. Although they had witnessed the penny dissolving in the acid and had no motive to harm that person, they obeyed the order and flung the acid at the person's face![1] What more convincing demonstration could there be of the power of hypnotic control?

With but a single group it is only a *demonstration* of what subjects will do in that setting. It is not an *experimental proof* that hypnosis is responsible for that surprising result. To implicate hypnosis as the causal element, we have to compare the behavior of hypnotized subjects with that of unhypnotized control subjects treated similarly except for the hypnotic induction. You might argue that there is no need for such a control group; common sense is the control condition! It is obvious that normal people—average college students—would not do those things, not without extreme coercion.

Obvious, maybe, but incorrect. The unhypnotized controls did exactly what the hypnotized subjects had done—they obeyed all three suggestions. Hypnosis was irrelevant to the outcome. Rather, the preferred explanation is in terms of elements of the situation *common* to both groups—the power of authority figures (scientists, professors) to elicit obedience in the context of the unique environment of the "scientific experiment." Accepting the role of subject places special *demands* on the person while he or she is functioning in that setting. The role of "subject"—passively subjected to the experimenter's manipulation—weakens independent assessment and relaxes usual constraints on behavior. These *demand characteristics* of the experimental setting may be sufficiently powerful to generate certain outcomes regardless of the treatment variables.

* Dr. Orne illustrates this point by asking friends to do twenty pushups. "Why?" is the standard reply. When he changes his request to "As part of an experiment I'd like you to do twenty pushups," "Where?" is the more typical reply.

To be sure, we are not saying hypnosis is not an effective tool for producing a wide variety of altered states of functioning. Rather, in this

---

[1] Precautions were taken to ensure that neither the subject nor the experimenter's assistant could be harmed in any of these tasks.

case it is not necessary to invoke a special, exotic agency because simpler explanations serve as well. Bodies that are heavier than air may fall to the ground because of "fear of heights," "reversed levitation," or "the curse of Spiro Agnew," but why the fancy inferences when "gravitation" is more parsimonious?

SOCIAL INFLUENCE WINS FRIENDS AND MAKES CONVERTS

To understand Patty Hearst's probable state of mind at the time she participated in the bank robbery, we must first determine the conditions surrounding what amounts to even more extreme behavior and attitudinal change—her earlier decision to give up her old way of life and become a soldier in the Symbionese Liberation Army. Was *that* decision "coerced"? Was she merely play-acting to save her life? Or had she made a conversion to a new ideology in the same way that religious converts choose to do?

The metamorphosis from Patty to Tania is accountable as an act of belief conversion resulting from the sustained operation of a combination of social influence conditions. Let us consider some of the variables at work in this case.

Initial position. Patty's political beliefs were not well informed, nor were they backed up by strong conviction. She did not have to be moved from a "right-wing" starting point; rather she was already somewhat left of center (it would probably have been more difficult to influence her parents to adopt a radical ideology).

Fear and anxiety. The conditions of her kidnapping and confinement in a closet made Patty justifiably afraid and anxious about her eventual safe return. By letting her out of the closet, not harming her, and treating her well, the SLA created unanticipated rewards that could be expected to induce feelings of gratitude. Her parents' failure to rescue her could have fed primitive anxieties about being abandoned by one's omnipotent parents. Even after her parents raised millions of dollars in ransom on her behalf, Patty rejected their efforts as "bad faith gestures."

Guilt arousal. Strong guilt feelings may have been induced in her because of her family's privileged position, the disparity between the Hearst wealth and the poverty of so many, and her life of noninvolvement in the "struggle of oppressed peoples." Racial guilt may have also been involved.

Isolation from old social support. The usual sources of support that Patty had relied upon for social rewards, feedback, and identity were severed.

Information control. The only ideas Patty was exposed to during this initial stage of her captivity were those contained in the philosophy of the SLA. There was no opportunity to independently assess their validity or seek informative counterarguments.

Persuasive communications. Patty was exposed to daily input of SLA rhetoric and the radical ideas of Fanon, George Jackson, and communist writers. These were presented to her directly, as well as overheard in the regular discussions of the cell members about the evils of capitalism, wars of liberation, and redistribution of resources.

Cohesive peer group. The eight members of the SLA were a cohesive unit sharing bed and board as well as beliefs. Their consensus defined reality in that situation; their approval became a powerful source of social reward, status, and recognition. Moreover, Patty could readily identify with them because most were her age and of similar backgrounds.

Communicator characteristics. The SLA members were practicing what they preached in not accepting the ransom money for themselves but, as in the Robin Hood legend, feeding the poor with what they got from the rich. They were dedicated and committed to their cause, and seemed knowledgeable to their politically naive captive. They had given up their freedom (and later their lives), knowingly becoming fugitives in the effort to achieve a goal beyond personal concerns. They were probably seen as trustworthy, expert, dynamic, altruistic, and attractive communicators who were also models of the message they proclaimed.

Illusion of free choice. Critical to inducing enduring change in Patty is the perception that the decision to join the SLA was of her own making. This perceived freedom of choice results in the discrepant behavior being accepted not as extrinsically forced but as self-generated. Once this happens, the new behavior will be maintained in the absence of surveillance or pressure—because it is one's own.

Evidence for conversion   What support is there for this analysis from statements by Patty, the Harrises, and prosecution witness Dr. Joel Fort? It was Fort's testimony that was most damaging to the defense Bailey had constructed.

From a manuscript prepared by Patty Hearst and William and Emily Harris, we learn something of the situation from the perspective of the principal actors. (Quotations are from a Chicago Tribune Press Service Report, *Chicago Tribune*, February 6, 1976.)

- From Patty:

  At first I didn't trust or like them . . . I thought he [Cinque] was crazy. I wasn't interested in learning anyone else's name or in talking to anyone. . . .

  After a couple of weeks I began to feel sympathy with the SLA. I was beginning to see what they wanted to accomplish was necessary, although at the time it was hard for me to relate to the tactic of urban guerrilla warfare. . . .

  What some people refer to as a sudden conversion was actually a process of development, much the same as a photograph is developed. . . .

  We ate all our meals together, though, and during these times, we would discuss different events, different struggles. At first I didn't say anything. I felt weird sitting and arguing with these people while I was blindfolded. After a while I began to participate in these discussions. I began to see . . . that U.S. imperialism is the enemy of all oppressed people. I opened my eyes and realized it was time to get off my ass.

- From William Harris:

  We had to help Tania understand what it meant to each of us to be a guerrilla so that she could bring it to a personal level in her own head. On her part, she had to convince us that she was being honest, objective and realistic. . . . At the last second before Tania took off her blindfold, Cinq reminded her that she could walk freely out the door and that we would help her return to her family and friends. We all wanted Tania to stay, but we wanted to make sure that she saw all her options and was making a strong choice with no regrets or indecision.

And from Dr. Fort's trial testimony, we begin to appreciate the perspective that emerges from a social-psychological orientation to the conversion of Patty Hearst.

> . . . One of the important frames of reference that I thought necessary for analysis of this situation is the social psychology area, particularly of attitude change and conformity . . . And, I did review the literature to the extent possible, books and articles, also consulted with a professor of sociology and two social psychologists [Zimbardo and Maslach] whose life work involves this area. . . . (*U.S.A.* vs. *Patricia Campbell Hearst*, 3/5/76, p. 3258)
>
> And each of these seven people [the SLA excluding Cinque], who interacted with the defendant and who came from comparable backgrounds, education and values and most of the same sex, that is, most of them being women, all of them went through an evolution. None of them, obviously, were born as adherents to an urban guerrilla philosophy or terrorist kind of ideology. In fact, more specifically, all of them made that evolution within relatively recent years. . . . (*U.S.A.* vs. *Patricia Campbell Hearst*, 3/8/76, p. 3304)
>
> To put it in kind of a cliché of American terms, we could say, how did a nice girl like that or a nice boy like that become an SLA member? (*U.S.A.* vs. *Patricia Campbell Hearst*, 3/8/76, p. 3303)

THE CREATIVE COMMUNITY PROJECT

YOU ARE INVITED TO PARTICIPATE IN A NIGHTLY OPEN HOUSE AND LECTURE SERIES, WITH DINNER AT 6pm AND MUSICAL ENTERTAINMENT BEGINNING AT 7pm, FOLLOWED BY LECTURES, A SHARING OF IDEAS AND REFRESHMENTS.

YOU MAY WANT TO ATTEND ONE OF THE FESTIVALS OR WORKSHOPS AT OUR 700 acre RANCH AND FARM IN MENDOCINO COUNTY, WITH WEEKEND AND WEEK LONG COURSES OFFERED.

A [Reverend] Moon for the Misbegotten

The conversion of Patty Hearst should raise for each of us the more personal question, "Would *I* have been able to resist the same social pressures were I in her place?" Then, at a societal level, we are forced to wonder whether or not many young people of the current generation could not be "guided" into extreme forms of conversion with much less fanfare and without being forcibly kidnapped. Perceptive *Newsweek* correspondent Shana Alexander thinks so. She writes:

> Could these gun-toting Barbie dolls be *our* children, we wonder? You bet. If this could happen to a family of upperclass Waltons like the Hearsts, it could happen anywhere. Every family today has its own Patty Hearst—girl or boy—dropped out, tripped out or thrown out, but gone and missed nonetheless. (*Newsweek*, April 29, 1974.)

An estimated 10,000 young Americans are numbered among the half million followers of one of the fastest growing religious sects in the United States—the Unification Church of Korean Reverend Sun Myung Moon. Religion and politics are intertwined in the writings of Reverend Moon. The earthly embodiment of Satan is communism. Political control of the United States (and other countries) must be seized to realize the goal of leading a holy crusade to rid the world of the evil of communism. (Interestingly, while the SLA hoped to seize power to spread communist ideals, Reverend Moon's disciples seek to seize power to exterminate those same ideals.)

An affiliate of the Unification Church is The Creative Community Project centered in San Francisco. The Project runs a communal house near the University of California's Berkeley campus (on Hearst Street!) as well as a 700-acre farm in Mendocino county. The farm is called the Eden Awareness Training Center, and is the largest of some 120 awareness training centers springing up throughout the United States.

Following what seems to be a chance encounter with a true believer, a potential recruit is invited first to dinner at the neighborhood house and/or to spend a weekend up at the farm. All quite low key, no hard sell here—just happy, smiling, attractive youngsters who would like *you* to be their friend and share in the good vibes they have discovered. "Why not give it a try, you've got nothing better to do for the weekend anyway, have you?"

Many weekend guests never return. They give up school, family, friends, religious beliefs, and their whole lifestyle to devote themselves to the goals of conquering evil and spreading goodwill. "Brainwashing" again is heard in the land as irate and bewildered parents accuse the Moon move-

"The last time I ever witnessed a movement that had

these characteristics — with a single authoritarian

head, fanatical followers, absolute unlimited funds,

hatred for everyone on the outside and suspicion

against their parents — was the Nazi Youth Movement,

and I tell you I am scared."

APA **Monitor,** June 1976. © (1976) by the American Psychological
Association: Reprinted by permission of APA and Charles Steacy.

ment of coercing their children into becoming "Moonies." After being initiated into the Unification Church, the Moonies become recruiters and trainees of newcomers, soliciters for funds, and workers in other capacities who promote and extend "the movement."

Washington Post columnist Jack Anderson reported on December 19, 1975 that at least one smiling young Moonie spent considerable time in and around the congressional office of former Speaker Carl Albert, who said she "just walks in here and sits down and chats." Albert told her the Moon movement was "stupid" and insisted she never lobbied him on any political issue. This smiling, polite Moonie was described by Albert as "just a nice girl, a very nice girl, a Jewish girl from New York. She got all hepped up on the Lord Jesus, and she just wants to share it . . . she's trying to convert me." Next to other standard reference books in his congressional library was a gold-trimmed deluxe edition of the catechism of Reverend Moon, *Divine Principle.*

One of our students spent a weekend at the Eden Awareness Training Center (for a class project) and, though he did return, his attitudes had been shaken up by the brief, two-day experience. He writes of the farm, "where people are trying to get their heads together to help mankind"; of the church, "seeking members all over the country and sending them to their training centers where they are loved by their heavenly brothers and sisters, away from the temptations of evil men." He was able to resist pressures to stay for the week (the movement had not effected the desired behavior change), but "his head" was not in the same place his body had returned to.

> When I arrived [back at the Stanford University dormitory] I was relieved to be on my own again, but also sad. People showed me love in Ideal City but I chose to return to a place where the programming was easier to avoid, with all my struggles, loneliness, and fair-weather friends.

We will examine Alex's experience in some detail later on in Chapter 6. Before doing so, however, we would like to make available to you some basic information about social influence processes. We think you will be in a better position to appreciate the dynamics of this particular experience if you bring to it a framework of general knowledge about the principles of attitude and behavior change.

What Are Attitudes, Anyway?

> *The concept of attitudes is probably the most distinctive and indispensable concept in contemporary American social psychology.* Gordon Allport

Did the Moonies fail in not getting Alex to make a behavioral commitment to stay on the farm? Hardly, if they influenced his attitudes as it appears they did. He may not join the movement himself, but his favorable comments and good feelings toward its members are likely to make him an unintentional recruiter. He spreads the word—"a satisfied customer is our best advertisement." The assumption is that a person's "satisfaction" (good feelings and belief about something) may have behavioral consequences (talking positively about the valued service or product).

Attitudes consist of these satisfactions and dissatisfactions. They are the core of our likes or dislikes for certain people, groups, situations, objects, and intangible ideas (such as communism or freedom of the press). Patty Hearst's new SLA attitude of dislike for American imperialism involved certain beliefs about the way Third World peoples were being oppressed and the necessity for armed liberation of those so oppressed. These cognitions were rooted in strong emotions and were stated in evaluative terms—"good," "bad," "desirable," "undesirable." Finally, these affectively loaded beliefs triggered action—"getting off my ass."

Attitudes have generally been regarded as either mental readiness or implicit predispositions that exert some general and consistent influence on a fairly large class of evaluative responses. Attitudes are thus internal, private events whose existence we infer from our own introspection or from some form of behavioral evidence when they are expressed overtly in word or deed. A verbalized attitude is called an *opinion*. In studying attitude change it helps to conceptualize attitudes as having three components: affect, cognition, and behavior. The affective component consists of a person's evaluation of, liking of, or emotional response to some object or person. The cognitive component has been conceptualized as a person's beliefs about, or factual knowledge of, the object or person. The behavioral component involves the person's overt behavior directed toward the object or person (see Fig. 1.1).

If attitudes are conceptualized in this way, we can see how techniques designed to change only one's emotional reactions toward some object or person would be attacking only one component of the attitude in question. Not only does this component conception of attitude suggest interesting methods of changing attitudes, but it also provides us with ideas about how to measure them.[2] The affective component could be measured by physio-

---

[2] The reader is referred to Postscript B for a more detailed analysis of attitude measurement, and to Bem (1970) and Audi (1972) for lucid presentations of the relationship among attitudes, beliefs, and behavior.

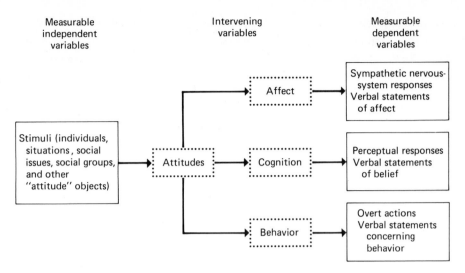

Fig. 1.1 A schematic conception of attitudes (after Rosenberg and Hovland 1960).

logical responses or verbal statements of like and dislike, while the cognitive component might be measured by self-ratings of beliefs or by the amount of knowledge a person has about some topic. The behavioral component could be measured by direct observation of how the person behaves in specific stimulus situations. In addition, attitudes are seen as enduring predispositions, but ones that are *learned* rather than innate. Thus, even though attitudes are *not* momentarily transient, they are susceptible to change.

How are these components relevant to any practical problem? Thinking of attitudes as underlying learned predispositions suggests that all the techniques that are known to increase or decrease learning should be applicable to producing change in attitudes. Rewards and punishments should be highly effective means of producing attitude change, and it should be possible to use them to predict the amount of generalized attitude change that will occur. In essence, all the techniques relevant to learning any materials should be relevant to learning and changing attitudes.

A practical consequence that follows from conceptualizing attitudes as enduring rather than momentary states is that it should be possible, by changing people's underlying attitudes, to produce longlasting rather than transient changes in behavior. For example, in overpopulated countries it would not be enough to have a change program that got the population to practice birth control for one month. What is required is a change lasting over many *generations*. It is assumed that if people's underlying *attitudes* toward birth control become very positive, birth control would be practiced for a much longer time. Hopefully, this positive attitude would be more likely to be transmitted from those directly influenced by the change program to subsequent generations than if only the overt behavior of using birth control devices was changed. Thus, if underlying attitudes are changed, more enduring and pervasive changes in behavior should be produced than if only the specific behavior in question is changed.

A practical consequence of thinking about attitudes as highly generalized predispositions is that, by changing attitudes, one should also be able to produce *many* specific changes in overt behavior. For example, in trying to produce changes in black children's self-conceptions, it is not sufficient to merely get these children to *say* they think more highly of themselves as black people, but rather the goal is to have the children behave toward themselves, toward other blacks, and toward whites in a host of changed ways. An efficient method of changing many specific behaviors at once would ideally be to change one or two underlying general dispositions or attitudes.

Our Attitudes and Yours

Former Attorney General Edward H. Levi once stated that the shockingly high crime rate in America was related to attitudes that tolerate crime. He believes the "main problem is the willingness of the country to accept that rate, because if we were not willing to accept it, enforcement against crime would be much better." Asked about solutions, he replied in a United Press release, "The main thing really—it sounds like not much but it's everything—is to change the attitude of the American people, this kind of strange tolerance of crime."

The attitude change process cannot be ignored, since it is so much a part of every human's life. Every day, each of us tries to influence someone's attitudes or is influenced by someone else's attempt to change our attitudes. Change agents come in assorted sizes, shapes, colors, and affiliations. Some have their banners unfurled, others peddle their influence in more devious, undercover ways. Knowledge of and insight into the influence process may help bolster your resistance to undesirable changes while increasing your freedom to choose meaningful new directions for yourself. In the chapters that follow, we will stress the pragmatic aspects of understanding the principles of attitude and behavior change.

Most books on attitude change are written from a formal, sterile, scientific point of view. Typically, they merely outline either theories or experiments on attitude change. The approach of this book will be a bit different. Throughout the entire book we will be asking you to put yourself into a specific situation and think how you would go about solving some practical problems involving attitude change. For example, we will ask such questions as, where would you look for methods or techniques to produce attitude change? How would you know you had produced the change you had hoped to produce? Is it change in existing attitudes or the formation of new attitudes that is required?

What questions must we ask to orient ourselves before seriously embarking on a program to change the attitudes of other people (see next page)? Where do we look for answers? What can we learn from the humanities, practical arts (law, politics), and social science? What findings do social psychologists offer that may be useful in building a technology of attitude change? Where do such findings come from? What are the features of an experiment? What is unique about an attitude change experiment? What do representative experiments actually look like? Can we increase our confidence in the results of experiments by learning to evaluate research critically? What help can theory offer in guiding our search for relevant knowledge and in making sense out of what we know? In this book we consider each of these questions in some detail. Once you are armed with critical appreciation of experimental methodology and theory, and know where to look for answers and what you are likely to find there, we finally consider several practical problems as they have been studied in real-life situations: psychological warfare, prejudice, police interrogation, supersalesmanship, reduction of coronary risk, and finally the conversion of the Moonies.

Our goal in all this is twofold: to turn you on to the potential value and excitement inherent in the study of attitude change, and to provide serious students with a primer that may be an impetus to further academic study.

BEFORE PASSING "GO," STOP AND ASK YOURSELF:

Before you become a consenting attitude change agent, it is wise to make up several sets of questions concerning the attitude change required. One set has to do with the nature of the change itself:

1. How specific does the change need to be? Does it involve one particular attitude, or a general set of attitudes?
2. How long does the change have to last?
3. How many people have to be changed—one, some, or many?
4. What is to be changed—how people think, how they talk, or how they behave nonverbally? Is it enough to produce unconscious change, or must the people be aware that they are changing?
5. Is change of some existing behavior or attitude required, or must a whole new set of behaviors or attitudes be created?
6. How will you evaluate your change program to know if it has worked?

Another set of questions deals with the control over the situation that you, as a change agent, would have:

1. To what extent do you control any communication media?
2. If you do exercise some control over the media, is it likely that people will tune in and remain interested in your message?
3. Are there other agents, trying to produce change in the opposite direction from you, who are competing for the attention of your audience?
4. What are the time limits you have?
5. How much money, resources, and so forth are available?
6. How will *you,* personally, be presented to the people whose attitudes or behavior you are trying to change? Will you be seen as an agent trying to produce change, or will you be seen as someone just interested in the problem?
7. Will you have control over the people who are available for change (are they a captive audience), or will they volunteer or select themselves?

Another set of questions you would surely want to consider deals with the consequences to *you* of accepting or not accepting a job as change agent.

1. Will you be required to have future interactions with the people you are trying to change? Will they get to know you as some obnoxious person who is always trying to influence them?
2. What is "your stake" in the problem topic? Are you biased on that topic? Are you committed to one side already?

3.   What about the consequences of being a successful manipulator? Will you be seen, and will you see yourself, as a hustler or a propagandist?

4.   How would you react to failure if your approach fails? (Will you learn anything from failure?)

5.   Might you yourself be changed by applying your own techniques?

The remaining sets of questions you might want to ask deal with the actual techniques of change that could be used, where to find and how to evaluate different techniques, and, finally, how to apply these change techniques to real problem areas. These are the main questions for which this book will attempt to provide some answers.

**considering
where
to
look
for
answers**

Suppose you were a reporter assigned to get a new angle on the Patty Hearst case. Instead of writing about your own ideas, you decide to find out what the public at large thinks. So, armed with notebook and tape recorder, you go out on the street, stop some passersby, and ask them "why would well-off kids become revolutionaries?" What sorts of answers would you expect to hear? Some actual responses to this question were the following:

> It's a guilt thing. You feel sorry that you have so much when there are so many disadvantaged people.

> It's a spoiled attitude. It's doing what you want because you've always done what you've wanted. It's just being spoiled.

> It's because they want to help people. They see all these people who don't have money and don't even have enough food to eat or a decent place to live.

Clearly, each of these individuals has a different way of explaining the behavior of the rich revolutionary—guilt, "a spoiled attitude," or altruism. Undoubtedly, other people would suggest still other answers. In and of themselves, these "explanations" are rather incomplete because they fail to identify the *process* by which the proposed factors affect behavior. However, they are interesting as examples of the ideas people have about how attitudes and subjective states influence and control overt behavior.

Each of us has a set of beliefs about influence processes—about what causes people (including ourselves) to change or to resist change. These beliefs shape our response to influence attempts and determine how we try to affect others. Psychologists have studied the nature of these beliefs about control by developing various scales to measure them. Some sample items from three major scales are presented on pages 46–47; you might want to see what *your* answers would be to the issues they pose.

The first scale (I-E scale) assesses the extent to which the individual believes that outcomes are determined by his or her own behavior (a belief in *internal* control) or by forces in the outside world (a belief in *external* control). It is interesting to note that over the past ten years the scores of college students on this scale have shifted toward a belief in external control. Why do you think this is so? One might speculate that such factors as the Vietnam war, increased crime, the Watergate scandal, and economic instability may make people feel as if they can no longer personally influence what happens to them.

The second scale (F-scale) was designed to measure an authoritarian personality syndrome. The authoritarian individual is characterized by the following cluster of beliefs about the control of behavior: a rigid adherence to conventional morality, a submissive and uncritical attitude toward idealized, moral attitudes, a tendency to reject and punish people who violate conventional values, and a preoccupation with power relationships (for example, leader-follower, strong-weak). Thus, *authority* and *morality* exert a strong influence on the attitudes and behavior of such an individual. (In Chapter 6 we will meet a prejudiced woman who typifies the high-F style of thinking.)

The third scale (Mach scale) is a measure of a person's general strategy for dealing with people. Originally based on the writings of Machiavelli (which we review later on in this chapter), the questions focus on beliefs

Niccolo Machiavelli,
1469–1527.

about people, tactics, and morality. People who score high on this scale have *relative* standards of behavior, and are very pragmatic and manipulative in their interaction with others. They have a "cool detachment" that allows their behavior to be guided by reason rather than emotion. In contrast, people with low Mach scores believe in *absolute* standards of behavior and are not manipulative in their dealings with people. They are prone to emotional arousal, and thus their actions are more likely to follow their heart rather than their head. High Machs have a power advantage over lows in face-to-face, affect-loaded situations where there are no explicit guidelines for how it is appropriate to respond.

Having reviewed some of the major types of attitudes that people have about control, you may be asking yourself, "but where do these ideas come from? How do people develop their own personal philosophies of the influence process?" To answer this, we will turn to two different sources of information—ourselves and others.

Know Thyself

In trying to understand the basis for our beliefs about control, we might best begin by looking at our own experience and development. Many different aspects of our life could have contributed to the formation of our personal belief system.

INTUITION

Cultural truisms and common sense may be one source of our ideas. Almost everyone knows that you can "catch more flies with honey than with vinegar." Also, it does not take much sophisticated reasoning to know that you can get most people to do something if you offer them enough money or some other reward. Stereotypes may also figure into our beliefs about effective and ineffective influence strategies; for example, many people mistakenly believe that you cannot reason logically with women because they are so "flighty and emotional."

OBSERVATIONS

Another source of information on influence processes is what we observe people actually doing. We might pick out a classmate who is very popular and notice what he or she says and does to attract so much positive attention. Or we might observe the techniques used by a political candidate to get people to shake hands, accept a leaflet, sign a pledge, or donate money. If we want to make an impression on the boss, we may borrow from the approach of the office go-getter who recently got a promotion.

Just as we get ideas about influence strategies by observing others, so we also learn by observing ourselves. For example, how do your parents get you to do something? Do they appeal to reason, sentiment, duty? Or what? Whatever works on you will certainly affect your philosophy of control. Similarly, you may eventually recognize the "lines" you are most susceptible to, and be able to figure out why. If you often find yourself buying things you do not need or doing things you do not want to do, you might begin to investigate the sorts of social pressures you are reacting to. Thus, we often learn about our feelings, beliefs, and attitudes by observing what we say and do.

FEEDBACK FROM OTHERS

Related to our observations of our own behavior is the feedback we receive about it from other people. Our observations of self can often be quite biased and distorted, and thus this feedback can be a very important source of information on our personal effectiveness. For example, someone might tell you that you "come on too strong," which reduces your power to influence. Or you might hear that your classroom presentation was "very thoughtful and well organized," which increases its persuasiveness. We continually receive feedback on our actions, and this is a major determinant of our ideas about influence and control.

SOCIALIZATION

Another guide for our behavior is the set of moral values and standards that has been inculcated in us by our family and by society's institutions (such as school and church). We each have a code of what is "right" and "wrong," and of what is to be most valued in our lives, and these personal standards influence many of our thoughts and actions. "Do unto others as you would have them do unto you," "honor thy father and mother," "honesty is the best policy," and "an eye for an eye" are all examples of such standards.

EDUCATION

In many cases our attitudes about influence strategies have been shaped by some specific training or education. You may have received job training on how to act with customers (for example, how to sell them something or induce them to leave a big tip). Political canvassers are usually given careful instruction in how best to present the arguments for their candidate. Books have been written that give lawyers numerous practical suggestions on how to more successfully persuade juries and clients (a few examples of these will be presented later in this chapter). Therapists, whose major function is to produce change in others, receive extensive training in how to guide and influence the behavior of their patients.

MEDIA

Finally, in these times your ideas about control are partially determined by what you see and hear in the mass media. Television, radio, newspapers, and magazines are all vehicles for showing you how people influence each other. The effective or ineffective techniques used by the president to get Congress to pass a bill are described by the media, as are the tactics that political candidates use to sway voters. Furthermore, the fictional interactions of the characters on television shows are also a source of information on how people are influenced (see Student Project #1 in Postscript D for a further development of these ideas). For example, the great controversy over TV violence centers around the argument that people may be learning to use aggression more often as a control tactic. (In Chapter 6 we will see an example of research that demonstrates the positive effectiveness of media in changing health habits to reduce heart disease risks.)

What Other People Know

Although we can learn much about influence processes by looking to our own thought and experience, an even greater source of ideas lies in the wisdom of others, both past and present. The attempt by one person to change the attitudes and behavior of others is an historically ageless tale. The story of Satan's temptation of Eve and her subsequent recruitment of Adam recurs in many forms in our literary heritage. Over the years, a wide variety of beliefs about personal and social influence in many different spheres of life has accumulated. Therefore, our consideration of control processes would profit from a search through the fields of history, religion, literature, and law, as well as of the behavioral sciences. Obviously, in a brief introductory text like this one, all we can do is suggest that such sources are worth your attention and illustrate why by providing a few examples. It will then be up to you to engage in further exploration of these fields and to develop additional insights into the process of influence.

HISTORY

For our present purpose it may be instructive to see what we can learn from two former masters of the persuasion process, Niccolo Machiavelli and Adolf Hitler.

Machiavelli

Communicator characteristics

> ... nothing is so apt to restrain an excited multitude as the reverence inspired by some grave and dignified man of authority who opposes them ... therefore whoever is at the head of an army, or whoever happens to be a magistrate in a city where sedition lies broken out, should present himself before the multitude with all possible grace and dignity, and attired with all the insignia of his rank, so as to inspire the more respect. (Machiavelli 1950, p. 251)

Disguised intent of persuader

> For he who for a time has seemed good, and for purposes of his own wants to become bad, should do it gradually, and should seem to be brought to it by the force of circumstances; so that, before his changed nature deprives him of his former friends, he may have gained new ones, and that his authority may not be diminished by the change. Otherwise his deception will be discovered, and he will lose his friends and be ruined. (Machiavelli 1950, p. 225)

Hitler

Tailoring the message to the audience

> The receptive ability of the masses is very limited, their understanding small; on the other hand, they have a great power of forgetting. This being so, all effective propaganda must be confined to a very few points which must be brought out in the form of slogans until the very last man is enabled to comprehend what is meant by any slogan. If this principle is sacrificed to the desire to be many-sided, it will dissipate the effectual working of the propaganda, for the people will be unable to digest or retain the material that is offered them. It will, moreover, weaken and finally cancel its own effectiveness. (Hitler 1933, p. 77)

Qualter, in his treatise *Propaganda and Psychological Warfare* (1962), describes further how Hitler devised a systematic program to effectively change the attitudes and values of an entire nation, a program in which every detail was turned to the advantage of the propagandist.

> Uniforms, bands, flags, symbols were all part of the German propaganda machine, designed by Hitler and Goebbels to increase the impact of strong words by evidence of strong deeds. Meetings were not just occasions for people to make speeches, they were carefully planned theatrical productions in which settings, lighting, background music, and the timing of entrances and exits were devised to maximize the emotional fervor of an audience already brought to fever pitch by an hour or more given over to singing and the shouting of slogans. ... (p. 112)

Adolf Hitler reviewing Hitler youth, Nuremberg 1935.

Kautilya

Although Machiavelli and Hitler are extremely well known to us, we should not assume that the Western tradition has a monopoly on theories of influence. In 300 B.C., long before Europeans were developing their ideas, a remarkable treatise on the art of government and diplomacy was written in India by a man named Kautilya. In addition to being a skillful writer and commentator, Kautilya was renowned as a maker of kings, so his doctrines are based on a great deal of practical experience.

Using temptation to assess persuasibility

> Assisted by his prime minister and his high priest, the king shall, by offering temptations, examine the character of ministers appointed in government departments of ordinary nature.
>
> The king shall dismiss a priest who, when ordered, refuses ... to officiate in a sacrificial performance [apparently] undertaken by an outcaste person. Then the dismissed priest shall, through the medium of spies under the guise of classmates, instigate each minister, one after another, saying on oath, "This king is unrighteous; well, let us set up in

his place another king who is righteous, or who is born of the same family as of this king . . . ; this attempt is to the liking of all of us; what dost thou think?" If any one or all of the ministers refuse to acquiesce in such a measure, he or they shall be considered pure. *This is what is called religious allurement.*

A commander of the army, dismissed from service . . . may, through the agency of spies . . . incite each minister to murder the king in view of acquiring immense wealth. . . . If they refuse to agree, they are to be considered pure. *This is what is termed monetary allurement.*

A woman-spy . . . may allure each prime minister, one after another, saying, "The queen is enamoured of thee and has made arrangements for thy entrance into her chamber. . . ." If they discard the proposal, they are pure. *This is what is styled love allurement.*

With the intention of sailing on a commercial vessel, a minister may induce all other ministers to follow him. Apprehensive of danger, the king may arrest them all. A spy, under the guise of a fraudulent disciple, pretending to have suffered imprisonment, may incite each of the ministers thus deprived of wealth and rank, saying, "The king has betaken himself to an unwise course; well, having murdered him, let us put another in his stead. We all like this; what dost thou think?" If they refuse to agree, they are pure. *This is what is termed allurement under fear.* (Kautilya's *Arthaśāstra,* pp. 15–16)

On acquiring communicator credibility and prestige

When the conqueror is desirous of seizing an enemy's village, he should infuse enthusiastic spirit among his own men and frighten his enemy's people by giving publicity to his power of omniscience and close association with the gods. Proclamation of his omniscience [includes] . . . pretensions to the knowledge of foreign affairs by means of his power to read omens and signs invisible to others when information about foreign affairs is just received through a domestic pigeon which has brought a sealed letter. Proclamation of his association with gods [includes] holding conversation with, and worshiping, the spies who pretend to be the gods of fire or altar when through a tunnel they come to stand in the midst of fire, altar, or in the interior of a hollow image; . . . performing magical tricks [such as] sending out volumes of smoke from the mouth on occasions of anger. Astrologers, soothsayers . . . together with spies and their disciples . . . should give wide publicity to the power of the king to associate with gods throughout his territory. Likewise in foreign countries, they should spread the news of gods appearing before the conqueror and of his having received from heaven weapons and treasure. (Kautilya's *Arthaśāstra,* pp. 423–424)

Even after 2,000 years, Kautilya's proposals for persuasion have a great deal of relevance to modern-day events. His recommendation of "magic tricks" to produce a powerful image of the king has an obvious parallel to the use of "Watergate dirty tricks" in the creation (and eventual destruction) of the public images of presidential candidates.

RELIGION

The belief in a god or the supernatural, as well as in a related dogma, can have a most profound impact on behavior. In addition to engaging in regular rituals of worship, people have been willing to risk humiliation, pain, and hardship because of their religious beliefs. They have even sacrificed their lives, as evidenced by innumerable religious wars and the deaths of martyrs throughout recorded history. Even today, the clash of opposing religious doctrines continues to be felt in such battlegrounds as Northern Ireland and Beirut. The strength of these beliefs attests in part to the ways in which they are developed and maintained.

Within religion, one of the most dramatic examples of persuasion is the sudden conversion. The individual undergoes a major change in attitudes toward God, toward other people, and toward self, and this is often reflected in significant behavioral changes. What sorts of influence attempts produce conversions?

Establishing a close personal relationship   Developing intense relationships with people is often the first step in converting them to your position. This technique was nicely articulated by General William Booth, the founder of the Salvation Army: "The first vital step in saving outcasts consists in making them feel that some decent human being cares enough for them to take an interest in the question whether they are to rise or to sink." (James 1936, p. 34)

Arousal of emotion   Many conversions are produced in mass revival meetings conducted by such well-known evangelists as Billy Sunday, Oral Roberts, Prophet Jones, and Billy Graham. These meetings are characterized by a high degree of emotional arousal, which is a result of the intensity of the gospel music and the exhortations. The evangelist will try to arouse strong feelings of guilt and fear in the audience by emphasizing their sins and wickedness and warning of the horrors of damnation. Then, by providing an opportunity for emotional catharsis and well-timed reassurance, he or she will direct the audience away from a life of self-indulgence and sin toward one of self-sacrifice in God's name.

Use of public commitment   A significant feature of mass revival meetings is the request for a public sign of belief—such as coming forward, taking a vow, making an overt pledge, or speaking out. Evangelists do not wait until their audience believes before requesting its members to act, but rather work on the now firmly established psychological principle (to be elaborated on in Chapter 3) that beliefs change *following* a commitment to behavior that is discrepant with the original beliefs. In fact, in the Old Testament the rabbis are enjoined not to make their parishioners or converts believe in God *before* they are asked to pray, but to have them pray first so that belief will follow.

The power of prayer   An influence technique that is unique to religion is that of prayer. By approaching God through word or thought, the person attempts to achieve a goal or bring about some change. This belief in the power of supernatural forces to intervene and improve one's life is often sufficient to effect changes in oneself. Thus, prayer can enable one to find peace and comfort, gain personal insight and understanding, and obtain the strength and inspiration to take some action. The personal consequences of faith and prayer are illustrated by the experience of pilgrims to Lourdes:

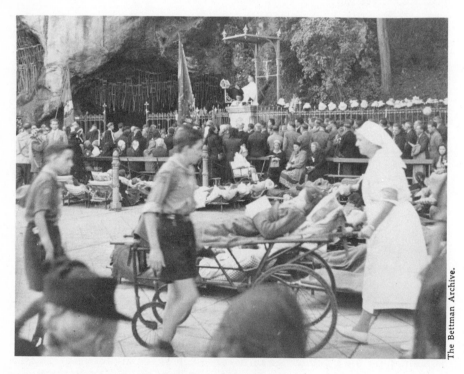

The Bettman Archive.

The Grotto Shrine of St. Bernadette, Lourdes, France.

On arrival at Lourdes after an exhausting, even life-endangering journey, the sufferer's expectation of help is further strengthened. He is plunged into "a city of pilgrims, and they are everywhere; people who have come from the four corners of the earth with but one purpose; prayer and healing for themselves or for their loved ones. . . . One is surrounded by them, and steeped in their atmosphere every moment of existence in Lourdes." Everyone hopes to witness or experience a miraculous cure. Accounts of previous cures are on every tongue, and the pilgrim sees the votive offerings and the piles of discarded crutches of those who have been healed. Thus the ritual may be said to begin with validation of the shrine's power, analogous to the medicine man's review of his cures in primitive healing rites. The pilgrims' days are filled with religious services and trips to the Grotto, where they are immersed in the ice-cold spring. Every afternoon all the pilgrims and invalids who are at Lourdes at the time, and they number forty or fifty thousand, gather at the Esplanade in front of the shrine for the procession that is the climax of the day's activities. (Frank 1961, p. 55)

Although some physical healing does occur, most of the sick do not get cured. Nevertheless, as a result of the prayers and rituals, almost everyone experiences a psychological improvement and feels more hopeful and self-confident.

LITERATURE

Literature is a rich and vivid source of ideas about the dynamics of both social and personal influence.

Initial identification with the audience   Marc Antony's classic funeral oration in Shakespeare's *Julius Caesar* is the best example of an explicit attempt to persuade an audience to alter its attitudes and modify its behavior. From an analysis of the techniques ascribed to Antony we may abstract several hypotheses about attitude change. The reader will recall the situation facing Antony and the goal of his persuasive communication. Cassius and the conspirators had persuaded Brutus to join them in killing Caesar in order to use Brutus' good reputation with the citizens to their advantage. At Caesar's funeral, Brutus, speaking first, justifies the assassination as a necessary act, done not from ambition or hatred, not from loving Caesar less, but from loving Rome more. The audience is swayed by his argument, and is set to oppose Marc Antony, whom they expect will give a pro-Caesar or anti-Brutus speech.

Antony purposely chooses to be the last speaker and begins with introductory remarks that confound the expectations of the crowd by affirming his essential agreement with their position. He has not come to praise

Caesar; his function is merely to bury him. He, like the crowd, must acknowledge that Brutus is an honorable man. Having created this intellectual basis for common agreement with the crowd, he then effectively proceeds by indirection and emotional appeals to force them to draw the conclusion that Caesar was unjustly murdered and that Brutus and the other murderers should be driven out.

Inner states as sources of influence   In one of his short novels, Dostoevsky presents a portrait of a man who falls prey to the compulsive behavior syndrome of gambling. The man speculates on the personal feelings and motives that cause him to risk all of his money over and over again in spite of possible disastrous consequences:

> But, noticing that red had turned up seven times running, by strange perversity I staked on it. I am convinced that vanity was half responsible for it; I wanted to impress the spectators by taking a mad risk, and—oh, the strange sensation—I remember distinctly that, quite apart from the promptings of vanity, I was possessed by an intense craving for risk. Perhaps passing through so many sensations my soul was not satisfied but only irritated by them and craved still more sensation—and stronger and stronger ones—till utterly exhausted. And, truly I am not lying, if the regulations had allowed me to stake fifty thousand florins at once, I should certainly have staked them. People around shouted that it was madness—that red had won fourteen times already! (Dostoevsky 1945, p. 100)

Although the gambler realizes what has become of him, he also believes that no external, social influence could moderate or change his inner compulsion:

> And now, more than a year and a half has passed, and I am, to my own mind, far worse than a beggar! Yes, what is being a beggar? A beggar is nothing! I have simply ruined myself! However, there is nothing I can compare myself with, and there is no need to give myself a moral lecture! Nothing could be stupider than moral reflections at this date! Oh, self-satisfied people, with what proud satisfaction these prattlers prepare to deliver their lectures! If only they knew how thoroughly I understand the loathsomeness of my present position, they would not be able to bring their tongues to reprimand me. Why, what, what can they tell me that I do not know? (Dostoevsky 1945, p. 118)

Using social reinforcements to obtain compliance

> The fascination that the police have for the thief is manifested by the thief's temptation to confess when he is arrested. In the presence of the examining magistrate who questions him, he is seized with giddiness: the magistrate speaks gently to him, perhaps with kindness, explaining what is expected of him; practically nothing: an assent. If only once,

Stock, Boston.

While some earn fame and fortune, most gambling addicts lose their self-respect along with their money.

just once, he did what was asked of him, if he uttered the "yes" that is requested, harmony of minds would be achieved. He would be told, "That's fine," perhaps he would be congratulated. It would be the end of hatred. The desire to confess is the mad dream of universal love; it is, as Genet himself says, the temptation of the human. (Sartre 1964, p. 175)

(In Chapter 6 we shall examine in more detail the techniques used by police interrogators to secure confessions.)

LAW

Trial lawyers have offered us dramatic descriptions of the myriad factors and seemingly trivial details to which they must be responsive in order to persuade a jury of twelve individuals to agree with their conclusion and reject that of their opponents. Louis Nizer's *My Life in Court* (1961) offers us much of value with reference to significant audience characteristics (such as sex, ethnic group, and social class) that must be taken into account in planning any communication strategy. He offers hunches about how to "size up" your audience (here, the jury), and how to assess their values and attitudes, and he suggests approaches that appeal to and exploit points of vulnerability. The following are some selected tactics used by Nizer.

Resistance to persuasion

When I am required to sum up first, I endeavor to prepare the jury so that it will not yield to the blandishments of my adversary. I remind the jury that he will have the last word and that I will not be permitted to reply. I tell them that I must depend on their recollections to correct any misstatement of fact which my opponent, who follows me, may make. I must rely on their discriminating judgment to reject any false arguments. Then, as I proceed to build my own case, I anticipate the contentions of my adversary. I announce his slogans and attempt to destroy them, asking the jurors to become my watchmen when they hear such sophistry, and reject it as an insult to their intelligence. (p. 434)

Eye contact

It is an early opportunity to look each juror in the eye and by sincerity and earnestness make contact with him. It is interesting to observe the bland look on a juror's face when you begin, perhaps even a cynical smile, and how he is caught up in the drama of your recital, his face responding properly with varying emotions of sympathy or resentment as the arguments make inroads upon him. Finally, when you walk up and back, and his eyes follow and are riveted upon you, the persuasive effort has begun successfully. (p. 42)

Of course, not all of the lawyer's persuasive techniques are directed at a jury. In many cases, settlements are reached by the lawyer's skill in influencing one or both of the opposing parties to accept a settlement.

Sex differences in claims settlements

When a client is not receptive to my advice, I frequently consult his or her spouse. I have discovered that women are far more willing to settle than men are. A man is easily tempted to risk everything on the chance that a jury might give him more. Most women prefer having the cash in hand. This is no surprise to those who know that men gamble more than women. It means, of course, that men will require more conditioning. Even if the plaintiff is a woman, you can usually be sure that she will require less conditioning than her husband. (Sindell and Sindell 1963, p. 308)

Assumptive technique

... Assume that you, as an adjuster, have made your presentation and your offer to the claimant. You don't ask him whether he would like to settle—you propel him towards settlement by asking such questions as "How do you want the check made out?" or "Do you want your full name on the check?" You don't ask him questions that he has to think about—you ask him questions that are easy to answer. Then you start to write out the check. The claimant may not really be ready to close—he may be wavering or he may want to think about your offer—but you have put him on the spot. He now has to take affirmative action to stop you from writing the draft, and unless he feels very strongly, he will just go along with you. The first thing he knows he is holding a draft and you are walking away with the release. (Hermann 1965, pp. 181–182)

Knowledge from the Behavioral Sciences

This brief survey of where to look for useful background information and ideas now focuses on the three disciplines in social science that have the most obvious and direct relevance to our general problem: anthropology, sociology, and psychology. Although at some points of intersection it is difficult to tell if a given piece of research belongs to one or the other of these areas, several critical differences stand out under most comparisons among them. The anthropologist interested in influence and persuasion would investigate various cultural and crosscultural dimensions, while the sociologist would focus on processes existing in society, in institutions, and within groups. In contrast, the psychologist's attention is directed at the individual human being. For example, some psychologists study individual feelings of rejection and low self-esteem. The sociological analogy would be the study of factors (such as assembly-line production and urbanization) that create feelings of alienation in a society, while the anthropological analogy would be how cultural norms of a reliance on fate and minimal achievement prevent people from moving beyond a subsistence economy. These three disciplines differ, then, in the unit of analysis (individual, group, or culture), in the variables and processes studied, and in techniques of investigation.

They are all on the scientific end of a continuum, the other end of which is represented by literature, humanistic studies, and arts. Thus they all propose formal techniques for gathering evidence that allow objective conclusions to be drawn independently of the personal biases of the investigator. They rely on controlled observation as a major method of collecting information about behavior, and hold their procedures and results up for public scrutiny, critical evaluation, and reproducibility.

ANTHROPOLOGY

In New Guinea, some aboriginal tribes still use stone axes in preference to more efficient and durable metal axes. This cultural lag in getting people to adopt new techniques that have been proven superior to traditional ones is fostered by a general resistance to giving up old ways of responding. From anthropological studies of this phenomenon across different cultures we may be able to come up with some general description of the conditions that maintain this resistance and the techniques that can be used to weaken or eliminate it.

Certain attitudes and values are often so widely accepted in a given culture that they are virtually truisms for all members of that culture, and rarely, if ever, are contrary points of view presented. As an example, consider the norms in our society about masturbation and homosexual intercourse. Not only are these practices viewed as bad or sinful, but it is often believed that engaging in such sexual activities will permanently impair one's later, "normal," heterosexual experiences. However, among the people living on the Melanesian Islands in the southwest Pacific, there is an entirely different set of sexual attitudes and behaviors (Davenport 1965). Unmarried males and females are kept completely separated, since premarital intercourse is strictly forbidden. It is believed that sex drives must be expressed, however, so young people are specifically encouraged to masturbate in order to satisfy their sexual urges. In addition, unmarried males engage in homosexual intercourse, with the full approval of the culture; this does not have any harmful effects on their later heterosexual activity.

Observations made by investigators are filtered through glass ground by biases in their own culture. Because of this, they may be unaware of, or misperceive, variables and processes that are important for their understanding of why people hold the attitudes they do. Within our own culture, this is the charge leveled against white middle-class reformers trying to produce change in lower-class black ghettos.

SOCIOLOGY

Many of the beliefs, attitudes, and behaviors we exhibit have been largely determined by the relevant groups in our life. Our family, friends, classmates, and work associates are only a few of the groups whose norms shape our own. These groups define what is right, socially appropriate, or "in," and produce adherence to these ideas through such techniques as social rewards, threats of punishment or ostracism, and various other pressures toward conformity. The impact of college peers on a person's political attitudes was clearly demonstrated in a classic study of women attending Bennington College in the late 1930s (Newcomb et al. 1967). The college atmosphere was highly liberal, although most of the women came from very conservative family backgrounds. The majority of women who became strongly involved in the college community adopted progressively more liberal political attitudes over the four-year period. In contrast, those who maintained strong ties with their families continued to keep their conservative attitudes. Twenty-five years later, Newcomb found that this college-induced liberalism had persisted. Why should this be so? One probable answer is that when these women graduated from Bennington they selectively chose new reference groups and mates who supported their liberal attitudes. Thus their friends, coworkers, and husbands maintained the initial influence of their college environment.

Other investigations have studied how certain groups, such as gangs, influence the occurrence of aggressive behaviors. These "subcultures of violence" value physical aggression as the acceptable response to any personal affront (whether real or imagined) and impose strong sanctions on those who deviate from this norm (Wolfgang and Ferracuti 1967). Violence is used to attain status and power, save face, and defend one's masculinity. It even appears in the subculture's games, such as "playing the dozens" (in which you and your opponent systematically insult one another).

> One of the tormentors will make a mildly insulting statement, perhaps about the mother of the subject, "I saw your mother out with a man last night." Then he may follow this up with "She was as drunk as a bat." The subject, in turn, will then make an insulting statement about the tormentor or some member of the tormentor's family. This exchange of insults continues, encouraged by the approval and shouts of the observers, and the insults become progressively nastier and more pornographic, until they eventually include every member of the participants' families and every act of animal and man. . . . Finally, one of the participants, usually the subject, who has actually been combating the group pressure of the observers, reaches his threshold and takes a swing at the tormentor, pulls out a knife or picks up an object to use as a club. This is the sign for the tormentor, and sometimes some of the observers, to go into action, and usually the subject ends up with the most physical injuries. (Berdie 1947, p. 120)

THE PSYCHOLOGICAL APPROACH

Within the behavioral sciences, the primary source of answers about attitude and behavior change is the field of psychology. As indicated before, psychologists focus their attention on the individual and on how he or she functions. Thus they are particularly well qualified to study the process by which a person receives various types of information and then responds to them.

There are many different sub-areas of psychology, but they can be generally classified into one of two orientations. The first orientation looks *inside* the person for answers about individual behavior, while the second orientation looks *outside* the person. In other words, in trying to understand why a person behaves in the way he or she does, some psychologists will investigate the person's unique, internal characteristics, while others will look to the external, social influences on that person. The "inside" approach is demonstrated by physiological psychology (which studies such things as the brain, hormones, and the nervous system), and by much of traditional personality and clinical psychology, which focus on the individual's stable or dispositional traits, personality structure, and mental disorders.

In contrast, the "outside" approach is used by social and experimental psychologists, who study how the individual is affected by such factors as the physical environment and the presence (real or implied) of other people. The behavioristic approach proposed by B. F. Skinner and others would also be characterized as "outside" since it looks only at the effect of external stimuli, rewards, and punishments on behavior and makes no claims about what is going on inside the person's head. As Skinner put it, ". . . the problems we face are not to be found in men and women but in the world in which they live, especially in those social environments we call cultures." (Skinner 1975, p. 49)

Although we can classify different areas of psychology as primarily "inside" or "outside" in approach, this does *not* mean that the orientations are incompatible. In fact, the trend in recent years is toward an *interactionist* approach, which studies how "inside" processes are affected by "outside" influences and vice versa. For example, the "outside" factor of peer pressure may cause people to adopt a group norm, but their style of adherence to that norm may be determined by the "inside" factor of personality traits.

While it is difficult to make an absolute distinction between "inside" and "outside" orientations, the distinction is still useful. The two approaches have very different implications in terms of the possible modifiability of behavior. That is, by looking in different places for the sources of behavior, "inside" and "outside" psychologists will arrive at different conclusions about (1) whether or not a behavior *can* be changed, and (2) if so, *how* it can be changed.

For example, let us consider the problem of violence and crime, which is of uppermost concern to many American citizens. "Inside" psychologists would try to solve the problem by looking for the internal, personal causes of violent behavior. Depending on their specialization, they might look for physical abnormalities (such as brain tumors, hormonal imbalances, or genetic anomalies), or they might look for psychological disturbances (such as mental illness, impaired intellectual functioning, or a low level of ego control or moral development). In contrast, "outside" psychologists would look for the external, social causes of violence. They might identify such factors as environmental stressors, group norms, models, and social rewards as the causes of aggressive action. Some "inside" approaches suggest that violence is inborn, while most "outside" orientations favor the theory that it is learned. If violence is inborn and personally caused, then society can control it by segregating violent individuals, providing acceptable means of expressing violence, or administering individual therapy. However, if violence is learned, then society can control it by removing the rewards for violence, by modeling (and rewarding) alternative nonviolent forms of behavior, or by reducing the impact of environmental stressors (such as poverty and discrimination). With the first approach, the question becomes "*who* causes violence?" while the second orientation asks "*what* causes violence?" Thus the type of question determines the types of solutions we will use to implement changes.

In this book, our orientation will be that of most other attitude change researchers—namely, an *interactionist* approach. We shall be looking at the "outside" situational conditions that affect "inside" attitudes, and at how, in turn, these attitudes affect overt behavior. We shall then point out how that behavior becomes an observable event that may influence other people's attitudes. Thus, the pattern of situation → attitude → action → new situation → new attitude, and so on, is our view of the continuous, interwoven process of social influence.

To illustrate our stance, let us return to the case study of Patty Hearst. Our analysis looked primarily at the social influences on an individual's behavior. We have not tried to figure out what was so special about Patty's personality or upbringing alone that caused her to act in the way she did (as many popular commentators have done). Instead we have pointed to the social and situational forces that influenced her behavior, such as informational input, group cohesiveness, and social reinforcement. Such an analysis points to the possibility that *any* of us would have responded in the same way that she did. Rather than viewing her behavior as an individual aberration, we should recognize that it tells us far more about the power of social influence than most of us have been willing to believe.

Up to this point we have been talking about social influence processes in two very disparate ways. On the one hand we have discussed very general scientific approaches, while on the other we have pointed to a number of very specific tactics for changing attitudes and behavior. What connects the abstract orientations to the concrete techniques is *theory*, and this will be the focus of our next chapter.

MEASURES OF ATTITUDES ABOUT CONTROL

There are several different psychological scales that attempt to assess a person's attitudes about influence and control: among them are the Internal-External Control Scale (Rotter 1966), The F-Scale (Adorno et al. 1950), and the Machiavellianism Scale (Christie and Geis 1970). Listed below are a few sample items from each scale:

The Internal-External Control Scale

Choose the answer that best describes your feelings.

(1) _____ a. One of the major reasons why we have wars is because people don't take enough interest in politics.

_____ b. There will always be wars, no matter how hard people try to prevent them.

(2) _____ a. In the case of the well-prepared student there is rarely if ever such a thing as an unfair test.

_____ b. Many times exam questions tend to be so unrelated to course work that studying is really useless.

(3) _____ a. The average citizen can have an influence in government decisions.

_____ b. This world is run by the few people in power, and there is not much the little guy can do about it.

(4) _____ a. Most people don't realize the extent to which their lives are controlled by accidental happenings.

_____ b. There is no such thing as "luck."

(5) _____ a. It is hard to know whether or not a person really likes you.

_____ b. How many friends you have depends upon how nice a person you are.

(6) _____ a. What happens to me is my own doing.

_____ b. Sometimes I feel that I don't have enough control over the direction my life is taking.

The F-Scale
True–False

(1) _____ Obedience and respect for authority are the most important virtues children should learn.

(2) _____ What this country needs most, more than laws and political programs is a few courageous, tireless, devoted leaders in whom the people can put their faith.

(3) _____ An insult to our honor should always be punished.

(4) _____ Most of our social problems would be solved if we could somehow get rid of the immoral, crooked, and feebleminded people.

(5) _____ What youth needs most is strict discipline, rugged determination, and the will to work and fight for family and country.

(6) _____ People can be divided into two distinct classes: the weak and the strong.

● ● ●

The Machiavellianism Scale
True–False

(1) _____ The best way to handle people is to tell them what they want to hear.

(2) _____ One should take action only when sure it is morally right.

(3) _____ Anyone who completely trusts anyone else is asking for trouble.

(4) _____ The biggest difference between most criminals and other people is that the criminals are stupid enough to get caught.

(5) _____ It is hard to get ahead without cutting corners here and there.

(6) _____ When you ask someone to do something for you, it is best to give the real reasons for wanting it rather than giving reasons which carry more weight.

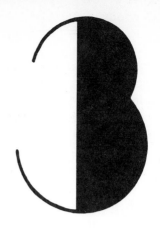

examining theories of attitude and behavior change

As we have seen, the process of social influence is not only widespread, it is ageless. The story of Adam and Eve is in part an account of the susceptibility of Eve to the guile of Satan-turned-Serpent and of Adam's vulnerability to Eve's persuasive arguments. There is no question but that some people are better able than others to convince, cajole, and sell themselves, their beliefs, and their snake oil. But does the power of persuasion lie in the mysterious and unlearnable talents of select individuals, or in the efficacy of the techniques of attitude and behavior change that these people happen to use? It is our position that an understanding of how social influence operates can be developed from knowledge of existing social science research and from current attempts to theorize about the mechanisms of attitude and behavior change. The practitioners of social influence—the hustlers, con artists, advertisers, professors, and so forth—merely have a better knowledge of these techniques than the average person.

In this chapter we shall explore several different approaches to ways of influencing attitudes and behavior. From the outset, we should make it clear why we are concerned with the attitudes people hold and not just the way in which they behave. At first glance, it might seem that attitudes are unimportant. For example, unless the birth rate were to decrease, even an extreme change in birth-control attitudes would not reduce the increased demand for food, energy, and space. In fact, some might argue that a reduction in birth rate is the *only* important issue.

Our interest in attitudes stems from two sources. First, as social scientists we are naturally curious about the way in which people think and the contents of those thoughts. It seems intrinsically interesting to know such things as whether and how many people favor capital punishment, think welfare should be abolished, believe in the second coming of Christ, have fantasies about killing themselves, and so on. Second, and more important, as social engineers interested in using what is known about interpersonal influence to solve social problems, we cannot afford to ignore attitudes. After all, it may be that we cannot change the birth rate without *first* changing people's attitudes toward birth-control practices. Furthermore, it is conceivable that any change in birth rate will not last unless it is accompanied by a major reorientation in beliefs and attitudes to sustain the change in behavior.

As can be seen, the utility of the concept of attitudes depends on the extent to which knowledge of any given attitude allows one to predict reliably that a given behavior will follow. This is an issue of much research interest to social scientists. For example, they wonder if worker satisfaction is related to job turnover, absenteeism, and on-the-job accidents. Other studies ask whether racial attitudes are related to behaviors toward minority groups, such as choosing to live in interracial housing, or offering jobs, hotel rooms, or assistance to members of particular racial and ethnic groups.

The general conclusion of these many studies is that there is *not* a one-to-one relationship between behavior and attitudes. There is a link, but it is a weak one. Predictions can be made, but rarely are they accurate for the individual case. There are a number of reasons why the link between attitudes and behavior, as typically studied, is a weak one. A person might hate his or her job as an assembly-line worker shelling peanuts, cleaning scallops, or riveting fenders, but the dissatisfaction could be overwhelmed by the need to support the family and the absence of other job possibilities with equivalent salary. Another individual might be prejudiced against an ethnic group, say Sicilians, without ever having had first-hand acquaintance with any member of that group. This person might then act tolerantly toward any (and maybe all) individuals of this category who represent specific "exceptions" to the abstract rule.

Sometimes attitudes are in conflict, as often occurs in various types of addiction where people knowingly engage in self-destructive behaviors because the immediate pleasure of the act wins out over intellectual concerns for negative, long-term consequences. In addition, attitudes and behavior might not seem to go hand in hand because of a difference in the meaning of the two experiences: students who do not believe in "cheating" occasionally seek or give "help" to other students when the need is great;

"ripping off the establishment" may not be perceived as contrary to an attitude against "stealing," and "wasting the enemy" has been construed by some military operatives as not inconsistent with the moral belief, "Thou shalt not kill." In short, although we may think two behaviors belong to the same attitude class, the person whose behavior we are studying may not. Our concern is with the person and not with *our* perceptions of what attitudes *should* be related to which behaviors. If we find that people who claim to be prejudiced against blacks are just as likely to give their seat on a bus to an old black woman as an old white woman, we throw out *our* conception that giving seats to people is an index of racial prejudice. The weak link between self-reported prejudice and "seat giving" is a fault in our conceptual system rather than an indication that attitudes are unimportant. It simply means that we failed to take into account the many other concerns of the "seat giver," such as appearing manly to his date, the respect the person has for older people, and so on.

There are other reasons for a weak link between attitudes and behavior. A particular action may be the product of many different attitudes; a given attitude may influence a variety of behaviors in different ways. Attitudes vary in how intensely they are held, in how salient they are to the person holding them, and in how central or peripheral they are to other attitudes and values that form a cluster or syndrome.

TABLE 3.1
Attitudes Against Abortion Do Not Exist in Isolation (Adapted from Prescott 1975)

	People with an anti-abortion attitude also tend to believe that:
With regard to pain:	1. Harsh physical punishment is good for children who disobey a lot. 2. Capital punishment should be permitted by society.
With regard to sex:	1. Prostitution should be punished by society. 2. Nudity within the family has a harmful influence upon children. 3. Sexual pleasures help build a weak moral character.
With regard to drugs:	1. Alcohol is more satisfying than sex. 2. Drugs are more satisfying than sex.
With regard to politics:	1. Conservatism is better than liberalism.
	Cultures that punish abortion also tend to:
	1. Practice slavery 2. Practice polygamy 3. Restrict the sexual experience of youths 4. Punish extramarital sex 5. Have dominant fathers rather than mothers

A good example of the latter point comes from a study relating attitudes about abortion to attitudes about pain, sex, drugs, and politics. Table 3.1 reveals that people who claim to be against abortion also believe in harsh physical punishment of children, are less liberal in their attitudes toward sex, and tend to be politically conservative. People in favor of abortion have an opposite set of beliefs. Similarly, a frequency count of different cultures that do and do not punish abortion reveals that those cultures that do are more likely to practice slavery and punish extramarital sex.

It should be clear from the above arguments that research that assumes a one-to-one relationship between a given attitude and a particular class of behavior is bound to find a weak relationship between the two. What is needed is an approach that recognizes the complexity inherent in the attitude–behavior link. One such approach, most suited to our applied orientation, shifts our focus from the single individual to the *population* as a whole. It also emphasizes changes or shifts in attitudes, averaged over the entire population, rather than whether one person's attitude is stronger than another person's. Even though we cannot predict the behavior of single individuals, we should be able to predict that people (in general) will *change* their behavior if we can *change* their attitudes of greatest relevance to the behavior in question. We cannot predict which people will change or how much each will change, but a change in the attitudes of the population should be accompanied by a change in the behavior of the population. Furthermore, given the interrelationships among attitudes, a change in one attitude may be accompanied by a change in *many* different behaviors. Therefore, focusing on just one type of action may lead to an underestimation of the impact of a change attempt.

Two aspects of the above orientation are important. One is that it emphasizes *population* characteristics rather than the behavior of single individuals. It claims attitudes will be primarily useful in predicting group averages and the percentage of people in a population who behave in certain ways. Second, it emphasizes *change*. By changing the attitudes of the population toward a particular product, political candidate, institution, and so on, we should expect a *change* in some population measure; for example, the number of General Motors cars sold each month, the percentage of people voting for Jimmy Carter, or the amount of money donated to the Catholic church.

Prediction of such group effects will often be sufficient for the purposes of the politician, entrepreneur, or propagandist. It is not sufficient, however, for purposes of therapy. Where the goal is to modify maladaptive habits and pathological response patterns, for example, in a person with an extreme phobia or a compulsion, the change must be specific. In such instances, we will have to shift our focus from attitudes to more specific information about the individual, information that will allow us to tailor a change attempt to that person. This kind of influence attempt is rarely a one-shot persuasive effort, of course; it almost always takes time to discover something about the person's reinforcement history, motivational hierarchy, sources of resistance to change, cognitive style, and language usage, and the external situations in which the new behavior will operate.

It is precisely because attitudes and behavior are related in complex rather than simple ways that we need some guidelines to help us understand this complexity and to steer us through the maze of variables and processes that could affect attitudes, beliefs, and action. A good theory does just that.

What Is a Theory?

Essentially, a theory is an abstract, symbolic representation of what is conceived to be reality. That is, a theory is a set of abstract statements or rules designed to "fit" some portion of the real world. A model airplane is, in some sense, a concrete theory of a real airplane. We can use the model plane to test how a real airplane will behave (fly) under various conditions, if we assume that the model "fits" with the real plane. If we subject the model airplane to certain air currents (as in a wind tunnel) and observe how it behaves, we should be able to predict from its behavior the behavior of a real plane subjected to similar air currents. The accuracy of our predictions (or hypotheses) will be a function of how well the model "fits," or represents, the real plane.

Just as the model is used to predict the behavior of the real plane, a set of symbolic statements could be created to do the same thing. In order to use a theory (set of symbolic statements) to predict behavior, we need two sets of rules. One set of rules has to relate some of the symbols (called conceptual independent variables) in our theory to aspects of the air current, and the other symbols (called conceptual dependent variables) to the behavior of the real airplane. These are the *correspondence rules*. The other set of rules (called *functional* relationships) must tell us how to manipulate the symbols or concepts of the theory so that we can derive the necessary hypotheses. In physical science theories, these rules are typically mathematical ones, or rules of abstract algebra and calculus. For example, if the symbol X represents some change in air current, and Y the initial position of the airplane before the change in air current, then the rule given for predicting the effect of the change in current on the behavior of the plane might be: $Y \times X =$ new position. Our rule here is: multiply X times Y to get the new position of the plane. Theories need not use *only* mathematical rules to tell us how to derive the effect that a conceptual independent variable will have on a conceptual dependent variable. In fact, most theories in psychology use rules of grammar and implicit semantics to suggest how to manipulate these symbols.

In summary, a theory is merely an abstract way of relating and simplifying some events and processes in the world. It should give the experimenter correspondence rules for relating conceptual variables to specific operations; that is, rules that allow a researcher to know how a specific event or thing in the world relates to concepts in the theory. It should also provide functional relationships that tell the experimenter how to manipulate and interrelate the various conceptual variables. Once they are so related, the experimenter can (deductively) derive specific hypotheses of an "if . . . then" nature. If a certain value of the independent variable occurs (for example, wind current) then the dependent variable should be affected in a given way (for example, the airplane's movement should change a given amount). Theories also incorporate a number of *hypothetical* variables and assumptions whose sole purpose is to relate the conceptual variables to each other. They are not directly related to operations, but rather to other conceptual variables that are themselves tied to specific operations. It follows, therefore, that these hypothetical variables can be validated only indirectly, even when the entire theory is supported by sound evidence.

How Is a Theory Useful?

A theory makes explicit what is meant by a conceptual variable. By allowing only certain correspondence rules, a theory limits the operations that can be used for a particular conceptual variable, and makes explicit what those operations must be. Furthermore, a theory, by using a set of rules and hypothetical constructs to relate conceptual variables, allows the experimenter to derive *new* relationships. That is, a theory suggests how events in the world ought to be related even *before* these events have been observed. For example, the movements of the known planets led astronomers to predict that there must be another planet at a given distance from the sun. This theoretically guided search subsequently uncovered the existence of the planet Uranus.

When an experimental test of a prediction is validated, then the entire theory from which it was derived receives support. In addition, this new empirical finding is related by the theory to a body of previously established results. Theories thus help to formulate a network of interrelated facts and principles that explain some portion of reality.

In summary, theories are vital in any systematic approach to understanding complex phenomena because of the following:

1 They can generate predictions about complex functional relationships between variables.

2 They integrate many empirical observations that, on the surface, may appear to be dissimilar.

3 They separate relevant from irrelevant variables, and provide schema for organizing the relevant ones.

4 They allow for the derivation of nonobvious predictions (that is, statements about reality that one would not make on the basis of intuition).

5 They explain why variables function as they do, often by postulating hypothetical processes.

In psychology, theories are designed to relate changes in stimulus conditions to changes in the behavior of humans and animals, just as the theory of aerodynamics tries to relate changes in air currents to changes in the behavior of aircraft. Theories of attitude and behavior change also try to relate changes in stimulus conditions, attitudes, and personality variables to observed changes in verbal and nonverbal behavior.

But there are relatively few explicitly stated theories of attitude and behavior change (see Insko 1967 for a survey of existing theories). Why should this be so, if theories offer so many advantages? The simplest explanation for the absence of theory in this area is that building a theory that accounts for human behavior is the most difficult of all intellectual activities. Not only does it require an unusual level of creative ability, but it demands other attributes of the theory builder. One must have the confidence (that is, *chutzpah*) to risk being wrong when offering one's simplified view of reality. Built into any good theory is a method of proof that will allow for the possibility of the theory being disproven. In fact, much of the research a theory stimulates is designed to prove it wrong, in part or completely, and this is as it should be. Thus while this intellectual activity may yield large rewards, the likelihood of failure is even greater.

Theories of Attitude and Behavior Change

Obviously we think theories are important, and we would now like you to see for yourself what some different theoretical approaches look like. We have selected five general theories that deal with attitude change and/or behavior change. They vary in many ways: for example, some are formally stated as theories (as in the theory of cognitive dissonance) while others are more informal summaries of relevant variables and hypothesized inter-relations (the Yale attitude change program and the social learning approach). Some theories emphasize rationality and information-processing capacities (the Yale approach again), others focus on motivational dynamics (the Michigan group dynamics approach). While the instrument of attitude change in one theory is persuasive communication, in another it is the power of discrepant group norms, and in a third it is reinforcement contingencies. Despite different assumptions about the process by which an attitude may be influenced and the unit of behavior that can be changed, all these theories offer valuable insights into the psychological mechanisms by which we can be influenced by other people and, in turn, exert an influence on them.

The remainder of this chapter outlines the following five major theories of relevance to us as potential agents of social change: the Yale attitude change approach, the Michigan group dynamics approach, the theory of cognitive dissonance, attribution theory, and finally, social learning theory.

THE YALE ATTITUDE CHANGE APPROACH

Spend a few minutes watching TV the week before a presidential election and you will see a major form of influence in action: the persuasive communication. Listen to a salesperson tell you about the virtues of buying a particular car and you will see the same technique again. In some sense, the professor who assigned this book also uses persuasive communications when he or she lectures. Attempting to influence another person by arguing, presenting facts, drawing conclusions, and predicting future consequences is one of the most frequently used influence techniques. It is also the technique most of us think of when the idea of influencing someone is mentioned.

Carl Hovland, a professor of psychology at Yale University, headed a team of researchers concerned with influencing the morale of soldiers in World War II and with changing attitudes of civilians towards various aspects of the war effort. After the war he gathered a group of students and colleagues around him and developed what has since become known as the Yale approach to attitude change. In this orientation, an attitude is seen as an implicit approach or avoidance response (a favorable or unfavorable reaction) to some attitude object. Thus, an attitude is the *affective* or emotional reaction people have to the attitude object; it is their liking or disliking for a person, object, group of people, or symbol.

Attitudes (the affective component) are influenced or changed by altering the opinions or beliefs (the cognitive or knowledge component) that people have. Thus we should be able to change people's *attitudes* toward abortion by changing their *beliefs* about the age at which a fetus becomes a living human being or by altering their beliefs concerning the right of a pregnant woman to decide what to do with her own body. It is further assumed that the learning of new information in a persuasive communication will change beliefs. An effective communication will raise questions about abortion ("Is a three-month old fetus a human?") and provide whatever answers support the appropriate belief. If the incentives or anticipated rewards for accepting the answer to the crucial questions are substantial, people will change their beliefs about the human nature of an unborn fetus. They will come to believe that a three-month old fetus is (or is not) human.

Usually, the support structure for accepting the new beliefs is presented as part of the persuasive communication. Continuing with the abortion example, it might be argued that a three-month old fetus does not have a soul and, therefore, that no religious rules are being violated. Alternatively, the mental and physical health of the mother might be noted. To the extent that these consequences are valued by most people, opinions about a three-month old fetus—and, therefore, attitudes toward abortion—should change.

A relevant example of the important relationship between people's beliefs and their attitudes comes from a recent study on birth control. In a survey of 201 lower-income mothers, Crawford (1973a) found that those who had more favorable attitudes toward birth control also held more positive beliefs about the consequences of birth control (for example, it prevents unwanted pregnancies, it reduces worry about becoming pregnant, it helps solve the population problem, it makes sex more enjoyable). Those who had only a few beliefs, or were uninformed, had less favorable attitudes toward birth control.

Attention, comprehension, acceptance, and retention The Yale approach specifies four kinds of processes that determine the extent to which a person will be persuaded by a communication. The first deals with *attention*. Obviously, if people do not attend to the communication, no matter how persuasive, well organized, logical, and appealing the arguments, it will not change anyone's attitude. One must first get the intended audience to listen to what one has to say. Advertisers raise the volume of TV advertisements to attract and keep the attention of the viewer. Sexy women and men are presented in proximity to the object that the advertiser is selling,

Charles Revson, Inc.   Courtesy Bahamas Ministry of Tourism.

again often to attract attention. Advertisements are placed in appropriate magazines and time slots on TV so that the largest number of potential buyers will see the ad. (See Student Project #1 in Postscript D.)

The second process deals with *comprehension*. Even if the audience attends to the message, it is worthless if the audience does not understand what is said. No matter how sexy the person who holds the tube of toothpaste is, people will not change their attitudes toward the toothpaste if they do not understand the argument that toothpaste enhances one's love life.

The third process is *acceptance*. Acceptance of the arguments and conclusions of a persuasive communication is the result of the rewards that are presented in the communication. If a better love life is not your thing, then the message will probably have little or no effect on your opinions and your attitude toward the toothpaste will not change. On the other hand, if a better love life is what you are after, then you may decide a different toothpaste is worth a try.

Finally, for the communicated message to be effective, it must be remembered. *Retention* of the major point of the communication is the fourth critical process determining the efficacy of a formal communication. Since the action demanded (or suggested) in the communication is typically to be undertaken at a later time (when you are shopping or about to make love), the message must have some staying power if it is to have any impact at all. Slogans, catch phrases, and unusual examples are among the features that aid in the retention of a message.

Who said what to whom with what effect? In the Yale approach, the variables that influence the acceptance of arguments are placed into four categories. As you will see, the categories provide a useful way of organizing influence techniques.

Source. The effect of a communication on a person's attitude depends in part on its source. Some types of communicators are better able to influence people than others. For example, communicators who are highly credible are more persuasive than those who have low credibility. The two major components of credibility are *expertise* (factual knowledge) and *trustworthiness* ("good" motives). Sometimes, communicator characteristics that are irrelevant to the content of the communication are important, such as the communicator's race, physical attractiveness, perceived similarity to the audience, social status, sex, and speaking style. Some of the conceptual factors that affect communicator credibility are given in Table 3.2, along with an example of how a student may assess himself or herself with respect to these dimensions and then design a persuasion attempt accordingly.

Communication. Obviously, characteristics of the persuasive message can enhance or reduce its effectiveness. A poorly constructed and boring message is bound to have minimal impact. More subtle style and structural variables are likely to have effects as well; for example, (1) the order in which arguments are presented—should the strongest come first or last? (2) whether it is a one-sided or two-sided message—should you refute your opponent's position as well as present your own? (3) the explicitness of the conclusions—should you draw the conclusion for your audience or should you let them draw their own? Then there are a host of content characteristics: will a rational or emotional appeal work better? Should "scare tactics" be used? Should the message be short and sweet or should you overwhelm them with arguments? How much in the way of factual information and examples should be provided? These are all factors that might affect the persuasiveness of a communication.

Audience. Audiences and individuals vary in how persuasible they are. People who cannot understand your arguments will not be affected by them. "Persuasibility factors" such as a person's intelligence, self-esteem, dog-

TABLE 3.2
Factors Affecting Communicator Credibility (A Specific Example of a Student Attempting to Persuade Others Not to Use Drugs) (Adapted from Hart, Friedrich, and Brooks 1975)

Conceptual Factors	Examples of Assets	Examples of Liabilities	How to Do It
Power	Not much. I might be able to show them that my speech could save their lives.	They see me as just another person in class, with no special power to reward and punish.	Dramatize the horrors of drug addiction; back it up with plenty of painful examples.
Competence	They know from Bob's comment in class that I made the dean's list last semester.	I've never told them about my interest in drug addiction. Could be starting from scratch with most of them.	Mention early in speech about my work with the Crisis Center. Get that *Time* article.
Trustworthiness	Some of them know I really followed through on the group assignment. They shouldn't feel that I'd trick them.	This will be a new topic for me. Most unlike my last speech on the campus election scandal.	Don't have much to worry about here. Might remind them that I stuck with them when the professor tried to spring a quiz on us!
Good will	My strong suit. By now the group knows that I'm majoring in social work—who could hate a social worker?	No problem as long as I stay with hard drugs. Can't come down hard on pot.	Many of them smoke, so I'd better steer clear of the marijuana issue or they'll see me as caring more about preaching than about them.
Idealism	They know that I'm always up in the clouds and generally aspire to the same things they do.	Got to be careful not to get too carried away with the moral stuff. Stick to the "fully functioning human being" idea.	Should probably stress our common goals early in the speech *before* I mention drugs.

Similarity	I've been in class with them all semester. They know I dress and talk like most of them.	Could be a problem if I come on like Ms. Know-it-All. Have to steer clear of my religious views on the subject with these heathens!	Better tie this in with Claire's speech on legalizing pot. This should build more common ground between me and them.
Dynamism	My biggie! They know that they can't shut me up when I get committed to a topic.	No problem! (As long as I remember not to talk too fast!)	Pace yourself, baby, pace yourself.

matism, authoritarianism, and prior knowledge about the topic should have some effect on the ease with which he or she can be persuaded. Also important are the initial attitudes, involvement, and commitment of members of the audience. For example, the recent rise in the use of the gag rule by judges in popular trials and the requests by defense attorneys to move the cases to different cities represent beliefs that jurors should not be biased before the trial by information supplied by the news media. Presumably, jurors who have initial opinions about the guilt or innocence of the defendant will be more difficult to influence by the evidence presented at the trial.

Audience reactions. Audience reactions to a persuasive message ought to moderate the impact of the message. Opportunity for counterargument, whether out loud or to oneself, could make even the most well-meaning appeals ineffectual. How many times have you argued to yourself while listening to a persuasive message? Some communications and communicators may be more likely than others to elicit counterarguing. For example, taking an extreme position right away or using the "hard sell" may sensitize the audience to the manipulative intent of the communicator and result in inattention or even active disagreement.

Review As you can see, the Yale approach provides a structured list of variables or factors that have a direct bearing on the impact persuasive messages have on attitudes. As a formal theory it leaves much to be desired. However, it does direct our attention to very specific procedures that can be used to enhance the effectiveness of any change technique that relies on persuasive messages. It also provides some insights into why advertisements are structured as they are and why the campaign tactics of different politicians take the forms they do. If the audience does not attend to, comprehend, accept, and remember the arguments, the message will have little persuasive effect.

THE GROUP DYNAMICS APPROACH

In contrast to the more rigid "who said what to whom" methodology of the Yale tradition, the approach developed by Kurt Lewin at the University of Michigan is based on a field-theory orientation. It assumes that the individual is more than an isolated, *passive* processor of information who "computes" his or her final attitude from logical combinations of arguments. Instead, the person is viewed as a social being, with an intimate dependence on others for knowledge about the world and even about himself or herself. Recall how Patty Hearst was dependent on SLA members for all of her information—about other people's reactions to her kidnapping, about political ideas, about social acceptance, and even about where the next meal was coming from. Given the dependence we all have on other people, the groups to which we belong (and even some of those we avoid joining) take on major importance in shaping our beliefs and attitudes.

In this group dynamics approach, a major factor that causes people to change their attitudes, beliefs, and perceptions of the world is the *discrepancy* that exists between an individual's attitude or behavior and the *group norm*. Other people do not have to persuade you by argument; they need merely to hold a position that is different from yours—and you have to be aware of that discrepancy and to need their acceptance, approval, and recognition.

Pressures toward uniformity: If you can't beat 'em, join 'em Some time ago it was fashionable to use terms such as "hip" and "cool," and later the popular slogan was "right on." The spread of slang expressions and other fads (such as the nostalgia craze) can be understood in terms of the concept of *pressures toward uniformity*. More specifically, Lewin and his associates postulated that, in groups, various pressures exist that cause people to behave, think, and even feel alike. One of these pressures is the tendency of people in a group to reject and dislike those who are very different from the rest of the group members. A person who expresses opinions very different from those of the remaining group members or who dresses very differently or who acts very differently will be rejected by most of the group members. The possibility of rejection from a valued group generally causes people to become more like the remaining members of the group. (See Student Projects #2 and 4 in Postscript D.)

A classic demonstration of the tendency for group members to reject a deviate is provided in a study conducted by Stanley Schachter (1951). Groups of students met to discuss whether a juvenile delinquent, Johnny Rocco, should be treated leniently or harshly. A typical group consisted of nine individuals, three of whom were confederates told to play certain roles. One of the confederates took the modal or normative position of the six real students (either lenient or harsh), one took a position diametrically opposed to the normative position, and one was a "slider" who began by disagreeing but was eventually converted to the norm. Ratings by the real students of how much they liked these three types indicated that the modal person was most liked and the deviate (the one who consistently disagreed) was least liked. This result supports the claim that groups will reject those who disagree with the norm. If the group satisfies other needs of the individual, the possibility of being rejected could well make people adopt the normative opinions of the group.

Pressures toward uniformity may operate directly on opinions or indirectly by changing the way we perceive the world. For example, it is generally well known that a stationary light in the dark will seem to "move" if there are no other external references (that is, if one cannot see anything else). This is termed the *autokinetic effect*, and has been used by Muzafer Sherif (1936) to study the role of socially developed reference points in perception. In a typical study, subjects estimated the direction and distance that a stationary light moved. Of course, different people saw it moving in quite different ways. Some said it moved only small amounts, others claimed they saw quite elaborate and large designs being traced by the light. Each subject developed his or her own range of apparent light movements. After several subjects were put together and required to make judgments one after the other, a new *group range* developed. Small-movement subjects increased the size of the movements they saw while large-movement subjects decreased the size of movements they saw. In short, their judgments became more uniform as influence processes within the group came into play.

A different paradigm, developed by Solomon Asch (1956), shows that social pressures toward uniformity can affect what one does even when an *objective* reference exists. Groups of male college students were told they were in an experiment concerned with visual judgment. Lines were drawn on cards and the subjects were told to judge which of three lines were the same length as a standard line. The three lines were different enough in actual length so that everyone could easily pick the line that was objectively the same as the standard. The experimenter would hold up the standard line and the three comparison lines, and then ask each student to give his or her answer. However, all but one of the students (who was always the last one to answer) were confederates. On certain key trials, the confederates all chose one of the wrong lines. On 37 percent of these "conformity" trials, subjects agreed with the obviously incorrect response. Only 25 percent of all of the subjects were never influenced by the group majority, while about 30 percent almost always agreed with the majority. Even in the face of objective standards, a group norm can influence our behavior.

Examples of conformity effects in your own life are abundant. It was not very long ago when long hair on men was a sign of homosexuality. Miniskirts were once the rage. The "twist" was being danced in even the most posh night clubs. Experimenting with LSD was an "in" thing to do. Sit-ins were a regular occurrence on campuses. Political activism was more important than law or medical school. In short, the ideas and attitudes that we often embrace as our own come from the groups to which we belong.

Where your head is at is where other heads are   When a discrepancy or inconsistency exists between one person's position and that of others, the individual moves toward the normative position. An attempt to understand how these pressures toward uniformity operate at the level of a particular individual was developed by Leon Festinger in his *Theory of Social Comparison* (1954). Briefly, the central idea of this theory is that people need to compare themselves to others in order to evaluate their own abilities and opinions. For example, suppose you wanted to know if you were a "fast"

"Well, heck! If all you smart cookies agree, who am I to dissent?"

Drawing by Handelsman; © 1972 The New Yorker Magazine, Inc.

© Gahan Wilson.

runner. Let us say you could run one-fourth of a mile in forty-five seconds. Does this make you a fast runner? To find out, you would need to compare yourself to other people. If others were able to run the distance in less time, you would be a slow runner. If, on the other hand, everyone else was unable to get below a minute, you would be a fast runner. It is impossible to determine whether you are a fast runner without such a comparison because the very concept of "fast runner" is relative. In order to evaluate most abilities we need social information—about how other people perform.

Of course, we do not evaluate our abilities by comparing ourselves to just anybody. For example, the fact that you can do more complex algebra problems than a four-year-old does not mean you are intelligent. On the other hand, if your score on a calculus exam is below that of 80 percent of your classmates, your self-evaluation may well decrease. Social comparison theory argues that we compare ourselves primarily to *similar* others. That is, we select comparison groups on the basis of their similarity to us.

Our attitudes, as well as our ability evaluations, are also influenced by social comparison processes. Because there is often no objective standard against which to evaluate attitudes (as "Is democracy better than socialism?"), we can do so only by comparing ourselves to other people. In order to find out whether one's attitude toward nuclear power is extreme, valid, rational, or justifiable, the individual must know what other people think. If everyone else claimed that nuclear power was the most dangerous energy source there ever was, an initially middle-of-the-road position might be seen as very favorable toward the issue.

To the extent that a discrepancy exists between one's initial position and the norm of a reference group, there will be a *need* to reduce the discrepancy by either changing one's position in the direction of the norm, trying to influence the group norm, or rejecting the group as irrelevant. In the case of the nuclear initiative in California, for example, several engineers who were in favor of the initiative but who worked for the regulatory agency (which was against the initiative) quit their jobs. They rejected the group to which they originally belonged because their position was irreversibly discrepant from that of the group norm.

Review As you can see, the group dynamics approach stresses the impact that group norms can have on our attitudes and behavior. Persuasive messages play only a minor role in this approach. In addition, unlike in the learning view of the Yale approach, in the group dynamics approach change occurs because it is *motivated* by various socially based needs—the need to compare oneself to others, the need to evaluate one's own abilities and attitudes, and the need to reduce discrepancies between one's own position and group norms. Essential to this process is the power of the group to reward a member for compliance and punish for deviance. When a group satisfies an individual's needs and helps him or her to attain important goals, that group exerts considerable power over the values, beliefs, attitudes, and behavior of that person. Thus a person changes his or her attitude to satisfy various personal and social needs or to reduce unpleasant motivational states, rather than because of the weight of the arguments presented in a persuasive message. By de-emphasizing the role of the persuasive message, the group dynamics approach points out how we might be influenced by less obvious events in our environment. It emphasizes subtle social pressures that can operate whenever we are in the presence of other people. When our behavior is changed by the operation of group pressures we describe the process as *conformity*.

COGNITIVE DISSONANCE THEORY

The notion that people cannot tolerate discrepancy between their own and other similar people's attitudes was subsequently extended by Leon Festinger in his *Theory of Cognitive Dissonance* (1957). Festinger retained the notion that discrepancies or inconsistencies cause an uncomfortable tension that people try to reduce or eliminate, but he assumed the discrepancy itself to exist entirely within the individual's own cognitive system. While groups and social norms might still play a role in creating discrepancies, dissonance could be a nonsocial phenomenon. The major inconsistency was between different cognitions that a person held. For example, a person who smokes has the cognition, "I am a smoker." Information about the negative consequences of smoking produces a second cognition ("smoking is related to lung cancer") that is *inconsistent* or *dissonant* with the knowledge that the person smokes. After all, if smoking causes lung cancer, why smoke? One cognition does not psychologically follow from the other; it is hard to believe them both at the same time.

Cognitions or cognitive elements are bits of knowledge ("it is raining"), opinions ("I like the rain"), or beliefs ("the rain makes flowers grow"), either about the environment or about oneself. According to cognitive dissonance theory, cognitive elements can be in one of three relationships: dissonant, consonant, or irrelevant. In the smoking example, the cognition "I like the taste of cigarettes" would be consonant with the knowledge that the person smoked, while the cognition "pork should not be eaten raw" would be irrelevant.

In considering the cognitive elements that have been presented, it should be noted that some of the elements are linked to the person's behavior and others to the environment. This implies that changes in the environment and in the person's behavior will produce changes in that person's cognitive elements. If he or she stopped smoking, the cognitive element "I smoke" would obviously change to "I don't smoke." Thus a critical point in the theory is that one of the ways in which a person can change a set of dissonant cognitive elements to a set of consonant elements is by changing his or her behavior, if that behavior comprises one of the dissonant elements.

Factors affecting the magnitude of dissonance   To increase its predictive power, the theory differentiates between situations producing more dissonance or less dissonance. The magnitude of dissonance that the human organism experiences is a function of three conceptual variables. The first of these is the *importance* of each of the cognitive elements. For example, if it were not important to our hypothetical smoker that he or she might die of lung cancer (because the person was eighty years old and had lived a full life anyway), then there would be little dissonance produced by the two cognitions, "I smoke" and "smoking is related to lung cancer." There would be great dissonance, on the other hand, if our subject did not want to die or become ill.

The second variable affecting the amount of dissonance a person experiences is more difficult to conceptualize. Up to this point, our hypothetical person has been walking around with only two or three cognitions in his or her head. Actually, the human organism knows, believes, and has opinions about many more things. The magnitude of dissonance a person is experiencing at any one time is therefore a function of the number of dissonant and consonant cognitions that exist at that time. More specifically, the greater the *ratio of dissonant to consonant elements*, the greater the dissonance that is felt. In the previous example of the smoker, there were two cognitions that were dissonant with each other. Adding a third cognition, "my cigarettes have less tar and nicotine than others," reduces dissonance by increasing the number of consonant elements. "I smoke" is consonant with "my cigarettes have less tar and nicotine than others." By making dissonance a function of the ratio of dissonant to consonant elements, the theory provides for a dramatic reduction in dissonance merely by the addition of one or two consonant elements.

What may be called *cognitive overlap* is the third variable that helps determine the amount of experienced dissonance. Cognitive overlap refers to the functional equivalence of the objects or activities represented by each cognition. For example, in a choice between a Volkswagen and a Ford Mustang, the two cars have more features in common than a new car and a new sailboat. That is, there are more cognitive elements functionally similar between two alternatives when they share comparable features. There is less dissonance when one chooses either of the cars than when one chooses the car over the boat, since in the latter decision, many functions served by the boat are not shared by the automobile. Thus the magnitude of dissonance aroused by a decision between alternatives is inversely related to their cognitive overlap (that is, the less they have in common, the greater it is).

Dissonance is more likely to occur in a given situation if one *commits* oneself to some course of action while remaining aware of one's *volition* to do otherwise. These two features of dissonance were added to the original theory by Brehm and Cohen (1962) in order to clarify some predictions from the theory.

Behavioral commitment (public action) is important in the theory for two reasons. First, the observer does not have to make questionable inferences about the person's *covert* decisions, thus permitting more certainty in defining the conditions under which dissonance occurs. Secondly, public action is more anchored in external reality (and "fixed" in time as a fact) than are private responses (thoughts, values, motives, intentions, and attitudes). As a result, it will be more difficult to change the cognition of one's public behavior than the cognition of one's private attitude. Thus, when dissonance exists between a behavioral cognition ("I spent an hour working on a task") and an attitudinal cognition ("the task was boring"), the theory can predict which of these two cognitions will change. The cognition pertaining to the behavior will remain the same, while the attitudinal cognition will change so as to agree with the behavior ("the task was actually rather interesting").

How to reduce dissonance   This last point raises the crucial issue of the importance of dissonance *reduction* in the theory. Once dissonance is aroused, there will be a *need* to reduce dissonance. This need to reduce the psychological tension created by inconsistency motivates a wide variety of behavior. It is only by observing the presence and characteristics of dissonance-reducing behavior that one can infer that dissonance must have been present. In other words, since dissonance and magnitude of dissonance are hypothetical states, there is no direct, independent metric of them. Rather, they can be inferred only from the antecedent conditions that *ought* (by theoretical definition) to generate dissonance, or from the theoretically derived consequences of what should happen if dissonance were present.

It is possible to reduce dissonance in many ways: (1) by attempting to revoke the decision, (2) by lowering the importance of the cognitions or the decision, (3) by increasing the cognitive overlap between cognitive elements (searching for or misperceiving aspects of functional equivalence), and (4) by adding consonant elements to change the ratio of dissonant to consonant ones.

To illustrate how these techniques might be employed in a simple example, imagine a professor who, after much mental conflict, gives up a position at one college for a position at another. Her old college has many good features that she loses in going to the new one, and the new one has a number of negative features that she inherits by her choice. These two sets of cognitions contain elements that introduce dissonance following the decision to change colleges. She can then attempt to reduce her dissonance in several ways:

1   By either seeing the new job as only temporary, or actually allowing herself to be persuaded back to her old job or to a third alternative
2   By changing her evaluation of the importance of those positive features of the old college and the negative features of the new (for example, it does not matter if the old college has more intelligent students; lack of research facilities at the new college is not so important because she can spend more time doing neglected library research)
3   By minimizing the differences between the ability of her colleagues at the two schools, between the faculty clubs, and so forth
4   By seeking out colleagues who like being at the new college and those who have also left the old one, or finding unexpected virtues related to being at the new college (like the availability of good delicatessens)

Dissonance-arousing situations   There are two classes of decision-making situations that the theory describes as areas of relevant application: forced public compliance and free-choice decision-making. In the first type of situation, situational pressures induce the person to behave in a way that is counter-attitudinal. For example, a student who is personally in favor of legalizing marijuana may be required to argue against legalization as part of a speech-class exercise. When the student presents the counter-attitudinal speech, some dissonance will be aroused. However, even greater dissonance will occur if the student volunteers to give this particular speech than if he or she gives it to avoid receiving an F in the course. The amount of dissonance that will be experienced in a forced-compliance situation, and therefore the magnitude of the pressure to reduce dissonance, is an inverse function of the *justification* for engaging in the compliant behavior. That is, the more reasons that initially exist for behaving in this way, the less dissonance there will be. In this example, the student could reduce dissonance by changing his or her attitude toward legalization of marijuana in the direction of the speech that was made, by denying that he or she made the speech, or by adding further reasons to justify this act of public compliance.

Of course, not all situations that confront humans force them to comply to some demands. Some situations involve free choice. However, dissonance can also be produced in these instances. In the forced-compliance situation, the greater the magnitude of initial justification, the *less* the amount of dissonance experienced. In a free-choice situation, justification is also an important variable but in a slightly different sense. For example, in a choice between one of two record albums, there are usually positive and negative aspects associated with each album. One album may have great songs, but the group singing them might not be good, while the opposite may be true of the other album. A choice is always a potentially dissonance-producing situation. After one album is chosen, the loss of the *positive* qualities of the unchosen album is dissonant with the knowledge that that album was not chosen. Specifically, if the album with good songs is chosen, then two dissonant cognitions are, "I like the group that sings on album A," and "I have chosen album B." It does not follow that album B should be chosen if album A has the preferred group. However, choosing album B is consonant with the fact that album B has the better songs. It is possible to derive the following prediction about justification from the above analysis. More dissonance should exist *after* the decision is made if the two alternatives are nearly equally attractive. That is, the less justification (the fewer reasons) one has for choosing one or the other alternative, the greater the dissonance. In this case, justification involves the difference in initial attractiveness of the two alternatives. For example, if one album is clearly superior in all respects to another, then choosing it produces very little dissonance.

When dissonance is produced following a choice, the main method of dissonance reduction is to *increase* the attractiveness of the chosen alternative and *decrease* the attractiveness of the unchosen alternative. In the record album example, the album that is chosen will be seen as more and more attractive. The person may claim that not only are the songs better, but he or she was tired of the other group and had too many of its records already.

Until the music lover completes this difficult choice, he or she is in a state of conflict. It is only after one album is chosen that dissonance (which is a *post-decisional* phenomenon) must be considered if we are to understand the changes in perception, attitude, and behavior that will follow.

Dissonance and religious conversion An example of dissonance theory comes from the discussion in the first chapter of the Reverend Moon cult. There we pointed out how people are invited to come voluntarily for a weekend retreat, how no one coerces them to believe in the philosophy of the movement, and how people are encouraged merely to join in the activities. These techniques are precisely those that should produce considerable dissonance: "I do not believe in this philosophy [Reverend Moon's]"; "I am behaving like others who do believe in this philosophy, even though there is little justification (force or pressure) for me to behave this way." An obvious way to reduce the dissonance caused by the inconsistency in these cognitions would be to change the first cognition to "I believe in Reverend Moon's philosophy."

Dissonance theory even provides an explanation for the strong emphasis that religious movements such as Reverend Moon's place on winning new converts. One mode of dissonance reduction is to increase social support (to proselytize) for one's beliefs and ideas. The magnitude of experienced dissonance should be enormous when people join religious cults, given the major change in lifestyle, the rejection of previously valued friendships, and the acceptance of new ways of behaving that are required. By getting other individuals who initially valued the same things as the cultists to reject their old ways and join the cult, those who are themselves recent converts can point to this additional social support to rejustify *their* own decision. They must have made the right choice, otherwise why would so many other people be choosing to join the group?

Using less to get more Another important implication of the theory that can be seen in the above example relates to the way it deals with *justifica-*

tion and *rewards*. For the first time, we see that it may sometimes be better to use less to get more.

When people are induced to publicly comply with decisions and actions that are contrary to their beliefs and attitudes, a private change in their attitudes is most likely when (1) they perceive that the discrepant action was engaged in freely (high choice), and (2) there was not sufficient external reward or anticipated punishment to "coerce" the action. When the justifications for discrepant behavior are barely adequate to induce compliance, the person cannot readily point to sources outside himself or herself as the instigators of the behavior in question. The locus of the public compliance, then, is more likely to be internal. When this occurs, the need to be consistent changes private events to bring them in line with the public commitment. Then values, motives, beliefs, perceptions, and attitudes may all be modified—sometimes dramatically so—to make them consonant with the public behavior. Might gets compliance, but not attitude change. To change attitudes according to dissonance theory, first induce behavior change under manipulated conditions of high choice and minimally adequate justification, then provide an opportunity for the new attitude to be expressed. *Voilà* a changed attitude.

Review Dissonance is always aroused by the discrepancy between two or more relevant cognitive elements, when one of these elements relates to the person's behavior (his or her choice or compliant act) and the other relates to the person's internal or external environment. The magnitude of dissonance is a function of the ratio of dissonant to consonant elements, the importance of these elements, and the cognitive overlap between them. The initial amount of dissonance will be a function of the number of reasons (consonant elements) for either complying with external demands or choosing one alternative over another. The greater the initial magnitude of dissonance, the greater will be the drive to reduce dissonance either by changing one or more of the dissonant cognitive elements or by adding new consonant elements. One can reduce dissonance either by changing one's behavior, by changing one's internal environment (attitudes and perceptions), or by making more ambitious efforts to alter the external environment.

ATTRIBUTION THEORY

> *The Watergate incident was Richard Nixon's fault. Everyone knows the man is a dishonest, manipulative individual whose ends justified his means. He should have come forward and accepted full responsibility for his actions. That a president could act that way makes it even more disgraceful.*

Placing the blame on the *individual* is common practice in our culture. We hold *people* responsible for their actions. We evaluate *people* according to standards. We explain bizarre behavior by inventing unseen processes that reside somewhere inside the person. Without establishing a satisfactory motive, we are reluctant to convict someone of murder.

The aim of attribution theory is to explain the way in which people try to account for human actions. Why do we not explain Nixon's behavior by pointing to his working conditions, the necessity for secrecy in world politics, the fact that his behavior was being openly criticized, the threats on his life, the pressures of presidential life, the fact that he was surrounded by advisers who were recommending even more secrecy (and acting in a paranoid fashion), or the fact that many others in politics were also engaged in one or another dishonest activity?

The theory attempts to describe the way in which most of us generate reasons for our own and other people's actions. It provides a description of part of our thinking process. It is, therefore, a *cognitive* theory. There are no motivational constructs in the theory (such as a *need* to reduce dissonance or *pressures* toward uniformity). Instead, it attempts to understand how we *perceive* the motives, intentions, and causes of people's actions. The theory does not tell us whether the motives we infer others to have are the true ones; it simply provides an explanation for the way in which we reach our conclusions about motives and other causes for a person's actions.

The origin of attribution theory can be traced to the influential writing of Fritz Heider, in *The Psychology of Interpersonal Relations* (1958). Heider formalized the ways in which people ("observers") try to make sense of the behavior of "actors." It is interesting to note that when ordinary people try to understand behavior, they are acting as naive *psychologists*. They observe people's actions in a given setting and proceed to actively search for the meaning of, reasons for, and causes of these acts. From observing these actions, they make inferences about intention and responsibility. Given any observed performance, our naive psychologist makes *attributions* about the relative contribution of ability, motivation, luck, and other potential causes to the outcome. Ultimately, then, Heider's approach is to examine the *phenomenal* (or conscious) experience of the individual in order to determine the cognitive categories used to explain other people's actions and the processes that govern when these different categories of explanations will be used.

Heider's formulation spawned surprisingly little research compared to the other theories we've mentioned. It remained for Harold Kelley (1967, 1972a, 1972b), Edward Jones (1965, 1971, 1972), and others to construct newer versions of attribution theory that were able to spark research interest.

Situation versus disposition   Most researchers classify all of the potential causes that we might use to explain someone's actions into two kinds: situational (or external) and dispositional (or internal). Situational attributions identify factors in the social and physical environment that are causing the person to behave in a particular way. For example, if we saw someone hard at work and explained this behavior in terms of the money that would be earned, the grade that would be achieved, or the praise that would be forthcoming, then we would be using situational attributions. Such explanations assume that most other people would act in the same way if they were in that situation—in other words, the person's behavior says more about the nature of the situation than about the person. Furthermore, it is assumed that without those situational factors, the person would not engage in the given behavior.

In contrast, dispositional attributions identify the causes of behavior as residing within the individual and thus reflect some unique property of that person. Explanations of someone's hard work in terms of personal attitudes, religious beliefs, or character traits would all be examples of dispositional attributions.

Having emphasized the situational versus dispositional dichotomy, two questions naturally arise. Which type of explanation do people use more frequently, and what factors or variables affect when one or the other type will be used? Attribution theory argues that people are more likely to explain another person's actions by pointing to what seem to be that person's dispositions, such as his/her intelligence, generosity, dishonesty, anger, mental ill health, and so on, rather than to aspects of the situation, such as the way others react to the actions, the amount of money paid to the person, and so on.

Factors affecting the use of dispositional versus situational explanations
With regard to variables that affect which type of explanation is more likely, attribution theory suggests four major factors. First, people are especially likely to make dispositional attributions when the behavior is *non-normative* and differs from the common mode of action. For example, suppose we see a student behaving rudely toward a very well-liked and respected professor. We are far more likely to attribute this atypical behavior to something special about the student ("an insensitive boor," "a pathologically shy guy," for example) than to attribute it to something in the situation (such as a remark made by the professor).

I did NOT call you a liar. I said you were intellectually dishonest!

Dispositional attributions also become more common the more often a person engages in the behavior. Our explanation for the behavior of someone who is *always* on time for class is that he or she is a punctual or compulsive person. We see the behavior as reflecting some consistent character trait, rather than occurring in response to variable situational factors (such as people who arrive on time for class get better seats, hear important announcements, have their previous class nearby, and so on).

Dispositional attributions will also increase if the same kinds of behaviors occur in many different situations. The only satisfying explanation for the behavior of a person who returns lost wallets without removing the money, does not cheat on exams, and never tells lies is that the person *is* honest. We believe that it *must* be something about the person because the behavior is so consistent across so many situations. Personality theory is, therefore, a theory of dispositional attributions.

Finally, attribution theory argues that dispositional explanations will be more frequent when the situational causes of behavior are hidden or perceived as weak. Subtle social pressures of the type we emphasize throughout this text are often ignored in favor of dispositional explanations. Telling us the "choice is up to you," even when someone has manipulated us into adopting a particular position, is a technique that causes many of us to then use a dispositional explanation for our behavior (the appearance of free choice = no situational determinants, which in turn implies it must have been something inside of the person).

Harold Kelley developed a way of summarizing the first three of these four factors, namely normativeness, temporal consistency, and cross-situational consistency. Examine Fig. 3.1. The rows of the cube represent people, the columns situations, and the layers different times or occasions. Let us suppose that person 1 is the individual whose behavior we are trying to explain. Suppose the behavior is "dancing the hustle." We ask, why is this person dancing? We would be more likely to infer that it was something about the music or another aspect of the situation that was the dominant cause of this behavior if everyone else was dancing as well (if a column of this cube was filled with the same event). Alternatively, we might be more likely to say it was person 1's unique attitude toward dancing (or some other internal attribute) that was the culprit if we observed person 1 dancing in many different situations, such as at home, at dances, and in the park (if a row of the cube rather than a column was filled with the same event). Similarly, we should be more likely to assume that it was something about person 1's feelings, abilities, and/or attitudes with regard to dancing if we observed him or her dancing to every song (or on every oc-

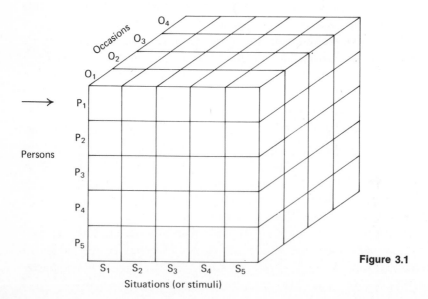

Figure 3.1

The Milgram shock box, with a compliant person becoming an obedient subject.

casion) that was played (if a layer of the cube was filled). Interesting questions arise when we have information about only *one* cell in the cube or when the same event occurs in both a row *and* an column of the cube. Since attribution theory is about the way we think, you can discover much of what it predicts by constructing hypothetical examples of your own and making inferences about the causes of *your* hypothetical actor's behavior.

Attributional biases   Attribution theory points out two ways in which our inferences about the cause of a person's behavior might be biased. First, we might believe that a person did something because of an attribute unique to the person (his or her attitude, motive, or mental state) when at least part of the *real* cause for that person's behavior was an aspect of the situation (or vice versa). In fact, any time we infer that a given action was primarily the result of either a disposition or an aspect of the situation, we are ignoring the obvious facts that behavior does not occur in a situational vacuum and that people bring things with them to the situation that affect how that situation will influence them. In other words, we ignore the fact that a person's behavior is always the result of *both* aspects of the situation and aspects of the person.

In the classic study by Stanley Milgram (1974) on blind obedience to authority, the majority of subjects continued to deliver, on demand, potentially lethal shocks to an innocent "victim" (confederate). Psychiatrists had predicted that such a reaction would be rare and indicative of abnormality. A large majority of students when learning of this experiment are convinced they would never have gone all the way, but would have been part of the brave, rebellious minority. Such attributional analyses underestimate the powerful social forces operating on the subjects in the situation, forces that would most probably cause *you* to react as they did. The danger of this bias in attributions is that it makes you more vulnerable to situational forces precisely because you do not acknowledge their potential power.

A consequence of our tendency to point to dispositions as the major causes of people's behavior is that it leads us to expect and perceive more consistency in the behavior of others than actually exists. We tend to be aware that we vary on most traits and behaviors "depending on the situation." We are not always generous or gregarious—it depends on a lot of things. But at the same time, we perceive *others* to be more situation-free and disposition-bound. And they, in turn, see us as consistent yet perceive their own reactions as dependent on the situation.

The second way in which our "naive" causal explanations are often biased is that they oversimplify the state of the world. Most of the time, our actions are *multiply* determined; that is, there are many different causes for any particular action. By pointing to Nixon's dishonesty as an explanation for the Watergate incident, people ignore many other factors that were also partly responsible for his actions. Any particular action is the result of many causes and our tendency to point to one or two of them to explain the action greatly oversimplifies the truth.

We know ourselves the way we know others   Attribution theory also suggests that at times we can overestimate the *consistency* in our own behavior, as well as that of other people's. Daryl Bem (1972) used this insight to offer an alternative explanation to cognitive dissonance theory—self-perception theory. He began by attacking the claim that people have attitudes that influence behavior. Instead, he argued that the responses we give on attitude questionnaires are often *constructed*, on the spot, as explanations for our own past behavior. Attitudes are not reflections of what we are predisposed to do, but leftover vestiges of what we once did. Behavior influences the development of our attitudes and other internal states because we infer the latter from our observations of the overt behavior and the context in which it occurs. Where the behavior is constrained or controlled by external forces it is not perceived as attitude-instigated. As perceived freedom of choice increases so that the behavior is free to vary, the observer infers that his or her attitudes, values, and needs are the cause of the behavior.

An experimental paradigm used in self-perception research (borrowed from dissonance research) requires that people write or give a speech that is against their initial position on a topic, a variable is manipulated, and post-treatment attitudes are measured. In one study, Snyder and Ebbesen (1972) required that college students write an essay taking the position that students should have *no control* over the courses they take in college. Half of the students were told the choice to write the essay was completely up to them, although it would help the experimenter out if they did so. The other half, however, were simply told they had to do it as part of the study. After completing the essays, the students were asked to indicate how much control they personally thought students should have. Those who were given a "choice" indicated that students should have less control than did those who were given no choice in writing the essay. Thus students in the "choice" group inferred from this isolated, fifteen-minute activity that they believed students should have little control over the courses they take. They obviously weighted this minor essay-writing activity, actually done to get a requirement of the introductory psychology class out of the way, very heavily when they then estimated their attitudes. Clearly, a single, recent, salient activity can be seen as more representative of the way one behaves than it actually is. (Chances are that the students in this study will never have to write a speech on that topic again nor had they ever done so before.)

With regard to our own behavior, it may be that we always infer what we believe from our most recent actions. Alternatively, it may be that for many issues and topics we are in exactly the same position when it comes to self-knowledge as we are when it comes to knowledge of other people. The students in the above study overemphasized the importance of the essay they gave because they had rarely discussed or even thought about the issue before. If this reasoning is correct, we might expect the effects of recent inconsistent behavior to be minimal when people have had a long history of prior action that is relevant to the topic. Getting active workers in the women's rights movement to write speeches in favor of sexism may very well have little or no effect on those people's attitude toward women's rights. When asked to report their position, they would have too many other activities to draw upon that would nullify the importance of the one speech in their estimation of what their attitude is—or ought to be.

Bem (1972) poses this type of argument in the following proposition:

> To the extent that internal cues are weak, ambiguous, or uninterpretable, the individual is functionally in the same position as an outside observer, an observer who must necessarily rely upon those same external cues to infer the individual's inner states. (p. 2)

For strongly held attitudes on which we have taken a public stand, we do not have to rely on external cues to tell us what we believe. The inference process of attribution is called into play when the situation is novel and unfamiliar, and when there has not been a strong public commitment or substantial investment of thought on the issues. Then you can bet that people come to believe in what they do rather than do what they believe.

Review Attribution theory directs our attention to some important general principles concerning the way individuals attempt to explain their own and other people's actions. The normativeness of an action, its temporal consistency and cross-situational consistency, and the obviousness of one or more situational constraints affect our tendency to infer dispositional versus situational causes for specific action. Influence strategies must be sensitive to a person's subjective interpretation because they constitute that person's view of reality. Similarly, knowledge of attributional biases tells us about sources of vulnerability to social influences that are often exploited without our awareness. Finally, an understanding of attribution processes makes clear the fact that we often greatly oversimplify the real causes of a person's behavior when we infer one major cause for the action.

SOCIAL LEARNING THEORY

If most of us do overemphasize the impact of dispositions on our own and other people's behavior, maybe we should look more carefully at the kinds of situational influences that can control the way people behave. Social learning theory attempts to do just that. It argues that there is a continuous reciprocal interaction among a person's behavior, events going on inside of the person (thoughts, emotional reactions, expectations, and so on), and the environmental consequences of that behavior. Thus, most human behavior leads to consequences that *feed back* on behavior, either maintaining or changing the probability of similar behavior in the future. For example, if every time you spoke to people they ignored you, the chances are that the rate of your initiating conversations would go down. On the other hand, if people acted interested and said you were a good conversationalist, it is likely that you would continue to seek out opportunities to talk to them. The theory assumes that the mechanism by which a person's future behavior is changed is a form of learning. The basic idea here is that the likelihood of a specific behavior is determined by the consequences the person expects will follow the performance of that behavior. If the consequences are positive or rewarding, the behavior is likely to recur. If they are negative or punishing (fear arousing, and so on), the behavior is not likely to recur.

Learning about relationships   Learning can proceed by any number of techniques. People can *directly experience* the consequences of their own behavior. When a black child asks a teacher about black history and the teacher ignores the child, the child will learn that if he or she wishes to find out about black history, asking the teacher (response) will not lead to answers (consequences).

People can also learn by looking. That is, they can see how other people's behavior is followed by specific consequences. Another black child in the same class will learn, merely by watching how the other child's questions go unanswered, not to ask questions about black history. This technique of learning by observation has also been called "modeling," "observational learning," and "vicarious learning."

People can also learn by listening or reading. They hear people talk about how specific behaviors and consequences are related. That is, they hear that if X is done, then Y will occur. From these symbolic rules they can learn that the behavior that X represents will probably be followed by the consequences that Y represents.

Other kinds of "if-then" relationships can also be learned. For example, one can learn which emotional states (sexual arousal, fear, and so forth) are likely to be produced by various stimuli. Such learning can proceed by direct experience, by observation of others, or by the hearing or reading about symbolic relationships between stimuli and emotional responses. For example, people can be emotionally aroused, either negatively or positively, by certain words such as "Jew," "cop," "commie," without having *directly* experienced negative or positive consequences when faced with the real people represented by these words. Thus, the word "hippie" can arouse a negative emotional state in some people simply because the word has been associated with other words that produce negative arousal, such as "bad," "dirty," "lazy," and so on. In more general terms, people can learn that certain stimuli are associated with other stimuli. When these stimulus-stimulus relationships are learned, previously neutral stimuli can come to arouse negative or positive emotions, or stimuli that were previously arousing can come to be neutral. Thus it is possible for some people to be emotionally aroused by what seem (to other people) to be neutral stimuli simply because they have learned a different set of associations for such stimuli.

Discrimination and generalization. When people learn "if-then" relationships, they typically do not learn them in a vacuum. They also learn the conditions under which these relationships are true. For example, children eventually learn that only when a stove is on (or has just been turned off) are they likely to be burned if they touch it. When the stove has been off for a long time, touching it will lead to a different set of consequences (not being burned). In this way, people *discriminate* among situations or stimulus events. They learn to expect *different consequences* for the same behavior when different stimulus conditions are present. Different behaviors occur in different situations because people learn to *expect* different consequences in the two situations. Necking in front of one's parents is not as common as necking in one's dorm room or car because the consequences are different in the two cases.

It is interesting to consider that people who act in ways we would call "crazy" often do so because they fail to discriminate among situations that most other people do distinguish. For example, kneeling in the middle of the street with one's hands folded praying to God might seem strange, but exactly the same activity in a church is judged to be quite normal. Similarly, urinating in a classroom is seen as extremely bizarre even though the identical activity in a bathroom is perfectly appropriate. The concept of discrimination does not imply, however, that everything a person does will be different in the two situations. It is perfectly reasonable to read in both classrooms and bathrooms. Only certain activities are not appropriate in both situations. When variations in stimulus situations are responded to in similar ways, the person is said to *generalize* across these situations. When the person responds differently to stimulus variations, it is said that he or she *discriminates*.

Reinforcements and standards   Anticipated consequences control the way people behave because some consequences are rewarding and others are punishing. However, it is important to remember that the value of various reinforcements is relative and not absolute. That is, what is rewarding for some people may not be so for others. Some people might be willing to work for hours to own a 1958 Chevy convertible. Others would not want the "pile of junk." The fact that you find a given object (or event) rewarding does not mean that the same object will be desirable to everyone else.

Social learning theory points out that we determine many of the consequences of our actions by the standards we set for ourselves. When we meet those standards, we reward ourselves with compliments, pats on the back, and/or special treats. Similarly, when we fall below those standards we punish ourselves by derogating ourselves or denying ourselves the things we like. In fact, depression and feelings of inadequacy may result from people setting such high standards for themselves that they almost always fail to meet them. Just as with more overt activities, personal standards can be acquired in many ways: via instruction, direct experience, or imitation of relevant models. In some cases, models will display standards that are different from the ones they impose on others. For example, parents who smoke and drink but tell their children not to are providing inconsistent standards.

Cognitive processes   In order for past consequences to have effects on future behavior, the individual must *remember* what happened as well as *expect* it to happen again. A person who starts to blush and stammer when speaking before a group is probably doing so because of memories of past criticism or embarrassing moments in this type of situation. Therefore, cognitive processes that affect how well we can remember our direct or vicarious experiences ought to affect how we behave.

Planning is another important cognitive activity that is likely to affect what we do. By anticipating the probable outcomes of different actions, we can develop alternative courses for future behavior. Such plans eliminate the necessity of figuring out what to do by trial and error. National defense and foreign policy often consist of elaborate "contingency plans." What would we do if . . . ? The kinds of consequences that are anticipated in these plans determine the response that is eventually chosen. In fact, in the realm of national policy, most of the disagreement centers on what the possible consequences of various actions *will* be, rather than on what the long-range goals *should* be.

Review of some specific change techniques   Figure 3.2 provides an excellent summary of the four major factors that affect a person's behavior (performance accomplishments, vicarious experience, verbal persuasion, and emotional arousal) and the kinds of events that control each factor. Basic to many of the modes of induction given in this outline are these four general techniques.

Direct reinforcement (or performance exposure) is one technique for changing behavior. The basic idea is that people will learn if they directly experience new consequences of their behavior. To get people to perform

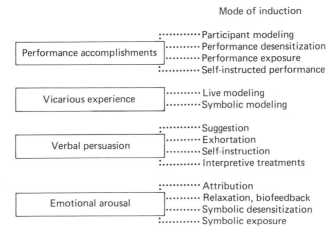

Fig. 3.2 Hypothetical and conceptual variables affecting performance: from social learning theory (adapted from Bandura 1976).

a complex behavior, this technique often requires that we "shape" people's responses by having them perform a graded sequence of steps of increasing difficulty. In this way, people come to learn new responses and to experience directly the consequences of these responses.

Extinction is another technique for manipulating behavior. In order to get people to stop a particular behavior, we merely prevent the consequences that they expect will follow their action from occurring, while letting them continue to perform the behavior.

Vicarious reinforcement and vicarious extinction whether live or symbolic are often useful techniques. The results obtained by using direct experience can sometimes be achieved more efficiently by having the person see other people performing in a certain way and receiving rewards or punishments as a result.

Instructions, rules, or communications (or verbal persuasion) can all be used to change behavior. The technique is to present the person with rules (or symbolic, verbally stated, response-reinforcement relationships) that are different from those the person believes are true. A related technique is to train people to present *themselves* with their own instructions, rules, and symbolic reinforcements or punishments. That is, train people to give themselves persuasive messages in particular circumstances.

Next we will examine whether these excursions into theory are fanciful or fruitful. We have already violated Sherlock Holmes' admonition that "It is a capital mistake to theorize before one has data." Having already done so, it remains for us to consider the nature of the data that have been collected from the research generated by each of the theories. In so doing, let us hope to be able to lay to rest such critical commentary on the virtue of theory as Voltaire's "Let us work without theorizing . . . 'tis the only way to make life endurable" (*Candide*), or Emerson's "The astonishment of life is the absence of any appearances of reconciliation between the theory and the practice of life" (*Journals*, 1844).

In the previous chapter we suggested that the only way to evaluate the ideas presented in theories was to conduct research. In this chapter, we shall examine some examples of the kinds of research that have been generated by people who are interested in attitude and behavior change. This examination represents our first careful look at attempts to systematically evaluate ideas about social influence.

reviewing representative research

Surveying for Golden Ideas

Most news programs predict with considerable accuracy who will win a political election when only a fraction of the vote is known. Such accuracy results from the fact that they use information about the behavior of people in exactly the same way that we have been urging you to do. They concentrate on *base rate* information that has been gathered in an unbiased or representative manner. Several different methods are used, including telephone polls of how individuals voted, analyses of voting records and demographic characteristics of selected districts, and specialized sampling procedures. All of these methods have the same goal: to select a small group of individuals whose voting behavior will be *representative* of the entire population. By examining the percentage of individuals who voted for a particular candidate in this sample, one can predict how the entire population will vote. Obviously, the key to this technique is the ability to observe accurately the relevant behavior of a sample of people who, in all critical respects, represent the population. Thus we can think of such surveys as providing us with an assessment of the population base rate of people's attitudes on specific issues.

Surveys are used for more than predicting how people will vote. For example, Elihu Katz and Paul Lazarsfeld (1955) used an interview survey technique to uncover the sources in a person's life that have the greatest influence on his or her decisions. They began with a series of questions posed to 800 families in the midwestern city of Decatur, Illinois (population of 60,000 at the time of the study). One of their most important findings was that each community within the city seemed to have *opinion leaders*. These individuals exerted a strong effect on the formation and change of many other people's opinions. So by altering the attitudes of this subgroup who serve as significant mediators of any persuasive attempt, it should be possible to change the opinions of communities at large.

This "two-step flow of communication" was nicely illustrated in a study of how doctors are persuaded to prescribe a new drug for their patients. Most of the doctors were unwilling to be innovators or accept the advice from drug salespeople directly. Rather, they waited to be persuaded by opinion leaders among their medical colleagues. Other doctors, who were willing to take more risk in being first to prescribe the drug, exerted a very powerful effect on the majority of doctors who had not been influenced by the sales pitch. Incidentally, in this study, a very interesting "nonobvious" measure of change was used: the actual druggist's records, which revealed the names of the doctors who prescribed the drug as well as when it was prescribed. Such a record allowed researchers to map the temporal pattern of social influence among doctors in this sample.

Surveys have also been used to determine what particular social problems people are concerned about. For example, two surveys of public opinion were conducted, one in 1949 and one in 1975, in which the respondents, who were all living in large cities (population over 500,000), were asked to name the worst social problem facing their community. Table 4.1 presents the results of both surveys. As can be seen, crime has moved to the top of the charts. Information such as this can be useful in deciding where to concentrate large-scale efforts for social and political change.

We often have our own intuitions about public opinion. The utility of surveys is that they sometimes contradict those intuitions. A recent survey of community attitudes toward local police was taken in a small Bay Area city in northern California (Crawford 1973*b*). People were asked, "How much respect do you have for the police?" and "Do you think there is any police brutality in the city?" At the same time, members of the city police department were asked to *predict* how people would answer these two questions. As you can see from Table 4.2, the police greatly *underestimated*

TABLE 4.1
**Survey of Attitudes about the Worst Community Problem in 1949 and 1975 by
Residents of Large Cities** (*San Francisco Chronicle*, July 28, 1975)

1975		1949	
Problem	*%*	*Problem*	*%*
Crime	21	Poor housing—slums	37
Unemployment	11	Transportation	31
Transportation—traffic	7	Unsanitary conditions	12
Education	6	High taxes	8
Poor housing—slums	5	Corrupt police	7
High cost of living	5	Crime	4
Drugs	4	Racial problems	3
High taxes	4	Juvenile delinquency	3
Unsanitary conditions	3	Lack of recreation	3
Ineffective police	3		
Juvenile delinquency	3		

the respect people had for them, as well as *overestimated* the public perception of the extent of police brutality. Had this survey not been taken, a department concerned with police-community relations might have spent considerable time and money attempting to change a negative public image that was actually nonexistent.

Unfortunately, the results of surveys do not provide a direct pipeline to the truth. As with every form of data collected, they must be interpreted with care. For example, as part of a project on legal decision making, Ebbe Ebbesen and Vladimir Konecni (1975) asked superior court judges to indicate what factors were most important in deciding how to sentence convicted felons. Several different survey methods were used. In one, the judges were asked to rate the importance of several factors, such as severity of the crime, prior record, the sentence recommendation made by the probation department, and so forth. In another technique, the judges

TABLE 4.2
Survey Results of Opinions about the Police (Adapted from Crawford 1973)

		Public opinion	*Predictions by police of public opinion*
How much respect do you have for the police?	A great deal	66%	24%
	Some	23%	30%
	Hardly any	11%	46%
Do you think there is any police brutality in the city?	Yes	32%	49%
	No	68%	51%

were given simulated cases that differed along various dimensions (for example, in some the defendant was convicted of forgery and had a prior record, in others the defendant was convicted of armed robbery and had no prior record). The judges were asked to give sentence recommendations exactly as they would if these were real cases. The results of these two survey methods were then compared to the sentencing decisions that the same judges made in comparable sentencing hearings in actual cases. To obtain this information, one team of observers sat in sentencing hearings and recorded what went on, while others coded the contents of the county clerk's files on each case.

The results were clear and quite provocative. The survey data did *not* agree with the actual decisions made by judges. In the simulated decisions, judges sent over 60 percent of all of the defendants to state prison. In real life, only 13 percent were sent to state prison. In the ratings, the judges claimed that severity of the crime was *the* most important factor, when in real life the probation department's recommendation seems to be the most important factor. In addition, while the extent of a defendant's prior record had only a minor effect on actual prison sentences, in the survey it was rated as the second most important factor. In short, the results of the survey presented a very different picture of the attitudes and opinions of judges from that obtained by observing the way they actually behaved in court.

There is many a slip between the practice and the preaching. We are often unaware of the variables that influence our behavior and, conversely, we often point to assumed sources of influence that can be shown to be ineffectual. When judges are asked what they would do in a sentencing procedure, their answers do not correspond with what they in fact do. This may occur because their concerns about their public image influence them more when they are in the courtroom than when they are evaluating a hypothetical case. In addition, decisions they make about particular flesh-and-blood defendants are likely to be more humanized and tolerant than those based on more stereotypic conceptions of a "felon." The above study cautions us to not rely too heavily on any one survey measure but to employ several different measures that together converge on the attitude under investigation.

Surveys are not inert measuring devices that leave no residue after being used. Often, the simple act of responding to opinion questions can *sensitize* people to arguments they would not have generated on their own. Alternatively, filling out a survey can be the act that cements and *bolsters* a person's previously amorphous position. The act of deciding where one stands on a previously unconsidered issue may even *create* new opinions and beliefs.

For example, in studying the impact of erotic films on sexual attitudes and sexual behavior, researchers have tried to assess initial level of experience by means of detailed sex questionnaires and check lists of photos of different positions of intercourse. These studies show that exposure to erotic films has no significant effect on subjects' attitudes. There were, however, some slight effects reported on sexual behavior—somewhat greater sexual activity at home on X-rated film nights. But surprisingly, the most arousing event in these studies turned out to be the act of filling out the questionnaires, which sensitized the subjects to sexual issues about which they were previously unaware. Or, by fantasizing about which of the ten coital positions they hadn't tried but might like to, the subjects got more turned on than they did watching other couples engaging in filmed erotic action (see Kutschinsky 1971; Mann, Sidman, and Starr 1971).

Surveys may have consequences other than the intended one of *gathering* information about existing beliefs, attitudes, and values. They may *provide* new information on issues that are unfamiliar. This occurred in the recent (1976) California election on the ballot initiative to declare a five-year moratorium on the building of new nuclear power plants in the state. Many survey respondents became aware for the first time that nuclear wastes present a major problem because they must be stored for thousands of years without leakage. "And how can they be protected against earthquakes?" one wondered. In a different vein, the results of the Kinsey surveys on the sexual behavior of the American male and female established, to some degree, social standards of what was acceptable common practice.

Survey results can often point out inconsistencies in opinions and beliefs that people already hold. Once the inconsistencies are made salient, they may cause major reorientations in a person's belief system. For example, Rokeach (1971) reports that he has dramatically changed the attitudes of college students merely by pointing out inconsistencies in the students' belief systems. After surveying student attitudes he reported back the result that students who had very positive attitudes toward equality (as a value) rarely said they participated in civil rights activities. When students learned of these results, not only did their attitudes toward civil rights change to conform to their positive attitude toward equality, but they were also more likely to join the NAACP and renew their membership in it if it had lapsed.

Politicians sometimes exploit survey results to create "bandwagon" effects by publicizing straw polls as forecasts of election victories. In fact,

sometimes primary *defeats* are distorted in order to create a propaganda effect. After a 1972 primary election in which McGovern received only 35 percent of the vote, campaign workers told the news media that this really amounted to a victory in a state that was initially so strongly against him.

The Value of Experimental Research

While surveys constitute one of the most common examples of research based on attitude theory, they are *not* experimental in nature. They do not and cannot tell us the variables and processes that influence people's attitudes and behavior. On the other hand, you may not be interested in whether dissonance or pressures toward uniformity really exist. You may care only about producing change. The underlying processes are then irrelevant. In this case, a catalogue of techniques for producing change with associated costs would be quite satisfactory, and the best strategy would be to select as many techniques as one's resources would allow and apply them all at once in a "total push" approach.

However, by putting all these techniques together, we would never be able to tell which of them were actually effective and which were not. If your goal is to know *why* people change, then more work is required. It is necessary to conduct *experimental* research in order to isolate the true causes and the mechanisms of behavior.

If you are not familiar with the features of the experimental approach, as compared to other forms of gaining knowledge, you should now read Postscript A before proceeding.

To review the essential features briefly, however, experiments attempt to eliminate all but one (or a few) explanation(s) for the way people behave in a given situation by *controlling* for the effects of variables that are not of immediate interest. For example, if an experimenter wanted to know whether it was the expertise or the trustworthiness of a communicator that was causing people to change their attitudes, one of these (for example, expertise) would be systematically varied with the other held constant. By *randomly assigning* people in the audience to either a high or low expertise condition, the experimenter can usually balance out existing individual differences (in intelligence, age, ego-defensiveness, and so on). There should be an approximately equal number of male and female, intelligent and unintelligent, attentive and inattentive people in both groups. Random assignment of subjects to experimental treatments prior to exposure to the independent variable is one of the most important characteristics of an experiment.

Experiments also always involve *comparisons*. In order to know whether expertise is an important factor in attitude change, we must compare the effects of communicators of different expertise. If appropriate comparisons are not made (against no-exposure control groups, treatments at different levels, base-rate changes), we cannot know whether it was the expertise or some other characteristic of the communicator, the communication itself, the audience, or something as irrelevant as the temperature in the room that was producing the result.

Another feature of experimentation is its heavy reliance on careful *observation* and *measurement*. If we are interested in knowing how group pressure affects people's attitudes, the first thing we must do is decide how we are going to observe or measure people's attitudes. Unless we develop objective procedures for measuring attitudes and behavior, we cannot tell whether our observations reflect real effects or our personal biases. There are many different ways to assess attitudes and behavior, as you will note when reading through the examples we use throughout the text as well as detailed discussions of this point in Postscript B.

Finally, experiments can be fun. The excitement of learning something no one else knows or of finding the answer to a personally important issue should not be overlooked.

The Yale Attitude Change Approach

Nothing is so unbelievable that oratory cannot make it acceptable.
Cicero, 46 B.C.

Although only one example of the Yale attitude change program will be presented, the procedures used in many of the experiments were similar enough that they can be characterized by this overview.

EXPERIMENTAL PROCEDURE

A message was constructed by the experimenter that advocated a position discrepant from that of the intended audience, and that contained supporting arguments, evidence, and implications. Usually there was only a single, relatively short message of unitary direction and organization. With few exceptions, the communication dealt with issues that were not ego-involving for the subjects. The attitudes were rarely socially significant ones, nor were they based on extensive prior experience or personal commitment. Carl Hovland (1959) cogently described the rationale for this feature of the attitude-change experiment: "We usually deliberately try to find types of issues involving attitudes which are susceptible to modification through communication. Otherwise, we run the risk of no measurable effects, particularly with small-scale experiments." Typically the source of the communication was explicitly stated. In cases where it was not, there was usually implicit endorsement of the message by the researcher. This legitimization of the message by the researcher's sponsorship may have increased the likelihood that subjects viewed the advocated position as one that was reasonable, or at least worthy of consideration.

The setting was always designed to guarantee the salience of the communication above all other possible stimuli. There were no competing messages, background distractions were minimized, and a serious, testlike atmosphere was created. Such experiments are novel situations for subjects, because they are often in an unfamiliar place (such as a laboratory), and they are engaging in unfamiliar behavior. Thus the usual social supports for their original attitude position are not available, since it is not possible for them to talk to other subjects, to question the experimenter, or to obtain more information than is given in the communication.

Subjects were most often college students who participated in order to obtain money or course credit. Once they were in the experimental room, they were a "captive" audience, with only "extrinsic" justification for being there. They did not come to hear a speech, but rather to obtain rewards that were totally irrelevant to the communication itself. They were generally more intelligent, more highly motivated, and better able to critically analyze the logical structure of a communication than were individuals from a noncollege population. With the use of captive audiences there was no problem of subject self-selection. That is, the audience was *not* composed of only those who came to hear this particular speech; rather, it was made up of people with a variety of attitudes toward the communication. However, there was always the possibility that there would be self-selection in exposure (attention) to some or most of the content of the communication.

Three general response measures were included in most of these experiments: (1) an assessment of the efficacy of the independent variable, (2) a measure of comprehension or retention of the message, and (3) a measure of attitude toward the position advocated.

For the first of these measurements, the experimenter collected information on whether or not the subject appropriately perceived the stimulus conditions defined as the independent variable. For example, was the subject made anxious by an anxiety-arousal manipulation, or were differences in communicator credibility between two sources accurately perceived by the subject? Whether the subject paid attention and learned the information presented was usually measured by multiple-choice, objective response tests of comprehension and retention of the message. These were administered some time after the message was delivered.

Attitudes toward the advocated position were determined by self-report opinion scales in which the subject described the degree to which he or she endorsed a particular verbal statement. Agreement or disagreement with the position were usually indicated by placing a response at some point along an *affective* dimension (often from "Like X extremely," through a point of neutrality, to the other end of the scale, "Dislike X extremely"). Opinions were often measured both before and after the communication, in order to obtain a measure of individual change. When they were measured only after the communication, they were compared with the after-only scores of a no-communication control group in order to determine what effect the communication had on those opinions. However, we might note here that when there was a pre-measure of attitude, the experimenter often tried to conceal the relationship between it and the subsequent experimental influence attempt. This was done by separating the two measures in time, or by using different physical locations, research personnel, and rationales for data collection.

The time spent in the entire experiment was usually short, less than one hour. The duration of the communication was brief, and the time between exposure to it and the measures of retention or opinion change was often a matter of minutes. Therefore, most conclusions must be limited to immediate or short-term effects, except in a few cases when the time dimension was purposely manipulated.

Now that you have a general idea about the typical structure of the Yale attitude change experiment, you are in a better position to review and evaluate a representative experiment in this area.

COMMUNICATOR CREDIBILITY

According to the Yale approach, the identical persuasive communication should produce greater attitude change when it is presented by a highly credible source than when it is presented by an uncredible source. Since trustworthiness is one aspect of credibility, Carl Hovland and Walter Weiss (1951) conducted an experiment that examined the role of the trustworthiness of a communicator in the effectiveness of a persuasive message.

The design of the study was quite simple. The subjects, undergraduate college students at Yale University who were in an advanced history course, filled out an opinion questionnaire a week before receiving persuasive communications. For some subjects, the communicators associated with particular communications were trustworthy, while for others they were untrustworthy. Immediately after the communications were presented, another opinion questionnaire was administered. Finally, a third opinion questionnaire was filled out one month later, to assess whether any effects would be lasting ones.

Keeping the overall design in mind, the details of the study were as follows. Five days after the administration of the first opinion questionnaire (designed to be a general opinion survey conducted by the "National Opinion Survey Council"), one of the experimenters entered the history class as a guest lecturer. The fact that he was a guest lecturer, who had never come to class before, was meant to dissociate his activities from the previous opinion questionnaire. He stated that he had been asked by the regular professor to discuss the psychology of communications with the

Washington Star Syndicate, Inc.

class, since so many of their attitudes and opinions were determined by what they heard and read. He then added that before he talked with the class, he wished to have "live data" from a survey that attempted to assess the role of newspaper and magazine reading as a vehicle of communication. After obtaining these data, he would discuss them with the class at a later session. The lecturer continued by summarizing what he wished the class to do: namely, read a few newspaper and magazine articles on controversial topics, which were based on the best available information. After reading the articles, the students would be expected to fill out a short questionnaire on their reactions to them.

Each student was then handed a booklet of four readings on four different issues:

A. Should antihistamine drugs continue to be sold without a doctor's prescription?
B. Can a practicable atomic-powered submarine be built at the present time (1950)?
C. Is the steel industry to blame for the current shortage of steel?
D. As a result of TV, will there be a decrease in the number of movie theaters in operation by 1955?

For each topic, respectively, the high and low credibility sources were:

High	*Low*
A. *New England Journal of Biology and Medicine*	Magazine *A* (a mass circulation, monthly pictorial magazine)
B. Robert J. Oppenheimer	*Pravda*
C. *Bulletin of National Resources Planning Board*	Writer *A* (a widely syndicated, anti-labor, anti-New Deal, "rightist" newspaper columnist)
D. *Fortune* magazine	Writer *B* (an extensively syndicated, woman movie-gossip columnist)

As a check on this manipulation, the perceived trustworthiness of each of these sources had been rated by students in the initial opinion survey.

For each topic there were both pro and con versions of the communication. Each booklet contained two pro and two con communications, one on each topic. One pro communication and one con communication were attributed to a low-credibility source, while the other two communications were attributed to high-credibility sources. All the communications on a topic were identical (thus controlling for the effects of characteristics of the communication) and differed only in the attributed source. There were a total of twenty-four different booklets, with different combinations of topic, source, and advocated position.

After the students had read the booklets, they were immediately given a second questionnaire that differed in format from the previous opinion survey. This questionnaire first asked general questions about the subjects' reactions to the articles and then asked for their own opinions. At the end of the questionnaire, there was a multiple-choice, factual quiz. The final questionnaire, given one month later, was identical to the second one (in order to assess delayed effects).

In considering the results of the experiment, we would first want to know how trustworthy the subjects judged the various sources. Did they indeed see the high-credibility sources as more trustworthy than the low-credibility sources? To answer this question, the ratings from the very first opinion survey can be used. The results can be seen in Table 4.3. A cursory glance at these results overwhelmingly confirms the hope that the high-credibility sources were seen as more trustworthy than the low-credibility sources.

TABLE 4.3
Percentage of Subjects Rating Source as Trustworthy
(Adapted from Hovland and Weiss 1951)

Topic	High credibility	Low credibility
A	95	6
B	94	1
C	81	17
D	89	21

What about attitude change? In order to consider the amount of attitude change produced, we have to be able to summarize the data. The summary technique used in this experiment was to take the percentage of subjects who changed their attitude (from questionnaire 1 to questionnaire 2) in the direction of the communication and subtract from that the percentage of subjects who changed in the opposite direction from the communication. Thus, if the communication were pro, the percentage changing in the pro direction minus the percentage changing in the con direction would be our measure (net change) of the amount of attitude change pro-

TABLE 4.4
Net Changes of Opinion in Direction of Communication for Sources
Judged Trustworthy or Untrustworthy by Individual Subjects
(Adapted from Hovland and Weiss 1951)

	Net change (percentage)	
Topic	Sources judged trustworthy	Sources judged untrustworthy
A	25.5	11.1
B	36.0	0.6
C	18.2	7.4
D	12.9	17.2
Average change	22.5%	8.4%

duced in the population. The net changes of opinion in the direction of the communication for sources judged to be trustworthy or untrustworthy are presented in Table 4.4.

These results show that the *difference* between the average (across topics) net change for the trustworthy sources and the untrustworthy sources was 14.1 percent. The probability of this difference being caused by chance is .03 (that is, it would occur by chance only 3 times in 100); thus this difference appears to be a real one. In other words, subjects are more likely to change their attitudes in the direction of a communication if they think that it came from a trustworthy source than if they think it came from an untrustworthy one.

But why does a trustworthy source produce more change? Do the subjects pay more attention to the speech and thus learn the arguments better? Data from the fact quiz in the second questionnaire indicated that there was no difference between the trustworthy and untrustworthy source conditions in the amount of information recalled about the communications. Apparently, trustworthiness affects the *acceptance* of the communicator's conclusions rather than attention to and comprehension of the arguments.

One virtue of this study is that the procedures and measures were quite consistent with the theoretical orientation adopted by the researchers. *Net change* in the population is precisely the right measure to take if one is interested in mass persuasion. In addition, the use of four different communicators and communications as well as attempts to influence people in both the pro and con direction increase our confidence in the *generality* of the trustworthiness effect. An interest in mass persuasion implies that one wants effects that will work across a variety of topics and trustworthy sources. Had but one topic and source been used, we could not know whether the results might generalize beyond the particular instances studied.

SO WHAT, IF WHO SAYS WHAT TO WHOM?

The Yale approach exerted its influence on social psychology for over twenty years. From the massive amount of experimental research conducted, we outline for you some major conclusions generated from these studies.

The persuader[1]

1 There will be more opinion change in the desired direction if the communicator has high credibility than if he or she has low credibility. Credibility is:

a) Expertise (skill, knowledge, and judgment relevant to correct stand on issue).

b) Trustworthiness (motivation to communicate knowledge without bias).

2 The credibility of the persuader is less of a factor in opinion change later on than it is immediately after exposure.

3 A communicator's effectiveness is increased if he or she initially expresses some views that are also held by the audience.

4 What an audience thinks of a persuader may be directly influenced by what they think of the message.

5 The more extreme the opinion change the communicator asks for, the more actual change he or she is likely to get.

a) The greater the discrepancy (between the communication and the recipient's initial position), the greater the attitude change, up to extremely discrepant points.

b) With extreme discrepancy, and with low-credibility sources, there is a falling off in attitude change.

6 Communicator characteristics irrelevant to the topic of the message can influence acceptance of its conclusion (for example, race).

How to present the issues

1 Present one side of the argument when the audience is generally friendly, or when your position is the only one that will be presented, or when you want immediate, though temporary, opinion change.

2 Present both sides of the argument when the audience starts out disagreeing with you, or when it is probable that the audience will hear the other side from someone else.

---

[1] Our organization and presentation of the material in this section is adapted largely from Abelson and Karlins (1970). Support for these propositions, as well as additional findings, can be found in the following: Hovland, Janis, and Kelley (1953); McGuire (1969); and Insko (1967).

3 When opposite views are presented one after another, the one presented last will probably be more effective. (The greater impact of what comes first is called a primacy effect; the greater effectiveness of the last message is a recency effect.) Primacy effects are more predominant when the second side immediately follows the first, while recency effects are more predominant when the opinion measure comes immediately after the second side.

4 There will probably be more opinion change in the direction you want if you explicitly state your conclusions than if you let the audience draw their own, except when they are rather intelligent. Then implicit conclusion drawing is better.

5 Sometimes emotional appeals are more influential, sometimes factual ones. It all depends on the kind of audience.

6 Fear appeals: The findings generally show a positive relationship between intensity of fear arousal and amount of attitude change if recommendations for action are explicit and possible, but a negative reaction otherwise.

7 No final conclusion can be drawn about whether the opening or closing parts of the communication should contain the more important material.

8 Cues that forewarn the audience of the manipulative intent of the communication increase resistance to it, while the presence of distractors simultaneously presented with the message decreases resistance.

The audience as individuals
1 The people you may want most in your audience are often least likely to be there. There is evidence for selective seeking and exposure to information consonant with one's position, but not for selective avoidance of information dissonant with one's position.

2 The level of intelligence of an audience determines the effectiveness of some kinds of appeals.

3 Successful persuasion takes into account the reasons underlying attitudes as well as the attitudes themselves. That is, the techniques used must be tailored to the basis for developing the attitude.

4 The individual's personality traits affect his or her susceptibility to persuasion; people are more easily influenced when their self-esteem is low.

5 There are individuals who are highly persuadable and who will be easily changed by any influence attempt, but who are then equally influenceable when faced with countercommunications.

6 Ego-involvement with the content of the communication (its relation to ideological values of the audience) decreases the acceptance of its conclusion. Involvement with the consequences of one's response increases the probability of change and does so more when source-audience discrepancy is greater.

The persistence of opinion change

1   In time, the effects of a persuasive communication tend to wear off.

a)   A communication from a positive source leads to more rapid decay of attitude change over time than one from a negative source.

b)   A complex or subtle message produces slower decay of attitude change.

c)   Attitude change is more persistent over time if the receiver actively participates in, rather than passively receives, the communication.

2   Repeating a communication tends to prolong its influence.

3   More of the desired opinion change may be found some time after exposure to the communication than right after exposure (the *sleeper effect*).

Group Dynamics

> *Let them exalt him also in the congregation of the people, and praise him in the assembly of the elders.* Psalms 107:32

One of the more interesting aspects of the group dynamics approach is its emphasis on the effects of active participation during group interaction. Thus, in one of the first attempts to show the power that group forces exert on individuals (Lewin 1943), housewives were asked to openly discuss the possibility of using organ meats (hearts, lungs, brain, liver, kidneys, and so on) instead of the more common cuts. (As with the Yale approach, these studies began during World War II when food rationing and conservation were important concerns.) A discussion leader guided the conversation so that the positive aspects of organ meats (such as their low cost and nutritional value) were discussed. Compared to a formal informational lecture on the benefits of organ meats, these active discussions left housewives who participated more favorable toward the idea and more likely to indicate they would try organ meats at home.

Actively taking a position in the presence of other uncritical (and sometimes supportive) people may be sufficient to exert a powerful impact on one's self-image (witness the example of converts to Reverend Moon's philosophy discussed in Chapter 1 and elaborated upon in Chapter 6). Many encounter groups also employ this technique. Some call it role-playing, others call it sharing, and still others refer to it as "interpersonal trusting."

THE INFLUENCE OF ROLE-PLAYING ON OPINION CHANGE

Irving Janis and Bert King (1954) conducted a careful experiment designed to assess the effect of role-playing in the presence of other people who were neither supportive nor hostile. As in Kurt Lewin's study of changing attitudes toward unfashionable meats, these researchers were interested in whether passive listening or active participation would have a greater impact on attitudes. By eliminating the group discussion and interchange that were present in that earlier study, they were able to focus more intensely on the question of active versus passive exposure.

Role-playing, like source credibility, is an extracommunication variable. That is, in testing the difference between role-playing and passive listening, the experimenter would want to make sure that the same communication content and structure were used for each method. In the previously described credibility study this was accomplished by attaching different source names to the same communication. However, for role-playing variables, the experimenter cannot merely ask some subjects to role-play and others to listen to a communication. This is because subjects who are role-playing may use persuasive arguments that are different from what the listening subjects receive. If this happened, the experimenters would not know whether a difference in attitude change was due to the role-playing itself, or to the different arguments used.

To control for this possibility and also maintain the idea of group participation, Janis and King used three communication topics, and tested subjects three at a time. Each subject had to role-play an attitude position on one topic and listen to the remaining two subjects role-play the attitude position on the other topics. Thus each subject passively listened to two communications. However, these latter communications were constructed from the role-playing speeches of the two other subjects. This point might be clarified by describing the procedure in more detail.

The overall design of this study was similar to that used by Hovland and Weiss (1951). Four weeks before the experimental sessions, an opinion questionnaire was administered to a college class. Embedded in the questionnaire were three key opinion items: the number of movie theaters that would be in existence three years hence, the total meat supply available to the United States in 1953, and the number of years it would take to find a cure for the common cold. The subjects' rating of the number of theaters, amount of meat, and number of years constitutes the opinion measure.

When the three subjects arrived at the experimental session, they were led to believe that they were taking part in a research project that had been designed to develop aptitude tests for assessing oral speaking ability. They were then given an outline that contained information relating to one of the three topics. The outline included arguments advocating lower numerical opinion estimates than those previously given by the subjects (thus constituting the discrepant position). With these outlines as a guide, the subjects were asked to give informal talks. While one of the three subjects gave a talk, the other two listened. Thus each subject gave one talk and heard two. After the third talk was completed, the subjects were asked to fill out a second questionnaire that contained self-rating items about performances and about their opinions on the topics.

The results of this experiment can be stated rather simply. For two topics (movie theaters and meat supply) the role-playing subjects changed their opinions more in the direction of the communication than did the passive listening subjects. For the common cold topic there was no difference in the amount of attitude change produced by the two methods. Furthermore, all of the changes in attitude were in the direction of the communications.

These results present a problem for us. If we wanted to use this role-playing technique to produce attitude change, we could never be sure that it would be the most effective method since, in this experiment, the role-playing technique worked for only two of the three topics. How can we determine why role-playing was less effective for the topic of curing colds? Fortunately, Janis and King used a good general technique at the end of each experimental session that supplied them with some hypotheses about this problem. The technique they used was an extended interview with each subject. After the subjects had completed the second questionnaire, they were interviewed about their reactions to the entire experiment. From the interview, the researchers found out that the subjects who had to talk on

Washington Star Syndicate, Inc.

the cold cure issue tended to be less *satisfied* with their role-playing performance than subjects who gave talks on the other issues. Thus the effectiveness of role-playing may depend on how satisfied the subjects feel with their performance. However, we cannot be sure this is true. It is only an interesting hypothesis based on informally gathered data. To check on its validity, a second experiment that *systematically replicated* part of the first experiment was conducted by King and Janis (1956).

The purpose of this second study was to see if the crucial factor in producing attitude change by role-playing was the satisfaction felt by subjects when they improvised well. To test whether such satisfaction was more effective than improvisation by itself, King and Janis conducted a three-group experiment. Only one topic was used (students were asked to believe that at least 90 percent of college students would be drafted after graduation, and once drafted would have to serve three years military duty). In one group, subjects used an outline to improvise a speech (which was tape-recorded by the experimenter). In another group, subjects merely read a similar prepared speech into a tape-recorder. In the third group, subjects silently read the prepared speech to themselves.

From the results of this experiment, the authors concluded that more attitude change was produced in the direction of the communication when the subjects improvised than when they either read aloud or to themselves. Furthermore, since subjects in the reading aloud condition were more satisfied with their performance than were subjects in the improvisation condition, King and Janis concluded that *improvisation*, or active participation, was more important than *satisfaction* in producing attitude change. In conclusion, these two studies seem to suggest that the role-playing of attitude positions counter to one's own can be a powerful technique in producing attitude change.

SOME RESEARCH FINDINGS ON THE POWER OF GROUPS

An isolated individual does not exist.
He who is sad, saddens others. Saint Exupéry, *Flight to Arras,* 1942

As with the Yale approach, the effects of groups on attitude and behavior change have been studied intensively. Here is but a small sample of some of the findings relevant to our current concerns. A more in-depth treatment is available in Kiesler and Kiesler's (1969) thoughtful presentation of research on conformity.

1 People's opinions and attitudes are strongly influenced by the norms and goals of groups to which they belong and want to belong.

A "smash-in," where college students mindlessly destroy an automobile— loving every destructive blow.

2 People are rewarded for conforming to the standards of the group and punished for deviating from them.

3 Groups are more effective in inducing conformity pressures on their members when they meet their members' social-emotional needs as well as fulfill instrumental goals.

4 Members of groups have more influence power over each other when they are part of groups that are high rather than low in cohesiveness.

5 The sheer frequency of communication by the group's members is a major determinant of interpersonal influence. People who talk most and say positive things are most likely to emerge as influence leaders.

6 The influence of neighbors increases with their proximity.

7 Groups may facilitate the release of normally inhibited behaviors in members by diffusion of responsibility, imitation, anonymity, and behavioral contagion. This *deindividuating* effect of being "submerged in the group" could lead to release of violent antisocial behavior or of restrained prosocial behavior, such as crying or being openly affectionate, depending on the circumstances.

8 The structure of communication networks within a group affects the way in which information is processed (filtered through a central position or shared by all in decentralized networks).

9 People who are most attached to the group are probably least influenced by communications that conflict with group norms.

10 Opinions that people make known to others are harder to change than opinions that people hold privately.

11 Audience participation (group discussion and decision making) helps to overcome resistance to persuasion.

12 Resistance to a counter-norm communication increases with the salience of one's group identification.

13 The support of even one other person weakens the powerful effect of a majority opinion on an individual.

14 A minority of two people can influence the majority if they are consistent in their deviant responses.

15 The need to maintain group consensus can lead to "group think," in which individual critical evaluation is suppressed and personal opinions are disregarded.

Cognitive Dissonance Theory

There are those who would misteach us that to stick in a rut is consistency —and a virtue, and that to climb out of the rut is inconsistency—and a vice. Mark Twain, "Consistency," 1923

Cognitive dissonance theory is well known for the nonobvious predictions about attitude change that have been derived from it. Consider, for example, the intuitively obvious claim made by the Yale approach that credible, trustworthy, attractive, and well-liked communicators ought to produce more attitude change than less attractive and less credible ones. Dissonance theory, combined with the role-playing method discussed previously, suggests an exception to the rule: a case in which a disliked communicator may be more effective than a liked one.

I'LL TRADE MY TUNA SANDWICH FOR YOUR GRASSHOPPER

Suppose you are "forced" to do something that you would rather not do— for instance, eat a fried grasshopper. Since most people in our culture would initially have the cognition, "I do not like fried grasshoppers, they're ucky," the knowledge that they were biting off the head of the grasshopper and chewing on the eyes could create dissonance under the right circumstances. Specifically, dissonance would arise if the justification for eating the grasshopper were minimal. There is probably more justification to comply to discrepant requests made by attractive, well-liked people than requests made by disliked, unappealing people. Therefore, greater dissonance should be experienced when the unpleasant behavior of eating the grasshopper is requested by a *negative* communicator than by a *positive* one.

An attempt was made to test this idea by using several different ways to induce Army reservists to eat fried Japanese grasshoppers. In one of the two most crucial conditions, a positive communicator made the request, while in the second, a negative communicator made the request. To control for the differences in general affect in these two conditions, a third group of reservists had a humorous experience while eating. To control for differences in respect between the attractive and unattractive communicators, a fourth group ate at the request of a respected (but not necessarily well-liked) group leader. Finally, in a fifth group subjects were not given a persuasive communication but simply requested to eat a grasshopper. To better appreciate the flavor of this study, we will describe the procedure in the author's own words.[2]

Procedure

All groups were brought into the reserve center's kitchen area by a sergeant and seated around a large table. Throughout the experimental period fresh coffee was available and the men helped themselves to it. The experimenter introduced himself, gave a brief statement on what the experiment was about, and had them fill out the first page of the questionnaire. The experimental variation was then introduced, after which they were exposed to the grass-hoppers. After they had finished eating, they finished the questionnaire. The experimenter then thanked them for their cooperation, asked them not to discuss the experiment with others, and excused them. The experiment lasted about forty minutes. The specific instructions and experimental variations in the five conditions were as follows:

In every group and experimental condition the experimental period started with the following statement being read by the experimenter:

Good evening. I am Dr. _____ and I am doing research for the Army Quartermaster on food acceptance. The Army wants to find out more about how the men feel about new, different, or unusual foods, because the new Army will consist of smaller, more mobile units than we had in World War II. These new units will be more on their own, without all the support personnel and field kitchens that we had before. So the kinds of food you'll have to eat, if you want to survive, may not be as good as they were before. You may have to eat food that you may not have eaten before, and live off the land more. So tonight we are going to find out what your attitudes and reactions are toward an unusual food that you might have to eat in an emergency. This food is grasshoppers.

After reading this statement, the experimenter handed out the three-page questionnaire and had the subjects fill out the first page, which included a rating scale on grasshoppers as a food. After they had completed the first page of the questionnaire, the experimenter then read the following statement in every group and in every condition: "This is a voluntary experiment, and no one has to eat grasshoppers if they don't want to." At this point, the instructions and procedures varied according to the experimental condition, as follows:

(a) Positive communicator. In this condition, the experimenter acted in a friendly, warm, permissive manner throughout the experimental period. Op-

---

[2] Smith, E. E. Methods for changing consumer attitudes: A report of three experiments. Project Report, Quartermaster Food and Container Institute for the Armed Forces (PRA Report 61-2), pp. 13–17, February 1961. Reprinted by permission of The Matrix Corporation.

Army reservists pondering the delights of eating a fried grasshopper.

erationally, this consisted of frequently smiling, referring to himself as Smitty rather than Dr. Smith, sitting on the counter rather than standing, saying that the men could smoke if they wished, that they should relax and enjoy themselves, etc.

In addition (in this condition as in the negative communicator condition), after stating that the experiment was voluntary, the experimenter said, "However, in order to get as many people as possible to try one, I will pay, right now, fifty cents to each person who eats one."

While saying this, the experimenter took a handful of quarters out of his pocket, showing them to the subjects, and paid fifty cents to every man who ate a grasshopper. It was explained that it was only necessary to eat one grasshopper to earn the fifty cents. After all those who wished to eat a grasshopper for fifty cents had done so and received their money, the experimenter said, "Now go ahead and eat."

(b) Negative communicator. In this condition, the experimenter acted in a formal, cool, official manner throughout the experimental period. Operationally, this consisted of ordering rather than requesting, telling the men they couldn't smoke, never smiling, standing in a stiff pose, replying in a sharp manner to questions, etc. In addition, the experimenter told the men in this

The slimy little beasties, two per order.

condition, as he had those in the positive communicator condition, about the fifty cents' incentive, and then proceeded as he had done in that condition.

(c) Respected leader. In this condition, after having made the statement that this was a voluntary experiment quoted above, the experimenter said, "I would like Sergeant _____ to tell you the importance of soldiers being willing to live off the land and eat strange foods."

At this point, a sergeant who had been selected on the advice of the officers as being highly respected by the men (in each case, a man with considerable years of experience as indicated by his hash marks and campaign ribbons) gave the men a talk in his own words on why they should learn to eat survival foods such as grasshoppers. In each case the experimenter had spoken to the sergeant prior to the experiment, and given him a rough outline of a survival talk that could be utilized. The sergeants took to this quite naturally, and generally used the same format, beginning with a statement as to the situation that soldiers often get into in which they are not amply supplied when pinned down by the enemy or isolated, and why it is necessary for them to eat strange and unusual foods that they would not ordinarily eat. They then gave examples of situations in previous wars in which they had eaten strange foods, stating that this had been necessary for their survival. They then concluded by stating that the men were fortunate to have this chance to learn to eat some of these survival foods. They concluded their talk by eating a grasshopper.

The experimenter suggested the survival approach to the sergeants but left it up to them to put it into their own words. This was done in order to make the leader influence condition, as a bench mark condition, as similar as possible to the manner in which influence attempts are normally made by NCO's to the men in the Armed Forces.

(d) Humor. In this condition, after having made the statement that this was a voluntary experiment quoted above, the experimenter stated, "To make this meeting more pleasant, I am going to play a record for you while you eat." The experimenter then put on the Bob Newhart record "The Buttondown Mind Strikes Back," at the particularly funny section on the "Grace L. Ferguson Airline and Storm Door Company." After the group had responded to the record with at least one good laugh, the experimenter presented them with an open can of grasshoppers and said, "Now go ahead and eat." The record continued to play until the men had finished eating.

(e) No influence control. There was no experimental manipulation in this condition, the subjects simply being told, after the statement quoted above that this was a voluntary experiment, "Now go ahead and eat."

Behavioral and attitudinal measures

The four major responses measured were: the number of grasshoppers eaten; attitudes toward eating grasshoppers (on a nine-point "hedonic" rating scale ranging from "dislike extremely" to "like extremely"); satisfaction with the group (on a twelve-item, seven-point Likert scale); and ratings of

TABLE 4.5
Mean Change in Attitudes toward Eating Grasshoppers
(Adapted from Smith, 1961a)

Condition	Attitude change
a) Dissonance, positive communicator	+0.1
b) **Dissonance, negative communicator**	**+2.5**
c) Leader influence	+0.4
d) Humor	+0.8
e) No-treatment control	+1.8

the positive and negative communicator (on a seven-point Likert-type scale of responses to the single item, "the instructor was friendly and courteous").

Results

For our present purposes we will look only at the results for the attitude change measure presented in Table 4.5. Dissonance theory argues that those who "chose" to eat the grasshoppers when the request was made by a negative communicator ought to have experienced the most dissonance. An easy way to reduce this dissonance would be to increase one's subjective liking for the grasshoppers. "If I'm not eating them because I like the person who made the request, I must be eating them because I like them." Indeed, exactly as predicted, the largest increase in liking of grasshoppers occurred in the negative communicator condition. In passing, it should be noted that the effects of the positive communicator, the respected leader, and the humor were *less* than those of the no-treatment control condition. That group serves as a baseline for the change in attitude due to merely being exposed to the opportunity to eat an unusual, disliked food.

Attribution Theory

> *If we have our own why of life,*
> *we shall get along with almost any how.*
> Nietzsche, *Maxims and Missiles*, 1888

You open the door to your house and see a man standing there with a gun pointed directly at your head. Your heart starts pounding, adrenaline pours into your automatic nervous system, you start to think about what to do (scream, run, attack, freeze?). Your blood pressure increases, your breathing rate goes up, blood rushes to your brain, your face turns white, and your mouth drops open. What emotion would you say you are feeling?

After applying to ten medical schools you have been rejected from nine. You are now holding an as yet unopened letter from your last hope. Nervously, you tear off a side of the envelope praying silently to yourself, wondering what you will do if it is a rejection. "We are pleased to inform you that you have been accepted." Your heart starts pounding, you jump up and down, your blood pressure goes up, adrenalin shoots into your automatic nervous system, blood rushes to your brain, you begin thinking how you should tell your parents, you start breathing heavily, and your face turns white. What emotion are you feeling?

Obviously, in the first case the emotion is fear. In the second, it is extreme joy or euphoria.

What is it about our experiences that determines the kind of emotions we feel? It is generally assumed by most people that their emotions are "wired-in" physical reactions to appropriate situations. Fear is different from happiness because one's body reacts differently to fear-arousing situations than to those that produce euphoria. If you reexamine our two examples, however, you will see that identical internal bodily reactions were described in *both* cases. The arousal was basically the same, but what differed were the thoughts that were described, the overt behavior, and the external situation. If different emotions were being experienced, it could not have been due to differences in the nature of the physiological arousal.

A substantial body of research indicates that there are few measures of physiological activity (or even patterns of responding) that can differentiate between different emotions. In other words, the state of physiological arousal is basically the same in euphoric and fearful situations. Even in sexual arousal, aside from such things as erections and blood volume increases in the nipples and vaginal region, the physiological arousal appears to be quite similar to arousal produced by other, nonsexy situations. All of this leads to the conclusion that our intensely different emotional experiences are caused by what we are perceiving, thinking, and doing.

Attribution theory provides a reasonable explanation for this state of affairs. Consider how a young child learns to describe his or her emotional states. All children cry at various times but how do they come to *label* or explain some of their crying as unhappiness and some of it as joy? The young child, just learning how to talk, must look to adults to learn the proper usage of words, including words that describe the internal, experiential world of the child. How does a parent know when to instruct, model, and reward the appropriate or accurate self-label? The only kinds of information to which the parent has direct access are the child's behavior and the situation in which the behavior occurs. The parent cannot see or feel the physiological arousal of the child; it can only be inferred. The parent uses the child's behavior (crying, laughing, running, shouting, and so on) and the situation (such as a broken toy, or a cartoon on television) to infer a label that appropriately describes the child's state. ("You're really upset, aren't you?"). As a result, the child may come to use the *same* cues employed by the parent to describe his or her own state. That is, the child might learn labels for experiences by observing his or her own behavior and the situation in which that behavior occurs.

Sound familiar? It is the same self-perception process that we outlined earlier, but now we are suggesting that self-descriptions of one's emotional state may be governed by variables similar to those that control self-descriptions of one's attitudinal state. In the first case, the self-description explains physiological arousal and possibly other "emotional behaviors." In the second case, it explains attitude-relevant behaviors (such as speech writing, choosing one record over another, eating fried grasshoppers, and so on). The basic process is the same in both cases, however. We use our own behavior and the situation in which the behavior occurs to make attributions about what we are feeling, as well as why we feel that way.

FINDING LABELS FOR UNEXPLAINED AROUSAL

Some of these ideas were tested in an ingenious experiment by Stanley Schachter and Jerome Singer (1962). They hypothesized that the same physiological arousal would be interpreted as very different emotional experiences (anger and euphoria) as a function of different situational cues. To demonstrate this, they attempted to produce physiological arousal in their subjects by injecting them with the drug, epinephrine. The situational cues were introduced via the emotional behavior of a model (supposedly "another subject," but actually a confederate of the experimenters). Some of the subjects were exposed to a model who was behaving angrily, while others saw a model who was behaving in a euphoric manner. Schachter and Singer predicted that these subjects, who had been physiologically aroused by the drug, would label this arousal according to the emotional cues presented in the situation by the model. Thus, subjects who saw the angry model would label their arousal as "anger," while those who saw the euphoric model would label it as "euphoria"—even though the source and nature of the arousal were the same in both cases.

This hypothesis is limited to those occasions when the true source of the person's arousal is unknown. Obviously, if the person had an appropriate explanation for the arousal, then he or she would not be searching the situation for cues as to an emotional label. In their experiment, Schachter and Singer tried to produce a state of unexplained arousal by deliberately misleading subjects about the effects of the injection. The responses of these subjects were compared with the responses of a control group of subjects who were given the correct explanation for their arousal—the injection of epinephrine. A second control group consisted of subjects who were given a placebo injection and thus, theoretically, should not have been experiencing any physiological arousal at all. With this general outline in mind, let us see how the authors actually tested their ideas.

Procedure Male subjects were told that the study was concerned with the effects of a vitamin compound ("Suproxin") on vision. After agreeing to participate, most of the subjects received an injection of epinephrine, which typically causes increases in heart rate and breathing, as well as tremor and a feeling of flushing. The Placebo control group received an injection of saline solution, which is a neutral substance with no side effects.

The subjects who received the drug injection were given one of three different sets of information about Suproxin's effects. In the *Informed* control condition, subjects were told (correctly) that the injection would make their hearts pound, their hands shake, and their faces get warm and flushed. In the *Misinformed* condition, the subjects were told (erroneously) that the side effects of Suproxin were a numbing sensation in the feet, itching, and a slight headache. In the *Ignorant* condition, subjects were led to believe that Suproxin would have no physiological side effects at all. (The Placebo group also received these instructions.) Thus, while subjects in the Informed condition had an appropriate explanation for their arousal, subjects in the Misinformed and Ignorant conditions did not. Presumably, these two latter groups of subjects would search the situation for information with which they could label their state of unexplained arousal, in which case the behavior of the model should be maximally effective in determining their mood.

After receiving the injection, each subject was asked to wait in the room for about twenty minutes (in order to let "the Suproxin get from the injection site into the bloodstream"). Another person (who had presumably also received the injection) was brought into the room to wait as well. This person was actually the confederate, whose job was to model either angry or euphoric behaviors. Theoretically, subjects who were experiencing unexplained arousal would use the model's emotional behaviors as cues for labeling their own emotional state.

In the *Euphoria* condition, the subject and confederate were left in a room that had a lot of material and equipment lying about in disarray. The confederate started to fool around with the materials, beginning by

Courtesy Philip G. Zimbardo, Inc.

Euphoric subject joins confederate in hula-hooping.

doodling on pieces of paper and then by crumpling up the pieces into "basketballs" and throwing them into the wastebasket. He made and flew some paper airplanes, and followed by shooting paper balls with a sling-shot made out of a rubber band. He then made a tower of manila folders and shot at that, and finally he picked up a hula hoop and started to twirl it. Throughout this routine, the confederate made comments about his activities and occasionally asked the subject to join in.

In the *Anger* condition, the subject and confederate were asked to fill out a long questionnaire while they waited in the room. The confederate began his routine by complaining about receiving an injection. He then started to work on the questionnaire at about the same pace as the subject. The first questions were fairly standard ones, but they then became more personal and insulting. The confederate began to complain about the questions and eventually became more and more angry about the information that was being asked of him. He finally became so upset that he ripped up the questionnaire and stormed out of the room.

Measures   While the confederate went through his twenty-minute routine, hidden observers scored the behaviors of the subject. In the Euphoria condition, the behavioral categories were: subject joins the activity, initiates new activity, ignores confederate, and watches confederate. The categories for the Anger condition included: subject agrees with confederate, disagrees, makes neutral comment, initiates agreement or disagreement, watches confederate, and ignores confederate. In addition, all of the categories were differentially weighted according to the amount of emotion that they implied (for example, +2 for agree, +5 for hula hooping).

After the twenty-minute waiting period was over, the experimenter returned to the room and asked the subject to complete a questionnaire about his reactions to Suproxin (since these could supposedly affect the vision tests). Two of the questions involved self-ratings of emotion. The subject was asked to indicate on a five-point scale: (1) how irritated, angry, or annoyed he felt, and (2) how good or happy he felt. In addition, he was asked to report the physical symptoms he had experienced. Physiological arousal was also assessed by taking the subject's pulse both before the injection and after the twenty-minute waiting period.

Results Subjects who had received the epinephrine injection reported experiencing more palpitation and tremor than did the Placebo control group. They also showed an increase in pulse rate, while the Placebo controls showed a decrease. Thus the epinephrine injection did produce a state of physiological arousal.

The extent to which subjects used the model's emotional behavior as a cue for labeling their own emotion was assessed in two ways: (1) self-reported emotion (the "angry" score was subtracted from the "happy" score), and (2) emotional behavior (a summed index of all the observational ratings). The results for the Euphoria conditions are presented in Table 4.6. As can be seen, the Informed subjects were *least* affected by the confederate's behavior, exactly as the researchers had predicted. The Informed subjects had an appropriate explanation for their arousal and did not need to use cues from the situation or the confederate to interpet their bodily state. In contrast, the two experimental groups lacking an appropriate explanation for the arousal (Ignorant and Misinformed) were *most* affected by the confederate. They reported the most positive emotions and engaged

TABLE 4.6
Self-Report and Behavioral Indices in Euphoria Conditions
(Adapted from Schachter and Singer 1962)

	Self-Report Index*	Behavioral Index**
Informed	0.98	12.72
Placebo	1.61	16.00
Ignorant	1.78	18.28
Misinformed	1.90	22.56

* The higher the score, the more positive the reported emotion.
** The higher the score, the more euphoric the behaviors.

TABLE 4.7
Self-Report and Behavioral Indices in Anger Condition
(Adapted from Schachter and Singer 1962)

	Self-Report Index*	Behavioral Index**
Informed	1.39	−.18
Placebo	1.91	.79
Ignorant	1.63	2.28

* The higher the score, the more positive the reported emotion.
** The higher the score, the more angry the behaviors.

in the most euphoric behaviors, presumably because they used the confederate's activity as a cue to label their own unexplained state as "euphoria."

Table 4.7 presents the results for subjects in the Anger conditions. (The Misinformed condition was included only for the happy condition and not for the angry condition.) Again, the subjects who lacked an appropriate explanation (the Ignorant condition) were most influenced by the confederate. They reported the least positive emotions and they displayed the most angry behaviors. In comparison, both the Informed and Placebo control groups had fewer angry responses.

Overall, the findings of this research show that people will sometimes rely on external information to decide what their internal feelings and attitudes are. When subjects lacked an appropriate explanation for their internal arousal, they looked to the immediate situation, and the other person in it, to find the cognitive label for their feeling state. However, this reliance on external factors did not occur when subjects either already had an explanation or were not experiencing an unexplained state of arousal.

This research made psychologists aware of the ready modifiability of affective states through manipulation of variables in the social situation. Emotion and mood were thus amenable to experimental investigation on the same terms as attitudes and behavior had been. Subsequent investigators have gone on to demonstrate that affective states could be altered simply by (mis)attributing their observable symptoms to external stimuli and events other than those actually producing the arousal. Thus, for example, fear of electric shock or test anxiety have been reduced when the person is led to believe that the arousal symptoms being experienced are the inevitable (and normal) consequence of a given pill (a placebo) or high-frequency noise. A variety of internal states have been altered by such attribution strategies, which locate the source of the arousal in nonpsychological or not personally relevant events. The surprising outcome of this body of research is how *insensitive* we are to internal events and how receptive to external ones. Oscar Wilde's *Picture of Dorian Gray* offered an insight into the duality of so-called inner reality and external appearances: "It is only shallow people who do not judge by appearances. The true mystery of the world is the visible, not the invisible." This perspective offers a natural transition to our last example of theoretically derived research.

Social Learning Theory

> The screams of the young boy could be heard up and down the hallway. Eyebrows barely moved as another screech pierced the air. They were torturing that poor mentally retarded boy, again—the one who keeps hitting his head against the floor unless you hold him close. Why can't they see that the boy just needs to be loved? I'm willing to take time out and feed him. It isn't that much of a bother to untie him from the bedposts so he won't choke on his food. If they would just put him under my care for awhile, I'm sure I could get him to stop eating the flesh from his fingers without his having to wear those extra-large motorcycle gloves. How can they possibly believe that intense electric shock will help? Don't they realize it will only make him withdraw more into himself and make it even harder for him to accept the love he needs?

This is a typical reaction to a particular form of *behavior modification* that uses principles derived from social learning theory. Dicky was a young boy who spent almost all of his time tied, in spread-eagle fashion, to the bedposts of his crib. He was self-destructive. He would bang his head against the floor over 1,000 times per hour if not stopped. He would chew away his own flesh.

Why does such personally destructive behavior occur, and how can it be modified? According to social learning theory, the answers to these questions lie not within the person but in the external world. For example, what are the typical consequences of Dicky's self-mutilating behavior? The attendants and nurses in the hospital grab him, hold him tight, and try to distract him by talking to him, rocking him, and so on. Maybe Dicky does these things to draw the attention of the otherwise busy attendants. Because life in the average home for the mentally retarded is not only boring but downright aversive, it may be that the little attention Dicky could get is a powerful reward.

While it would be possible to test this attention explanation by preventing attendants from engaging in their usual social conduct, it could be potentially dangerous to wait out the required number of self-mutilations before the responses (or the child) were extinguished. Therefore, the behavioral engineers decided to make the consequences for self-mutilation extremely aversive by shocking the boy immediately following every self-destructive act. Within a few trials, Dicky stopped banging his head and chewing his flesh. More importantly, since he no longer spent his time tied up in his padded crib, he was, with appropriate positive reinforcement, able to develop more normal social behaviors.

The case of Dicky is an example of behavior change that can be understood in terms of social learning principles. Let us now look at two studies that deal with verbal and emotional responses, as well as responses that seem less "abnormal."

THE EFFECTIVENESS OF DESENSITIZATION AND MODELING TECHNIQUES

The first experiment was conducted by Gordon Paul (1966) and the second by Bandura, Blanchard, and Ritter (1969). Both of these experiments involve a technique called desensitization. Essentially, it is a learning technique in which subjects learn a new set of *emotional* responses to an old stimulus. For example, a fear-arousing stimulus can become a neutral or positive stimulus, or vice versa. In the case of fear, a subject is first taught how to relax completely (a response that is incompatible with fear). After this training, symbolic representations of the fear-arousing situation are presented in a graded hierarchical form, from very nonarousing to very arousing, *while the subject remains deeply relaxed.* In this way, once the training is complete, the fear-arousing stimulus comes to elicit relaxation rather than fear responses.

In the first study, subjects volunteered to participate in the experiment because they were afraid of speaking in public. These subjects were randomly assigned to one of four conditions: desensitization, insight (traditional clinical therapy), an attention-placebo control, and a nontreatment control group. The insight condition consisted of various forms of the traditional long-term client-therapist interview. At the close of the interview, the therapist provided the client with an insight into the nature and cause of the speech phobia. The subjects in the attention-placebo control group were provided with useless placebos (said to reduce tension and anxiety) along with warm and understanding attention centering around the subject's "problem." The final control group received only a pre-post measure of the dependent variables. There were three before-after treatment measurements on all subjects: (1) ratings by unbiased observers of the subject's ability to actually give speeches in public, (2) self-report measures of anxiety during speeches, (3) physiological measures of arousal (heart rate, and so on).

The results can be stated quite simply. The desensitization, insight, and attention-placebo condition produced highly significant reductions in self-reported anxiety that were greater than those for the nontreatment control group. On the other hand, only the desensitization group almost completely eliminated the overt fear of speaking in public. Only in this group were almost all of the subjects able to speak in public without overt signs of fear or physiologically measured affective arousal. Stated another way, verbal self-ratings of fear (affective reactions toward public speaking) were changed equally well by each of the three treatments. However, actual public speaking behavior and the physiological measures of fear were affected only by the treatment derived from the social learning approach (desensitization).

Why should such a result be found? What makes verbal self-ratings equally sensitive to each treatment, while the nonverbal measures are affected only by one? The answer lies in the nature of the treatments. Each of them includes a large degree of verbal activity on the part of the subjects and experimenter. In the attention-placebo treatment, subjects are essentially *told* not to be fearful and given placebos that are supposed to make them less fearful. In the insight therapy treatment, the subjects are again *told* not to be fearful, and are also supplied with reinforcement from the therapist whenever they label themselves as less fearful. Thus in both these treatments, subjects are given reinforcement and attention for *talking* about themselves as being less fearful. On the other hand, subjects do not learn how to be less fearful (to actually relax) in these two treatments. In the desensitization treatment, however, subjects *do* learn how to be less fearful when faced with symbolic fear stimuli (usually verbal descriptions of public speaking). Once they learn not to be afraid, they correctly label themselves as less fearful.[3] Subjects receiving the other two treatments learn only how to *rate* themselves as less fearful, but not how to *be* less fearful in public speaking situations. From this study we can see how one class of behavior (attitudes, or self-ratings) can be controlled by one general set of stimuli, while another related class of behavior can be controlled by a different set of stimuli (the desensitization procedure).

The second study compared the desensitization technique with live modeling and with a no-treatment control (as well as other conditioning

---

[3] It should be noted that by labeling themselves as less fearful *after* giving a speech in public, the subjects are behaving in a manner predicted by dissonance theory. That is, they are bringing their attitudes (self-descriptions) in line with their behavior.

techniques). The purpose of this study was to determine which treatment method would produce the most behavioral change, and which treatments would also change self-ratings. Subjects were initially selected because they were highly fearful of snakes. The live modeling group saw a model handle a snake without showing any signs of fear while doing so. The desensitization group associated verbally presented snake stimuli with relaxation. The results demonstrated that live models produced a greater increase in *overt* handling of snakes than either the desensitization group or no-treatment control group. On the other hand, verbally stated attitudes were affected by both desensitization and live modeling.

Why should both of these treatments affect self-ratings, but only one treatment affect overt behavior? As in the previous study, the answer lies in the specific details of each treatment. In the live modeling treatments, subjects learn that "*if* people touch snakes, *then* nothing bad happens to them." That is, they learn that punishments are not likely to follow the handling of most snakes. However, in the desensitization treatment, subjects learn to relax while thinking about or hearing about snakes, and they do not *necessarily* learn that touching snakes will not lead to punishment. That is, they learn to relax when they hear, read, or think about snakes but not when they actually have to touch one. Thus we should expect all subjects to label themselves as less fearful on a questionnaire, or when *thinking* about how fearful they are of snakes. However, on the basis of the goals of the different treatment procedures, we should expect the desensi-

Courtesy Philip G. Zimbardo, Inc.

A person with a snake phobia learns to handle a snake through modeling.

tized subjects to be less able to actually handle a snake than the modeling subjects, who have learned snakes are not harmful.

These two studies demonstrate quite clearly that (1) social learning techniques (modeling and desensitization) can greatly affect attitudes and overt, nonverbal behavior, and (2) changes in attitudes are not necessarily accompanied by changes in behavior. In social learning terms, the consequences of thinking about a feared object may be changed quite drastically without changing the consequences of overtly interacting with the feared object. People can say they do not fear talking in public when they are sitting alone in a room filling out a questionnaire, but when they are on a stage speaking in front of an audience, their reactions may be entirely different. Therefore, techniques designed to change only the way in which people talk about their behavior, or their feelings, may not necessarily produce changes in their overt behavior or physiological reactions.

REDEFINING ATTITUDES AS BEHAVIOR

Social learning theory has no difficulty explaining the fact that attitude ratings and behavior do not change together. In effect, the social learning approach denies the utility of the concept of "attitudes." What it does, instead, is discuss how different classes of behavior (one of which is self-ratings) are controlled by different sets of consequences (contingencies).

Let us see how this would explain the lack of consistency found in different measures of the same attitude. As a specific example, suppose that the attitude in question were, "birth control should be practiced." One way to measure a person's attitude on this topic would be to ask whether or not he or she agreed with this statement. Another measure might be the number of times this person, in fact, used birth control techniques. Chances are that if we were to record both these measurements, they would not correlate with each other. That is, people might say that they agreed with birth control, but they might not themselves use birth control techniques. A social learning approach explains this "inconsistent" result by assuming the following: people expect that verbally agreeing with the above statement about birth control will be followed by different consequences than actually not practicing birth control. The different consequences seem obvious. The important point here is that what seem, on an intuitive basis, to be measures of an underlying attitude toward birth control are, in fact, merely two different classes of behavior that are controlled, not by an attitude, but by the consequences of the behaviors.

When would the social learning approach expect verbal statements to match nonverbal behavior? Essentially, it would predict a match whenever a person expects similar consequences for both kinds of behavior, or (to put it another way) whenever he or she does not discriminate between the two kinds of behavior (or between their *consequences*).

In summary, a social learning approach discards the concept of attitude in its attempt to understand and produce changes in behavior. Instead, it determines the class of behavior that is to be changed (verbal, nonverbal, emotional responses, and so on). Then it tries to specify what the person has learned and what is therefore controlling his or her present behavior. Once these crucial bits of information have been found, the technique (modeling, direct reinforcements, persuasive communications, and so on) that is most likely to produce a change in such information is applied. Stated another way, by changing the expected consequences for engaging in the crucial behavior, or by changing the associations with a crucial stimulus, we can change *any* specific behavior, regardless of the general class to which that behavior belongs.

In this chapter we have presented a spectrum of experimental research that stems from the five theoretical approaches outlined previously. It was our intention to illustrate how ideas are generated by theories and how, in turn, those ideas can be translated into testable hypotheses and concrete operations. We learn from these studies not only that it is *possible* to modify behavior, change attitudes, and manipulate mood states, but also something about the particular variables responsible for such alterations in the human condition.

However, before we put our faith, energy, and money into translating these experimental results into practical tactics and strategies, we want to be certain that they are reliable (can be replicated) and that they stand the test of critical evaluation. Accordingly, the next phase in our journey takes us to the land of the skeptics, where naive junior authors and seasoned principal investigators alike have been known to be denounced with critical relish.

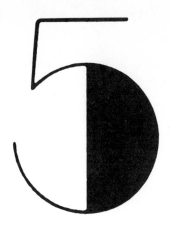

critically analyzing selected attitude change research

"Put her to the dunking test!" shouted the Grand Inquisitor.

"Begging your honor's pardon, but what, pray tell, is the 'dunking test' that I am to be put to?" the trembling young suspect implored.

"Witches can't drown. Therefore, anyone suspected of being a witch is strapped into a dunking chair and immersed three times in a tub of water. If she fails to drown, we have proof positive that she is a witch. Then we burn her at the stake." The Grand Inquisitor smiled grandly.

"Your demonstration, almighty sir, though quite dramatic, is lacking an important element for it to be widely accepted as an unbiased experimental test of your hypothesis—forgiving my impudence for implying a criticism of your most wonderful reasoning."

"And what is that?" flushed the Grand Inquisitor.

"You don't have a control group," the suspected witch replied. The Lesser Inquisitors grimaced and a hush came over the crowd. Growing bolder as she saw the Grand Inquisitor was weak on this aspect of experimental design, she continued: *"Without a comparison group of those people not suspected of witchcraft, your definition is circular and your test is not worth the tub it's held in. If I may be so brash, good sire, I would suggest that the appropriate paradigm involves preselection of subjects suspected of witchcraft and those who are not so suspected. Give both groups your assessment instrument. Then compare the survival rates in both groups. If you do not find more survivors in your suspected-witch group*

than in your not-suspected-witch group, then either your test is no good, or your suspicions are no good, or, of course, both."

"But if I do it the correct way, as you suggest, and fail to reject the null hypothesis, then either everyone's a witch or everyone drowns!" cried the Grand Inquisitor.

"To be sure, your eminence. And you would look stupid in either case."

"Uppity broad," muttered the Grand Inquisitor, "but right. Empty the tub!"

Scientific Method Requires Constructive Criticism

There should never be uncritical acceptance of anyone's conclusions about human behavior, be they Grand Inquisitors or just behavioral researchers. One of the virtues of the scientific method as used by psychologists lies in its encouragement of attitudes of openmindedness toward one's own work, of responsiveness to constructive criticism, and of the provisional, never absolute, nature of all "truth." Truth is for now, given the available information and subject to revision when better evidence does not support the current generalization.

We will apply a critical approach to five studies in order to demonstrate the level of concern and attention you must bring to the serious evaluation of any scientifically gathered evidence. Four of the studies have just been described to you (uncritically) in the previous chapter, while the fifth study is new. We believe that many important aspects of design, execution, analysis, and interpretation will be illustrated by an intensive examination of these particular studies. Our guiding principle is that the only experiments worth such a thorough, critical evaluation are those that contain ideas of potential theoretical value. A trivial idea does not merit the time and effort required by this kind of intensive analysis. Experiments that are interesting and valuable demand that, as part of their evaluation, the critics make concrete suggestions about how to clarify the ideas and how to retest them appropriately. From constructive criticism come ideas for improvements in design, procedure, or analysis that might better test the hypothesis under consideration. Sometimes the sensitive critic can discover a better explanation of why a particular result occurred or an expected one failed to materialize. To criticize for its own sake is to engage in a game of intellectual masturbation with a rather limited and introverted gratification.

Communicator Credibility Revisited

Of all the conclusions derived from experiments on attitude change, one that is considered fairly basic and reliable is Hovland and Weiss' (1951) conclusion that a communication is more effective if attributed to a credible source than it is if attributed to a noncredible one. This research, which derives from the Yale approach to attitude change, was described in some detail in Chapter 4. Let us now reconsider it more critically.

Do the obtained results support the interpretation of communicator credibility? If the data presented in Chapter 4 (in Tables 4.3 and 4.4) are recast as *difference* scores and rearranged in order of most to least attitude change (as in Table 5.1), then we can draw several conclusions that differ from those of Hovland and Weiss.

First, there is additional support for the relationship between trustworthiness and attitude change. In general, as the difference in perceived trustworthiness between communicators increases, the relative effectiveness of the trustworthy communicator also increases. However, to look at the data in another way, large absolute differences in the independent variable (78.2 percent difference in trustworthiness) result in but small differences in the dependent variable (only 14.1 percent difference in attitude change).

It is legitimate, then, to inquire whether this weak effect is significant. It appears from the authors' report that it is *statistically* significant; that is, with the sample size studied (244 observations), and the presumably small variability in response, a difference of 14 percent would occur only three times in one hundred by chance. Thus, we may be reasonably confident in concluding that this is not one of those chance occasions, but rather that

TABLE 5.1
Difference Scores (High Credibility Condition–Low Credibility Condition) for Percentage of Net Attitude Change and for Percentage of Subjects Judging Each Source as Trustworthy* (Adapted from Hovland and Weiss 1951)

| | Difference Scores for: | |
Issue	Net attitude change	Perceived trustworthiness
B. (Atomic subs)	35.4%	92.4%
A. (Antihistamine)	23.4%	88.8%
C. (Steel shortage)	10.8%	63.9%
D. (Future of movies)	− 3.3%	68.2%
Average difference	+14.1%	78.2%

* The reader should note that the latter is a measure of the subject's *interpretation* of the independent variable manipulation and not the difference between treatment groups.

this difference is due to the operation of a systematic psychological process that is repeatable under comparable testing conditions. It appears that we are dealing with a variable that has considerable theoretical value for an understanding of how attitudes are influenced by communications.

But can we go one step further and conclude that this finding has practical significance? Can we utilize it and incorporate it into a technology of attitude change? We can, on the one hand, if we simply consider that a difference of 14 percent in a national election would be enough for a candidate to be victorious.

On the other hand, in order to demonstrate a measurable effect upon attitudes, the researchers had to create extreme differences in communicator credibility that, nevertheless, gave only a slight edge to the credible source in producing attitude change. In real-life situations, where the naturally existing differences between communicators would be much less extreme, would there still be the same enhancement of the communication by virtue of its attribution to a slightly more credible source? Some of the data suggest that there would not.

One of the positive features of the design of this study is the use of four different attitude issues. If it can be demonstrated that the experimental manipulation had the same effect for all of them, then any conclusions drawn are not limited to the content of a particular, arbitrarily chosen topic. Instead, they are "topic-free" and have a wider range of generalizability. However, this is not the case in the present study, since (as can be seen in Table 5.1) there are different patterns of attitude change for the different topics. The positive relationship between trustworthiness and attitude change is sizable for one issue (B—practicality of atomic subs), moderate for another (A—prescriptions for antihistamines), but weak and probably not even statistically significant for a third (only 10.8 percent for C—blame for the steel shortage). When we examine the fourth issue used (D—the effect of TV on movies), the generalization breaks down altogether—an untrustworthy communicator is slightly *more* persuasive than a trustworthy one!

We may conclude from this that the relationship is *specific* to the type of issue used, or that only huge differences in trustworthiness lead to meaningful differences in attitude change. Such limitations on this generalization are hard to accept because the generalization is so intuitively reasonable (a more credible communicator *ought* to be more influential). Several lines of inquiry are now open to us. We can consider whether the variable of trustworthiness is a major component of credibility, or alternatively, we may question whether the specific operations used in this research to define credibility really tap the essential components of this construct. Another approach is to scrutinize the experimental situation for variables that may have been operating to minimize or distort the effect of credibility on attitude change. Such variables (artifacts) would account for the "slippage" between the big independent variable effect and the small dependent variable result.

All the World's a Stage . . . and We Just Role-Players

As we discussed earlier, role-playing in the presence of others seems to be an effective persuasion technique. In encounter groups or group therapy sessions, participants are frequently asked to actively adopt the role of another person (usually someone with whom they are having interpersonal difficulties). The goal of this technique is to produce changes in the participant's perception and evaluation of this other person—for example, "Now I see why he always puts me down—he's not very confident about himself." Sometimes just watching another member of the group enact a role may vicariously produce changes in perceptions and attitudes. For some people and some issues it may be necessary to personally enact the role and to experience what it feels like to be on the other side of the fence. Role-playing and improvisation are also used to make people more tolerant of a given contrary position by having them publicly espouse a set of opinions with which they initially disagree.

The conclusion derived from the body of research on role-playing is considered to be one of the most reliable in this area of attitude change: active participation is more effective in changing attitudes than is passive exposure to persuasive communications. Although the studies vary considerably in the form of role-playing utilized (from debate to psychodrama), they share the minimal requirement of the technique, which is that the subject become involved in the attempt to present, sincerely and convincingly, the attitude position of another person. The self-persuasion that occurs as a consequence of effective role-playing is also interesting because it does not fit the traditional attitude-change model. The change in attitude is the result of one's communication to *oneself* of a counter-norm position.

One of the few systematic attempts to explore those variables in role-playing that influence attitude change has been the series of studies by Irving Janis and Burt King, previously described in Chapter 4. You will remember that these investigators attempted to understand their earlier empirical finding (that "overt verbalization induced through role-playing tends to augment the effectiveness of a persuasive communication") by isolating the variable of *improvisation* from that of *satisfaction* as the major determinant in the acceptance of new ideas.

The data in Table 5.2 led them to conclude that subjects who were required to improvise a speech contrary to their own position adjusted their attitudes to conform with their role behavior more than did subjects who were required to read a prepared speech opposing their own position. This result occurred even though both the improvised and prepared speeches contained similar arguments and conclusions.

If we examine the values of net opinion change for each of the five items, and also note the meaning of the *combined index* of change, it becomes clear that two conclusions, rather than only one, are warranted by these data. Improvisation *is* more effective than the other treatments on items 1, 2, and 3, but it is *not* on items 4 and 5. These two clusters of items differ in the degree to which they are informationally and factually based (1 to 3), or self-relevant (4, 5). Other research in this area has also failed to find a significant effect of improvisation on attitude change when the opinions measured were self-descriptions of the subject's expectations or feelings. Thus, the authors' general conclusion must be limited to one class of opinion items. However, it is reasonable to presume that there may be a two-stage process in which a person first intellectually incorporates new information into his or her repertoire of verbal responses, and then subsequently accepts it at a personal level. In the brief time span used in the present study, only the first stage of this process may have been revealed by the measurements.

What about the satisfaction explanation? Is there any evidence that active participation has its effect because those subjects are more satisfied with their performance? The evidence clearly refutes this alternative. Subjects in the nonimprovisation condition rated themselves as more satisfied with their performance than did those in the improvisation condition, but they changed their attitudes less. In the nonimprovisation group, 96 percent of the subjects felt that their "performance was at least satisfactory," while only 63 percent of those in the improvisation group felt satisfied (a very significant difference of 33 percent, $p < .01$).

But this is only an indirect way of ruling out the "satisfaction hypothesis." Rather than basing conclusions on correlational data, a better strategy would be if "the experimenter differentially administered social rewards and punishments for the purpose of varying the satisfaction variable under conditions in which improvisation was held constant." (Janis and King 1954, p. 182)

This is exactly what these investigators did, by randomly dividing the subjects within the improvisation group into three equal subgroups. Subjects received either positive, negative, or no evaluative feedback after their speech. This manipulation had the expected significant effect of altering self-ratings of satisfaction, but had no effect on attitude change.

While this finding convincingly eliminates satisfaction as a reasonable hypothetical process in this particular attitude change paradigm, it raises two problems of interpretation, one of internal validity and one of external validity. Remember that one-third of the subjects in the improvisation condition were told that they did not improvise well. If this manipulation of satisfaction had been successful, it should have made about 33 percent of the subjects in the improvisation group feel that their performance was not "at least satisfactory." This is precisely the difference previously reported between the *entire* improvisation and nonimprovisation groups. Put differently, 33 percent fewer subjects in the improvisation condition were satisfied than in the nonimprovisation condition, *not* because they had to improvise, but because the experimenter told 33 percent of the subjects that their performance was not satisfactory.

The question of how these results compare to other established findings in psychology comes to the fore when we note that reward and punishment (the feedback manipulations) following a behavior (emitting counter-norm statements) had no subsequent effect upon that behavior—or at least upon acceptance of those statements—contrary to basic principles of reinforcement.

The final point we would like to note is the active versus passive exposure effect. These investigators, although primarily interested in the variable of improvisation, nevertheless include in their design a systematic replication of the conditions for retesting the active participation main effect they established in their previous study. However, if you re-examine Table 5.2 you may be surprised to see that the basic finding, the superiority of active over passive exposure, is *not* found. Indeed, silent reading is slightly more effective in changing attitudes than is active participation that involves public reading. To explain such a result, we could look to the specific conditions of testing used in this study. These may have introduced variables, not present in previous studies, that changed the expected main effect. For example, it may have been that the instructions given the public reading subjects (nonimprovisation treatment) focused their attention on the *mechanics* of speech delivery rather than on the *content* of their speech. The passive controls might have been attending more to the content, since public speaking was not of concern to them. On the other

TABLE 5.2
Net Percentage Change in Opinions Related to Exposure and Improvisation
(Adapted from King and Janis 1956)

Opinion topics	Exposure: Improvise:	Active Yes	No	Passive Silent read
1. Estimate of required length of service for draftees		41	27	5
2. Estimates of college students' chances of being deferred		44	26	25
3. Estimates of college students' chances of becoming officers		70	47	45
4. Expectations concerning the length of *one's own* military service if drafted		59	46	50
5. Expectations concerning the length of one's own deferment before being drafted		50	26	55
Combined index: percentage influenced on three or more of the five opinion items		87.5	54.5	65

* *p*-value is statistically significant.

hand, improvisation subjects would have to be interested in the content, since they had to generate it, as well as in its mode of delivery. *Post hoc* analyses such as this are of value if they correctly direct us to hitherto unsuspected sources of variability in our procedures, or if they lead to explicit hypotheses that are then tested in new experiments.

To conclude the analysis of this experiment on an optimistic note, it might be said that improvisation was in fact more effective than it appears from the data presented. If the essential ingredient in improvised role-playing is "sincerely advocating the role," then attitude change should be greatest for those subjects in the improvisation condition who did role-play sincerely. In the present study only 47 percent felt that they gave the "impression of being 'sincere.' " This is important because the experimental demand "to improvise" will be met very differently by individual subjects according to their intelligence, verbal fluency, shyness, experience with the issue, argumentativeness, preparation time and other variables. The importance of creating experimental conditions that make improvisation more probable is emphasized by Jansen and Stolurow (1962): "the relative ineffectiveness of improvisation might be explained by the fact that improvising is not an activity which can be done on request, but has to be developed with great care and can be expected to appear only after careful preparation." (p. 22)

To Know Grasshoppers Is to Love Them

The predictions derived from dissonance theory often go counter to our intuitive notions of what causes attitude and behavior change. Most of us feel comfortable with the idea that a positive, credible communicator will elicit more change than a negative, noncredible one. However, dissonance theory argues that in some circumstances the negative communicator may be the more effective change agent. In the previous chapter we saw how this hypothesis was tested in a particularly imaginative experiment in which Army reservists were induced to change their attitudes about eating fried grasshoppers (Smith 1961a and b). Looked at uncritically, the results seemed to support the dissonance prediction—there was greater attitude change in the negative communicator condition than in the positive communicator condition. However, this study is beset by a number of problems of experimental design and procedure that may preclude our unqualified acceptance of the findings—or require a better experimental setting in which to serve up the grasshoppers.

DESIGN PROBLEMS

The positive and negative communicators may have been perceived by the subjects in ways that the experimenter had not expected. When the "positive" communicator, a man with authority and expertise, acts cheerful, informal, and permissive in an Army setting, the reservists are likely to react with caution, even suspicion. When the "negative" communicator acts cool, official, and stiff, this is just what soldiers expect and they feel relatively comfortable. Thus, subjective reactions to these different communicators may not have been very different as measured by a check on the manipulation. A further difficulty would be the varying interpretations put by the subjects on the offer of fifty cents (an inducement? a bribe?).

In the respected leader condition, this man was selected by *officers' ratings*, rather than by the subjects themselves. Obviously, a discrepancy may have existed between the subjects' perceptions and the officers' perceptions of what a respected sergeant was! In addition, the sergeant concluded his "own words" talk to the men by eating a grasshopper. If he was, in fact, respected by the men, the men would be likely to imitate him and eat a grasshopper. On the other hand, if he was not respected (as was likely), his act may have been perceived as "calling their bluff," "an attempt to show them up," and so on. This latter alternative, coupled with the likelihood that Army reservists seldom listen to speeches by their non-coms, would lead to minimal effectiveness of this technique.

The failure to fit the humor manipulation into some overall rationale that would be meaningful to the subjects makes it a source of confusion to the men. As soon as they give one good laugh, a can of grasshoppers is shoved at them and they are told to eat! Contrary to the experimenter's expectation, the humor manipulation should produce the most ambiguity (a funny record is being played by a doctor during an official reserve meeting)—and very little attitude change.

The no-treatment control group may have been partly persuaded to eat grasshoppers by the original communication, which gave logical reasons for eating them. You might call this the "soft sell." Also, the high degree of choice (whether to eat grasshoppers or not) in a normally authoritarian environment may have made the subjects feel relatively autonomous, self-satisfied, inclined to try the strange food, and thus more receptive to the possibility of liking it.

PROCEDURAL PROBLEMS

Contagion and the unit of measurement

Since the subjects were tested in groups of about ten men (buddies from the same unit) who sat around a large table, they were in a free-interaction situation. Thus the behavior and attitudes of any one person could be directly influenced by the other subjects rather than by the particular experimental manipulation. Whether the person ate grasshoppers or not, and whether he changed his attitude or not, might be a function of uncontrolled, extraneous events that happened to take place in that group at that time. For example, suppose one popular leader within the group said, "I'll eat a grasshopper. Come on, you guys—what are you, chicken?" We might expect that all of the men in this group would eat a grasshopper as well. A *social comparison* process would be operating here, in which each man would be observing the reaction of the others and comparing himself to this normative baseline. As a result, the data might better reflect social *contagion* or public *conformity* behavior than responsiveness to the communicator's persuasive message. The men might all eat the undesirable food given this group pressure, but would you expect them to then find it more desirable or not?

When this study was replicated (to be described subsequently), some of the subjects were tested in groups, while others were separated from each other and tested individually. The results for these independent, individual subjects were comparable with Smith's (1961a) findings and supported the dissonance hypothesis (see Fig. 5.1). In contrast, the nonindependent, group subjects behaved very differently depending on what happened in their particular group when the request was made to eat the grasshopper. In one group, a soldier who ate a grasshopper immediately clutched his stomach, yelled out that it tasted like "shit," and pretended to be nauseous. Few others ate, as you might expect, but those who did changed their attitudes very positively. In the other groups given the identical treatment, there was more kidding about the grasshoppers. After one soldier ate a grasshopper and challenged the others to do so, they all ate, but few of them changed their attitudes of dislike of the ugly creatures. Can you explain how dissonance theory would account for the greater change in the first group and the lesser change in the second?

Measurement of attitudes

Initial position artifact. If subjects are *randomly* assigned to different treatment groups one should expect that their initial attitudes will be comparable *prior* to the introduction of the influence attempt. If there are sizable differences between group means even before subjects are exposed to the

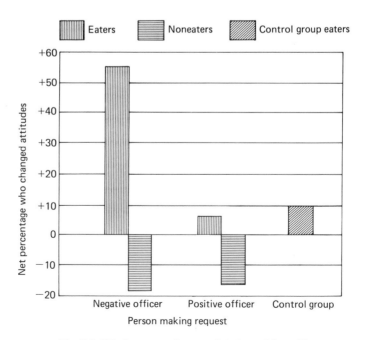

Fig. 5.1 "We love grasshoppers" (adapted from Zimbardo et al. 1965).

independent variable, then it is impossible to determine whether post-influence behavior is caused by the independent variable alone, or by its interaction with different initial attitudes. On the other hand, if initial rating differences are found, one might look to the experimental situation to see if there were any sources of influence operating *prior* to the initial measurement of attitudes. In the present study, it is obvious that the latter was true. Before the first measurement, all men heard what amounted to a brief introductory speech on the purpose of the study. Included in the remarks was a discussion of the need for a mobile army and the need to eat unusual foods, especially survival foods. After having stated that the Quartermaster Corps was sponsoring this research on *food acceptance,* the speaker ended with a statement that the experimenter wanted to find out the men's attitudes and reactions to grasshoppers. This is clearly a persuasive communication, the response to which depends largely upon the perceived credibility of the communicator and related situational characteristics (like whether there are others, such as sergeants, nodding in agreement with the statement). It is not surprising, then, that when pretest attitudes were measured just after the initial speech, the ratings of those in the positive communicator condition were more favorable than the ratings of those in the negative condition. Secondly, those in the respected leader condition were more favorable toward eating grasshoppers than those in the no-treatment condition. As shown in Table 5.3, both of these effects were greater *before* the manipulation of the independent variables than *after* it!

Sensitization and guinea pig effects. In the present study it was very likely that some subjects perceived a *manipulative intent* on the part of the experimenter. This possibility is enhanced by the procedure that was used.

TABLE 5.3
Mean Change in Attitudes toward Eating Grasshoppers (Adapted from Smith 1961a)

Condition	Pretest*	Post-test	Attitude change	Percentage of subjects eating
a) Dissonance, negative communicator	2.8	5.3	+2.5	50%
b) No-treatment control	3.2	5.1	+1.8	88%
c) Humor	2.8	3.6	+0.8	100%
d) Dissonance, positive communicator	4.0	4.7	+0.6	95%
e) Leader influence	4.6	5.0	+0.4	90%

* On a nine-point scale where 9.0 is "like extremely," 5.0 is neutral, and 1.0 equals "dislike extremely."

The subject was first told that the experiment concerned attitudes and reactions to grasshoppers and was asked for his current attitude. He was then asked to eat a grasshopper and, finally, to state his "new" attitude. Each person was given a three-page questionnaire and was told to indicate his initial attitude toward only one thing—grasshoppers—on the first page. He held on to this questionnaire while the induction took place (without opening it?) and then put his post-attitude rating in the same booklet. The subject is clearly sensitized to the food to be eaten, which is made highly salient, and he is also sensitized to the fact that the experimenter is interested in whether attitudes toward grasshoppers *change* after exposure to them. Thus attitude change may be a function of (1) the subject's willingness to comply with the apparent purpose of the experiment, (2) the tendency to resist the experimenter's attempt to manipulate and make guinea pigs of the subjects, or (3) a combination of these reactions. When added to the previously noted differences in the pretest ratings, these reactions yield simply uninterpretable data.

One might question the validity of the measurement of liking for the positive and negative communicator on similar grounds. The simple statement to which the men had to respond was a double-barreled item ("friendly and courteous"), loaded to yield a positive response. Furthermore, it was administered and collected by the same communicator whom each soldier was supposed to be rating. Added to these biases are the points we raised earlier about the relationship of the communicator manipulations to the general Army context. Thus it should come as no great surprise to you to discover that *all* subjects rated the communicator as very positive. Where a rating of 7.0 is maximum positiveness, one group averages 6.8 (positive treatment), while the other group averages 6.4 (negative treatment). Even though this mean difference is statistically significant ($p < .01$), can we conclude at a conceptual level that we have a *positive* and a *negative* communicator? Or do we only have two levels of a very positive communicator?

THE GRASSHOPPER REPLICATION

For a theory to be adequately evaluated, the hypotheses derived from the theory must be tested by experiments that are procedurally well executed. Because the Smith study had a number of flaws in design and procedure, it is not an adequate test of the dissonance predictions. Therefore, Zimbardo, Weisenberg, Firestone, and Levy (1965) decided to redo the study, retaining what was best about it (the basic paradigm) but correcting its faults. As in the Smith study, attitudes toward eating a highly disliked food —fried grasshoppers—were measured before and immediately after an inducement to eat the food. The communicator adopted a friendly, positive role for a randomly selected one-half of the subjects and an unfriendly, negative role for the others. The respected leader and humor conditions of the original study were eliminated since they were not relevant to the test of the basic prediction derived from dissonance theory.

Communicator characteristics   Because the communicator in both experimental roles was an officer in the college's ROTC program, it was possible to determine how he was usually perceived by means of responses on an alleged officer-rating survey. From the personality trait profile that emerged from this analysis, a set of experimental role behaviors was developed. In addition, *both* the positive and the negative communicator had to be perceived as possessing a number of positive traits necessary for effective execution of the experiment. Thus the communicator had to be seen by all subjects as conscientious, capable, well organized, concerned about the reactions of the subjects, and industrious.

Positive role. The communicator (playing the role of an experimenter) interacted with his "assistant" according to a prearranged script in which, for the positive condition, he gave politely phrased requests to the assistant, called him by his first name, responded to a "mistake" by the assistant with equanimity, and in general was considerate and pleasant. But at all times it was clear that he was the person in charge of the experiment and in control.

Negative role. The negative condition demanded that the communicator be perceived as an unpleasant person one would not want to know, work with, or work for. This perception of the negative communicator was largely induced by his quite formal interaction with the assistant. The assistant mistakenly brought in the "wrong" experimental food (a tray of eels in aspic instead of grasshoppers) just as the communicator was in the process of talking to the subjects in his most pleasant manner. The communicator suddenly blew up and said, "Oh, dammit, can't you remember the schedule? That food is for the next group. . . . Let's get with it and hurry up about it!" As the assistant left, obviously embarrassed, the communicator shrugged his shoulders disgustedly, then *reversed his role behavior in front of the subjects* and proceeded again in the same pleasant tone as previously.

Procedure   The subjects first completed a nine-point attitude scale of degree of liking for a wide range of food items, including the fried Japanese grasshopper. Following the initial attitude measurements, the subjects were assigned to the various conditions in the experiment. Differences in the communicator's role behavior commenced as soon as the subjects entered the experimental room. After they completed a hunger and eating habit

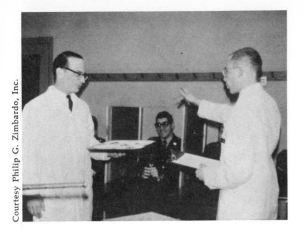

The "negative" communicator putting down his assistant.

questionnaire, heard a talk about the needs of the new mobile army, and witnessed the assistant's "mistake," a plate with five fried grasshoppers was placed in front of each of the men. The experimenter tried to induce the subjects to eat a grasshopper, although maintaining that their action was completely voluntary. Every subject had to make some overt response whether he chose to eat or not, but that response could be seen only by the experimenter.

Control groups were also used, in which subjects were not given an inducement or opportunity to eat a grasshopper. However, their attitudes were measured before and after a time interval equivalent to that of the experimental groups.

Post-compliance measures The final ratings were made in the *absence* of the "experimenter-communicator." An alleged civilian liaison told the subjects that he wanted to evaluate various aspects of the experiment and get more information from them. At this time the experimental subjects completed the following:

1 A post-measure of attitudes toward a number of foods, including grasshoppers

2 A measure of willingness to endorse eating grasshoppers (a second measure of attitude, more linked to action)

3 Checks on the experimental conditions of choice, pressure, and so forth (assessing some of the general experimental conditions)

4 Several indexes of evaluation of both the communicator and his assistant (assessing the independent variable)

Results The main results of the study are the attitude change scores from the pre- to post-measures of liking for fried grasshoppers. However, other information is also important. For example, in all groups about 50 percent of the men ate the grasshoppers (the mean being two grasshoppers). Thus there was no initial difference in overt behavioral compliance. Also, results from a rating scale indicated that the subjects felt they had complete freedom of choice in eating the grasshoppers. Furthermore, it appears that the manipulated differences in the communicator traits were perceived by the subjects exactly as intended.

The attitude change results are presented in terms of the net percentage of subjects who increased their liking for the grasshoppers (see Figure 5.1). If the dissonance theory prediction is correct, the subjects who ate the grasshoppers for the negative communicator should have increased their liking more than those who ate the grasshopper for the positive communicator. This was exactly the result, with the absolute effect being quite large—50 percent more change in the negative than in the positive communicator treatment. This result was, of course, statistically significant. The control groups (without the discrepant commitment) showed practically no net change in attitudes. This result replicates, with the proper controls and a somewhat improved procedure, the earlier findings we had questioned before.

Happiness Is Not Unexplained Arousal

The Schachter and Singer (1962) study was one of the first major experiments within an attribution theory framework. The original thinking behind it argued that the same undifferentiated state of physiological arousal could be interpreted as either anger or euphoria, depending on the cognitive label attached to it. Although this conclusion is a provocative one, is it in fact supported by the evidence?

A careful inspection of the reported findings suggests that the best answer is no. The initial data analysis reveals no significant difference in self-reported emotions between the experimental conditions and the placebo control groups. According to the experimenters' theory, the Placebo and Informed groups should be experiencing neutral emotional states, since the Placebo group is unaroused and the Informed subjects already have a non-emotional explanation for their arousal. However, in the Anger condition, these two groups have the most extreme self-ratings of emotion. Although the experimenters point to the predicted overall pattern of means within each emotion condition, this pattern is not very dramatic in absolute size. As shown in Fig. 5.2, the differences between groups are *less* than one

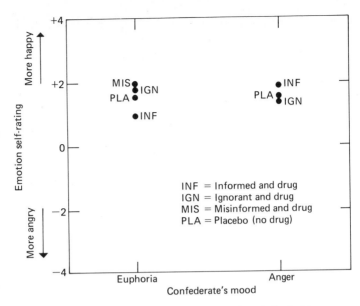

Fig. 5.2 An absence of effect in affect (adapted from Schachter and Singer 1962).

single scale unit on a nine-point scale! The theory also requires absolute differences in emotion ratings between the experimental groups of the Euphoria and Anger conditions. That is, subjects experiencing unexplained arousal should feel happy in the Euphoria condition and angry in the Anger condition. However, as can be seen in Fig. 5.2, *all* of them reported feeling slightly happy.

The behavioral data are not much more convincing. Although the pattern of mean scores for "anger units" is in line with the experimenters' theory, the *size* of this response is not. The low mean score for subjects with unexplained arousal could conceivably represent merely *one* instance of verbal agreement with the angry confederate's position over nearly twenty minutes of interaction! This pallid behavioral response hardly justifies the contention that these subjects were displaying behavior symptomatic of an "angry" emotional state. One "right on" does not qualify as an outburst of anger.

METHODOLOGICAL CRITIQUE

When a set of experimental data fails to support the theoretical hypotheses, it may reflect some flaws in the design and/or procedure of the study, rather than an incorrect hypothesis. The weak results in the Schachter and

Singer study might suggest that some methodological artifacts are obscuring a much stronger finding. Let us look first at the operations utilized in translating hypotheses into experimental manipulations.

Design problems

The arousal variable. One of the major problems in the experiment centers on the use of epinephrine to produce physiological arousal. This drug has different effects for different people, especially when the dosage is held constant (as it was in this study) and not adjusted to variations in each subject's body weight. As a result, there was no experimental control over the onset, intensity, or duration of the arousal. Some subjects may have felt strongly aroused, while others might not have experienced any physiological changes. If subjects did experience arousal symptoms, but these were not concurrent with the confederate's actions, then the subjects would be unlikely to perceive the confederate's moods as even remotely appropriate in labeling their own.

A further problem involves the probability of subjects attributing their arousal to the injection, in spite of the experimenter's statement that it was only a vitamin supplement without side effects. Receiving an injection and suddenly experiencing arousal are two rather unusual experiences (especially in a psychology laboratory experiment). When they occur in close proximity, it is quite likely that people will assume that one caused the other or that they are somehow related. To be sure, 26 percent of the subjects in the Euphoria condition reported being "self-informed" about the injection, in addition to 13 percent of the Anger subjects. We do not know how many others did not report what they perceived.

The emotional label variable. The Euphoria and Anger conditions varied in more ways than just the mood of the confederate. As a result, there are so many factors that could have affected the subject's response that it is not possible to make meaningful behavioral comparisons between these two conditions. In the Euphoria condition, the confederate was physically active, while in the Anger condition he sat quietly for most of the time. If the subject joined in the "euphoric" activity, he might then have had an alternative explanation for his physiological state ("I'm feeling aroused because I've been running around and hula-hooping it up"). No such "activity" explanation existed in the Anger condition.

Another, more serious, problem involves the different reasons given or assumed for the confederate's behavior. Since there is nothing inherent in a messy room that should cause people to experience euphoria, the confederate's playful behavior may tell the subjects more about his particular personality than about the appropriate way to respond to a situation. This *dispositional* interpretation is made especially salient by the confederate's own statement that "this is one of my good days." (Schachter and Singer 1962, p. 384). From the subject's point of view, whatever is causing the confederate to feel euphoric is something unique to him and not something the subject might share. Thus there is no basis for a common cognitive explanation. In contrast, the Anger condition does provide some relevant situational demands. The confederate's anger is directed at a long and insulting questionnaire that the subject is also completing. Thus there is a clear situational factor that is causing the confederate to feel angry and could conceivably be affecting the subject as well.

Procedural problems

Further methodological difficulties involve the dependent measures, which were either confounded, ambiguous, or absent. Because there was no assessment of the emotional label variable, it is not known how the subjects actually perceived the confederate's mood—as "euphoria" or "anger" or some other emotion. For the variable of physiological arousal, two measures were used—one direct (pulse rate) and one indirect (self-report of physiological symptoms). However, neither of these measures provides an accurate assessment of the ongoing course of the arousal. They were taken after the entire session was over and are confounded with any physical activity on the part of the subject.

There are additional problems with the two measures of the subject's emotional response. One measure was a self-report of emotional feeling, while the other involved a series of behavioral ratings made by hidden observers. For the first measure, subjects were asked how "good or happy" they felt, and also how "irritated, angry, or annoyed" they were. Rather than presenting these scores separately, the experimenters subtracted each subject's "anger" rating from his "happiness" rating to yield an index of emotional feeling (the mean scores are presented in Fig. 5.2). The meaning of such scores is unclear, since the same score could result from totally different emotional states. For example, a person with a "happy" rating of 2 and an "angry" rating of 0 (no anger) would have a total emotion score of 2— but so would someone with a "happy" rating of 4 and an "angry" (or annoyed or irritated) rating of 2. The compound phrasing of the emotion statements could mean that subjects were responding "good" and "irritated," which are not justifiably translated into the more extreme polarities of "euphoria" versus "anger." A further problem with these two self-report ratings is that they were the only dimensions of emotion that were measured. If subjects labeled their arousal in terms of other emotions, there was no way of assessing it. In addition, there were no measures of the reasons given by the subjects for their emotional state, nor was there assessment of their emotional level at the start of the study.

Several problems plague the interpretation of the measure of overt behavior. First of all, different ratings were used for the Euphoria and Anger conditions, so that no direct comparisons can be made. Secondly, various behaviors were arbitrarily assigned different weights (for example, flying paper airplanes was +3; disagreeing with the angry confederate was −2, and so on). In the Euphoria condition, each weight was then multiplied by an estimate of the amount of time spent by the subject in that activity (although, inexplicably, this was not done in the Anger condition). For both conditions, these weights were then summed into a single, overall index whose meaning is not at all clear. Does this composite score reflect many low-scoring behaviors or a few high-scoring ones? Did the subject spend a lot of time in a few activities or just a brief moment in many? Such questions are crucial in determining whether or not subjects truly "caught the confederate's mood," as the theory predicted they would. As indicated earlier, some of the data show that they did not.

THEORETICAL CRITIQUE

Although there are numerous flaws in the method used in this study, they may not be entirely responsible for the lack of strong findings. It is also possible that there are difficulties with the theoretical formulation on which the research methodology is based.

Alternative cognitions   One problem involves the researchers' narrow conceptualization of the cognitive labeling process. They postulate that "cognitions arising from the immediate situation as interpreted by past experience provide the framework within which one understands and labels his feelings"(Schachter and Singer 1962, p. 380). Although they make a passing reference to "the past," it is clear from their elaboration of this statement and their experimental test that they view "the immediate social situation" as the primary, if not exclusive, source of emotional cognitions. They do not consider the possibility that a person will search his or her memory for past events or prior comparable situations that could provide an appropriate explanation for the current state of arousal. Subjects might have tried to recall similar situations in which they had felt aroused (such as being in a testing situation or visiting a doctor). They might have then used these memories to derive an appropriate emotional cognition ("I must be getting upset about the tests they are going to do, since I always worry about failing" or "I've never liked getting stuck with needles by doctors, so that's why this injection bothers me"). In other words, subjects may have indeed searched for an appropriate cognition, as the theory predicts, but they may have relied on sources of information other than those limited to the confederate's behavior within the immediate social situation. If so, this would explain the relatively weak impact of the confederate's mood.

Negative arousal states Another area of criticism centers on the conceptualization of unexplained arousal as an affectively *neutral* state that can be molded into either a positive or negative emotion. The idea that unexplained arousal is neutral seems intuitively correct only for someone who is experiencing such arousal for the first time (such as a child). He or she must look to other people and/or the situation to make sense of this strange and puzzling experience. However, the concept does not seem to apply as well to older people who have had numerous experiences pairing arousal with emotional labels and with appropriate arousal instigators. For them, the physiological and cognitive factors are completely entwined with most emotion-inducing situations. Therefore, if they were to feel aroused without knowing why, it would not only be an unusual experience but probably a disturbing or even frightening one, since they would feel a loss of control over their internal states. Indeed, the concept of unexplained arousal is very close to the clinical definition of "free-floating anxiety," which is always characterized by negative emotional affect. One could argue that subjects in the Schachter and Singer paradigm who experienced unexplained arousal had a negative emotional response as a consequence of it. If so, then their search for an appropriate cognitive label would not be the unbiased one proposed by Schachter and Singer. Rather, it would be *biased* toward cognitions of *negative* emotional states.

TWO NEW EMOTION REPLICATION STUDIES

Given the theoretical impact of the Schachter and Singer study, one would expect that independent replications of it had already been done in the decade since it appeared. However, until very recently, no such replications had seen the light of publication. This may have been due to the methodological complexity of the experiment, involving as it does a team of a medical doctor, observers, and a trained confederate for each subject. Another problem centers on the use of drugs in research, especially where deception about the drug is involved. Also, replications may not have been done because psychologists believed in, and wanted to accept as valid, the dramatic conclusions and implications of the study.

Nevertheless, it is essential that such an important theory be independently tested and replicated, especially when there are so many flaws in the original study. Therefore, two different experiments were designed to replicate and extend the Schachter and Singer findings. One experiment involved an exact replication of the original paradigm (Marshall 1976) while the other used a new procedure as a modified replication of the hypotheses (Maslach, in press).

Hypnotically induced arousal The Maslach experiment used an hypnotic induction to create physiological arousal. This technique produced marked physiological changes in the subjects, and allowed for a greater degree of control over the onset and maintenance of the arousal state. The arousal symptoms were hypnotically conditioned to a specific cue and introduced at the appropriate time during the procedure. The lack of an explanation for the arousal was produced by a posthypnotic suggestion of amnesia. Thus subjects experienced physiological arousal but did not know why it was occurring and did not remember that it was due to a hypnotic suggestion. In control conditions, subjects varied in whether or not they were hypnotized, given the arousal cue, or given amnesia for the arousal suggestion.

The confederate behaved in comparable ways in the two emotion conditions (for example, chatting with the subject, reviewing the test materials). Only the confederate's obvious emotional state (happy or angry) was varied, and manipulation checks showed that subjects perceived these emotions correctly. The types of reasons given for the confederate's emotion were also comparable in the two conditions and were ones that subjects could share (such as upcoming exams). Furthermore, the confederate's behavior appeared appropriate and believable.

A large number of dependent measures were added to the experiment, including physiological recording of arousal responses, questionnaire items on perception of the confederate's mood and reaction to the confederate, a battery of emotion scales, a common behavioral rating scale (used by hidden observers), and a clinical interview.

Results. In all cases, subjects who were experiencing unexplained arousal reported *negative* emotions, regardless of the confederate's mood. The control subjects, who were either unaroused or who had an explanation for their arousal, reported neutral or slightly positive emotions. The consistently negative internal state of the experimental groups occurred in spite of the fact that there were systematic differences in overt, external behavior. That is, subjects behaved in a happy, prosocial way with the happy confederate (smiling, talking and so forth), and in a somber, nonsocial way with the angry confederate (avoiding talk or eye contact). However, these *behavioral* responses did not always correspond with *affective* responses. Subjects separated their private feelings from their public behavior, and rarely used the confederate's mood to label what they were feeling. In searching for an explanation for their negative emotions, subjects went beyond the immediate situation (and the other person in it) to draw upon both their current life situation (outside the experiment) and their past experience.

Thus, the conclusions of this experiment (as graphically illustrated in Fig. 5.3) are: (1) unexplained arousal generates a *negative* affective state (regardless of the confederate's mood) and not the assumed neutral one; (2) because of this negative affect, people will be *biased* in their search for cognitions appropriate to negative emotional states; and (3) this cognitive search process is *extensive,* and is not limited to the immediate situation.

Drug-induced arousal   It is possible that Maslach's experiment did not reproduce the original pattern of findings of the Schachter and Singer study because it used a very different procedure involving hypnosis. Therefore, the Marshall (1976) experiment was designed to be a more exact, faithful replication of the original paradigm. Epinephrine injections were used to create a state of physiological arousal, and the confederate followed the

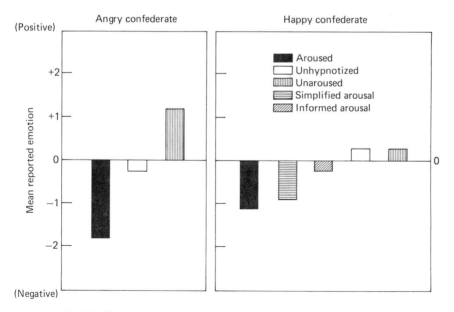

Fig. 5.3 The negative emotional consequences of unexplained arousal regardless of the confederate's mood.

same routine outlined in the initial study. Marshall added some slight modifications to improve the basic paradigm, such as conducting the experiment in a physical therapy room of the Student Health Center. This provided an appropriate setting for the drug injections and the vision tests, and made the presence of hula hoops and other equipment seem reasonable. He also included a wide variety of improved dependent measures, such as continuous physiological recording via telemetry and both pretest and posttest self-reports of emotion.

Only a euphoric condition was used because that is where the Schachter and Singer predictions and Maslach's part company. They agree on the anger condition consequences: unexplained arousal should result in negative emotional states in the presence of an angry confederate. Schachter and Singer argue that this is so because of the confederate's mood; Maslach argues that it is because of the nature of unexplained arousal.

Results. Even with this ideal procedural replication, Marshall also found *no* empirical support for Schachter and Singer's conclusions. Subjects who had received the standard (.5cc) epinephrine injection, along with an "inadequate" explanation of its side effects, did not differ from placebo controls in either emotional affect or behavior. To see if differences would emerge if the arousal were more intense, Marshall increased the epinephrine dosage level, adjusting it to the body weight of each subject. These subjects did experience more intense physiological arousal (at a level comparable to that of the hypnotized subjects in the Maslach study). But they reported a *negative* emotional state, exactly like Maslach's subjects and unlike the reported findings of the original study. Furthermore, Marshall replicated Maslach's finding that the subjects' public behavior was affected by the confederate's mood, but that their private feelings were not.

Thus, taken together, these two replications cast serious doubt upon the validity of the original conclusions about arousal and emotion. Instead they point in a new direction—study of the effect of unexplained arousal on emotional pathology. This is one way in which critical analysis can lead to solid new paths rather than being merely a source of complaints that existing paths are inhospitably muddy.

Shedding Fat by Word and Deed

The principles derived from social learning theory are currently being applied in programs to treat a wide variety of personal problems. One such problem, which is a major source of concern for many Americans, is obesity. The difficulties involved in effectively losing weight, and then maintaining that loss, are all too well known, especially to anyone struggling with the physical and psychological consequences of obesity. Indeed, there is now a remarkable obesity industry in this country, which includes diet books, diet foods, diet clinics, and "fat farms." Despite a huge investment of money and effort, these programs are far from delivering what they promise. Recent evidence suggests, however, that the use of behavior modification techniques might be particularly effective in this area of self-control.

An interesting study by Penick, Filion, Fox, and Stunkard (1971) directly compared two programs in the treatment of obesity: one was a behavior modification program while the other used supportive psychotherapy. Both treatments were carried out once a week in a hospital setting for a period of three months. The subjects were thirty-two people (twenty-four females and eight males) who were at least 20 percent overweight. Fifteen people were randomly assigned to the two behavior modification groups, and the remaining seventeen people participated in the two psychotherapy comparison groups. Most of the people were middle-class private patients who paid in advance for the entire program, although six of them were lower-class welfare patients who had been referred by a state rehabilitation agency and whose fees were paid by the state. The goals of both treatment programs were: (1) a significant loss of weight, and (2) the development of self-control with regard to obesity-related behaviors.

RESULTS

Overall, all four treatment groups showed a loss of weight (which was measured on a weight scale and not on a self-report scale). However, the *median* weight loss in the behavior modification groups was greater than that of the therapy control groups. At the end of the three-month program, 53 percent of the behavior modification patients had lost more than twenty pounds, and 13 percent of them had lost more than forty. In contrast, 24 percent of the therapy control groups had lost over twenty pounds, but none had lost as much as thirty or forty pounds. A follow-up several months later revealed that the patients had continued to lose weight (instead of the usual experience of rapid regaining of weight after treatment). However, the behavior modification groups continued to surpass the others. Twenty-seven percent of them had now lost more than forty pounds, while 12 percent of the comparison groups had done so. The message seems

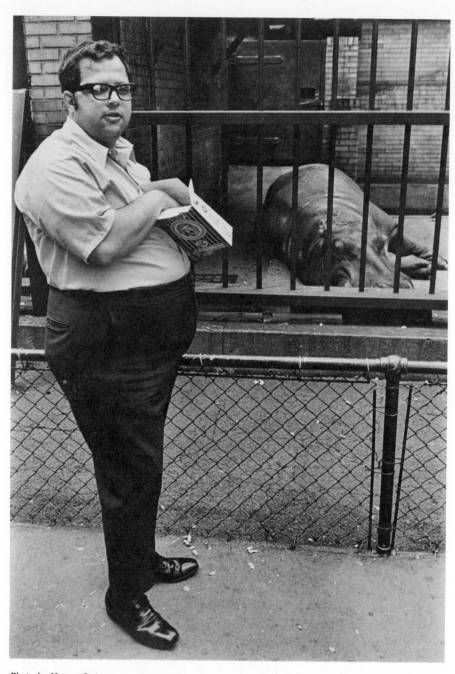

Photo by Harvey Stein.

clear as to where to begin if you want to take off a lot of unwanted fat—go behavior mod.

CRITIQUE

Impressive as these overall results are, a closer analysis of this study raises a number of questions about the effectiveness of the behavior modification program. First of all, the pattern of data is not as simple and clear-cut as it seems initially. Although the two treatments differ in *median* weight loss, there is no statistically significant difference in *mean* weight loss. Thus, depending on what measure is used, there either is or is not a difference between the two programs. The explanation for the lack of a mean difference can be seen in Fig. 5.4. The *variability* in weight loss for the behavior modification group is much greater than that for the therapy control group. In the former group, some people lose a lot and some lose a little (one person even gains!), while in the latter group everyone loses a moderate amount.

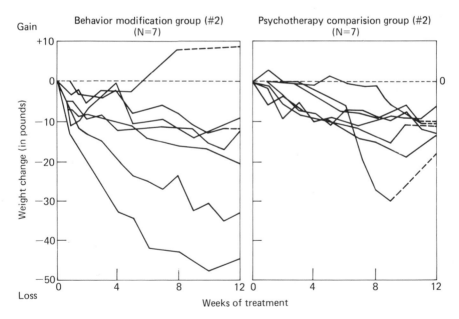

Fig. 5.4 Weight changes of patients given behavior modification or psychotherapy treatments (adapted from Penick et al. 1971).

Clearly, the behavior modification treatment is working for some people but not for others. Why might this be so? A review of the specific techniques used in this program may shed some light on this perplexing result.

Daily records   Patients had to keep daily records of their eating behavior—how much they ate, when and for how long—as well as of the situational circumstances. This is a very time-consuming and inconvenient task, and some patients may have found it quite aversive, while others may have seen it as part of the "treatment" variable and not just a baseline measurement.

Control of discriminatory stimuli   Whenever patients ate, whether it was a meal or a snack, it had to be done in one place (such as the dining room). They had to use a distinctive table setting (a particular placemat and napkin), and they had to eat alone and without doing anything else (such as reading or watching TV). Since this was a troublesome procedure, which was not monitored by the experimenters, it is not clear how often or how well it was followed—or what effect it had on the subjects' family lives.

Techniques to control eating   Patients were told to do certain exercises to get them to eat more slowly, such as counting each mouthful of food and placing utensils on the plate until the mouthful was swallowed. The subjects' word is all we have of whether or not they did what they were supposed to, or thought they did, or remembered accurately after the fact that they did.

Reinforcements   When patients successfully used the above techniques or resisted eating even when tempted, they awarded *themselves* a certain number of points. These points were later converted into money and donated to the group. At the beginning of the program, each group decided how to use its money: one group donated it to the Salvation Army and the other group gave it to a widow with fourteen children.

Negative reinforcements included losing points for failure to control eating and flavoring snacks with castor oil to make them taste bad. In addition, each patient kept a "fat bag" in the refrigerator, which contained sixteen pieces of suet. The patient tried to visualize this as his or her personal fat. For every pound lost, one piece of suet was removed; for every pound gained, one piece was added. If a patient lost the entire fat bag, the group gave her or him a prize, as well as extensive praise.

A number of problems are evident here. First of all, the allocation of points was based on self-reports of one's efforts (which could have been faked or distorted). Secondly, the conversion of one's hard-earned points into money that the group then gives away may not have seemed so charitable and reinforcing to some of the participants. For example, some people might have wished to keep their "winnings" for themselves (particularly if they were not well off financially). Or they may not have been happy with the group's decision about the money, but would have had to go along reluctantly because of majority rule, group pressure, and other sources of influence. People who were shy or who felt they had low status may have felt particularly "pushed around." In either case, the point technique may not have been a source of incentive motivation for them, or it may have been of mixed value.

Although the goal of the behavior modification program was the development of self-control, the use of *group* techniques may be the effective factor operating here. Group modeling, group praise, and group decision making were all major components of this treatment. How important were these aspects of the program in the actual achievement of weight loss, as opposed to the more individual techniques? Unfortunately, no answer to this question can be provided, since none of the techniques was assessed separately. All we know is that the entire program worked, and very well for at least some people. However, we do not know which parts of the program were actually effective in producing change—one, some, or all of them.

The question then becomes, "what do you care about—getting the change or knowing how you got it?" From the point of view of the patient, it does not matter which parts of the program worked, just so long as *something* works. From the point of view of the therapist and experimenter, however, it *does* matter which parts are effective. Such knowledge can help them design better weight-loss programs by indicating which factors are critical and need to be refined and intensified. It can also reduce their costs by pointing out what factors are ineffective and superfluous and therefore could be eliminated.

In passing, we cannot help but point out that the results of this study could lead to two very different TV commercials for weight reduction: to buy "Behavior Mod" or pay for "Psychotherapy."

> Tired of being called "Fatstuff"? Behavior Mod will help you become the attractive, energetic person you've always admired in trim-line models. Recent research from a major university convincingly demonstrates that, on the average, patients who follow a Behavior Mod program lose significantly more weight than those treated by the best other "traditional" therapeutic approach. The doctors who reported their remarkable results in a medical journal go on to tell us—"and it never returned." [Fade from hippopotamus transformed into a panther.]

. . .

> Want to discover the real you waiting to be liberated from the dungeon of obesity? Psychotherapy Persuasively Pummels those Pounds off your Paunch. A recent study by a team of medical researchers convincingly proves *no* other known treatment that was compared to psycho-

therapy was *more effective* in controlling weight loss. Psychotherapy is your ONLY way to new freedom through a new figure.

. . .

Facetious though these examples may seem, they have their parallels in the everyday abuse of research applied to the marketplace. But research on attitudes and behavior may also be used for the betterment of the human condition—to inform and guide our decisions. We turn next to consider a range of "real-world" applications of social influence based upon the psychological theories and empirical results with which you are now acquainted. The determination of whether the practice is a good use or unethical abuse of the principles of attitude and behavior change is one that must concern us all.

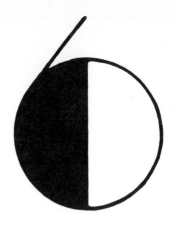

translating principles into practice: the tactics and strategies of change

We can now step out of the rarefied air of psychological theory and the purified atmosphere of the laboratory to look at relevant situations in our own lives. This does not mean that the behavioral sciences have already amassed a large enough body of reliable data or developed theories comprehensive enough to explain how variables interact to change attitudes. On the contrary, there is a real need for both better theory and more compelling data, but the practical problems facing us today are in dire need of solution. We must proceed with what we know, and hope that the scientific analysis of the attitude change process will develop concurrently with the practical analysis of realistic concerns.

In this concluding chapter, then, we want to examine a number of practical attempts to change attitudes and behavior —attempts that start out with a desired, often specific, goal in mind. In so doing, we will be emphasizing the problem-centered orientation we proposed right from the beginning of this book. In addition, we hope that you may begin to see how the applied and pure approaches may interact to the mutual benefit of both.

Attitude Change and Assessment: The War Babies

Attitude change research was born in the 1940s in response to practical problems created by World War II. In a similar way, the psychological assessment of intelligence was given an impetus in this country by pragmatic concerns emerging during World War I. The earlier concerns centered on identifying and rejecting draftees whose mental abilities were too low, while those with above average capability were sent to special training programs. This task was complicated because of the substantial number of recent immigrants with a poor command of English. The development of nonverbal performance tests to measure intelligence (The Army Alpha and Beta Tasks) helped to resolve this selection problem. As a consequence, the Wechsler-Bellevue Intelligence Scale now incorporates both verbal and performance measures in the assessment of IQ.

The new problems faced by the military in World War II were of a more social-psychological nature. They were those of assessing the social-personal attitudes of bomber crews, evaluating the effects of persuasive films on soldiers, determining reactions of white soldiers toward Negro infantrymen in their division, getting housewives to change the food habits of their families, and so forth. In July of 1941, the Secretary of War issued an order that no surveys of attitudes of enlisted men could be undertaken because of their possible "destructive effect on morale." Nevertheless, a study was done the day after Pearl Harbor, and it showed that the evidence gathered from attitude questionnaires pointed out critical weaknesses in certain military practices much better than did the previously used officer's reports. The latter were impressions of a haphazardly selected, biased sample of informants—the worst kind of evidence. Samuel Stouffer (who headed a group of psychologists working for the Research Branch of the Information and Education Division of the War Department), in his studies of the attitudes of American soldiers (1949), noted that relatively little use was made of controlled experiments to evaluate the effect on attitudes of propaganda and changes in military procedures. This was due largely to a lack of good criteria for evaluating when these subtle changes in attitude occurred.

A scientific approach to communication and attitude change developed directly out of this wartime research, under the direction of Carl Hovland. He had worked on experiments in mass communication (see also Hovland, Lumsdaine, and Sheffield 1949) while in the army, and later, as mentioned in earlier chapters, inaugurated the Attitude Change Center at Yale University. This center, in turn, became the major academic site for research on attitude change and for the training of students and young social psychologists (P. G. Z. among them). As we have seen, the general theoretical orientation of the Yale School continues to be a significant frame of reference for understanding the impact of communications on attitudes.

Preaching and Practicing

We now ask you to consider with us the following range of problems, from which will be drawn practical, concrete illustrations of attitude and behavior change programs in action. Is "creating an image" a *new* Madison Avenue approach? In what sense is our educational system a propaganda mill? What does psychological warfare propaganda look like, and how can it be detected? How can mothers be persuaded not to serve their babies home-made foods in favor of buying Brand *X*? How can the prejudiced attitudes of a given woman toward a minority group be changed? How can the police get you to change your attitude against self-incrimination and thereby confess to a crime that may deprive you of your freedom or life? How can a person's need for freedom and self-assertion be incorporated into a persuasion program? Can heart-disease risk be lowered by social influence? Finally, we ask, is mass conversion achieved by means magic or mundane?

CREATING AN IMAGE, OR "PACKAGING" THE COMMUNICATOR

Television has made us aware of the extensive use of public relations firms to promote the campaigns of political candidates. Hair style, clothes style, and speech style are modified to fit an image fashioned by opinion polls,

"It was either the knish in Coney Island, the cannoli in Little Italy, or that divinity fudge in Westchester."

Drawing by Levin; © 1976 The New Yorker Magazine, Inc.

advisers, and media experts. Thus former President Ford was trained to use hand gestures, albeit woodenly, when making key points during TV speeches. This image management strategy was first used many years ago. An enterprising public relations man (whose pseudonym was Ivy Lee) was hired to change the prevailing stereotype of John D. Rockefeller. Mr. Rockefeller was generally considered a self-aggrandizing robber baron. A complete image reversal was called for, one in which the public would view him as a philanthropic, kindly gentleman. The strategy was deceptively simple: one of the most effective techniques was to publicize pictures and stories of Rockefeller giving shiny new dimes to every child he met in the streets. It is tougher on the tummy these days with urban politicians having to appeal to diverse ethnic constituencies. The TV image comes to mind of suave John Lindsay, New York's former Mayor, making the rounds eating knishes, pizza, Polish sausage, ribs, fried bananas, and egg rolls, topped off with an all-American hot dog from Nathan's delicatessen.

EDUCATION: HIDDEN PROPAGANDA FOR THE ESTABLISHMENT

Traditionally, *propaganda* is defined as an attempt to influence public opinion and public behavior through specialized techniques. It is contrasted with *education*, in which there is also an attempt to change attitudes and behavior, but through information, evidence, facts, and logical reasoning. In an ideal sense, educators teach students not *what* to think, but only *how* to think. In this way, propagandists differ from educators because they intentionally try to bias what people see, think, and feel in the hope that they will adopt their viewpoint.

But are there concealed, subtle forms of indoctrination in education that cloud these neat distinctions? Think back to the examples used in your textbooks to teach you the purely objective, academic discipline of mathematics. Most of the work problems dealt with buying, selling, renting, working for wages, and computing interest. These examples not only reflect the system of economic capitalism in which the education takes place, but are also an endorsement or subconscious legitimization of it. To illustrate, take an example that might be used to make concrete the arithmetic operations involved in dividing 90 by 60. "John wants to borrow $90, but Joe can only lend him $60. What percentage of the amount he wanted does John obtain?" The same conceptual operations could be equally well learned with a different illustration, perhaps less likely in our country: "John earns $60 a week for his labor from Company X. Medical and health authorities are agreed that the weekly cost of living for a family of four is $90. What percentage of a decent, acceptable minimal wage does Company X pay John?"

While such an example may seem farfetched, consider the complaints of the black community that textbooks in all areas omit reference in word or picture to the reality of black history, black culture, or even black existence—except as related to slavery and primitive native customs. Such an omission fosters the majority attitude among black and other minority children that their race (and they as members of it) is insignificant. If this is not an intentional goal of our educational process, then its impact should be assessed, and correctives considered.

A travel film shown in a geography class shows how Russian children are indoctrinated to salute the picture of Lenin that is in every classroom. Chinese children are likewise seen as little automatons forced to sing patriotic songs and give their allegiance to their communist rulers. When *you* sang the Star Spangled Banner, saluted the American flag, and pledged allegiance to the United States while a portrait of Kennedy, Johnson, Nixon, or a latter-day president looked down approvingly on your elementary classroom, were you really free *not* to do so?

PSYCHOLOGICAL WARFARE

The problem of comparing the concealed purpose of a communication to its obvious manifest content is one of our central tasks in analyzing propaganda used in psychological warfare (the organized use of propaganda, or nonviolent persuasion, against a military enemy). The purposes of such propaganda are as follows:

1 *Conversionary*—to weaken or change the emotional, ideological, or behavioral allegiance of individuals to their group (army, unit, village, nation, and so on)

2 *Divisive*—to split apart component subgroups of the enemy to reduce their combined effectiveness (the Allied propaganda tried to make German generals think of themselves first as Catholics; the Vietcong propaganda stressed the subordinate status of blacks in America to create further dissension in the ranks)

3 *Consolidating*—to ensure compliance of civilian populations in occupied zones

4 *Counteracting*—to refute an effective theme in the propaganda of the enemy

Examples of German propaganda Imagine how the morale of American soldiers might have been affected in World War II by such German propaganda leaflets as shown on the next three pages. (See Linebarger 1954 for a good analysis of the psychology of warfare.)

WHAT TO DO

✝ REMEMBER, the Kreuzotter [pronounced CROYTS-otter] is about two feet long, dark grey in color, with small black crosses running the length of its body.

✝ IN THE DAYTIME avoid rocky areas where the Kreuzotter may be hiding. If you must walk among rocks, watch carefully for the snake, for it is well camouflaged. If you pass close to it, it may strike.

✝ AT NIGHT take all possible precautions to keep the Kreuzotter out of your tent. When you awaken in the morning, look around carefully, be sure it is not near before you get up.

✝ IF BITTEN do not get panicky. Do not run. Open the wound and bleed it immediately. If this is impossible, use a tourniquet. Send for aid at once.

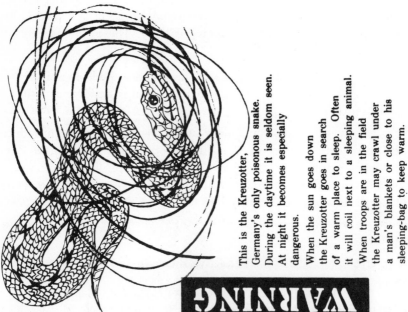

This is the Kreuzotter, Germany's only poisonous snake. During the daytime it is seldom seen. At night it becomes especially dangerous.

When the sun goes down the Kreuzotter goes in search of a warm place to sleep. Often it will coil next to a sleeping animal. When troops are in the field the Kreuzotter may crawl under a man's blankets or close to his sleeping-bag to keep warm. In the morning, if the snake is disturbed, it may strike.

WARNING

Maneuvers The Easy Way

The psychiatrists were right when they said life is what you make it.

Take this maneuver. It can be rough and miserable, or it can be a soft touch for any guy with an imagination.

For example, when you're standing around in the chow line waiting for cold salmon and beans, why make matters worse by griping about it.

GIVE YOURSELF A BREAK AND THINK ABOUT THE GOOD OLD DAYS.

Why Complain?

Instead of cold
salmon and beans

remind yourself about
a real mouthful,

Instead of grime and
mud in the field

Sunday dinner with fried chicken
mashed potatoes, cole slaw, cherry
pie

remember all those

weekend parties with the boys,
football games, drive-in
theaters

Instead of night
guard and details

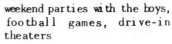

think about

Saturday night dates with
soft lights and soft shoulders -- and no curfews

THIS MANEUVER SHOULDN'T GIVE YOU ANY TROUBLE
AT ALL. ALL YOU NEED IS A LITTLE IMAGINATION.

BETTER BUY BABY FOOD, DON'T DARE MAKE IT AT HOME!

The scare tactics in these German propaganda examples seem a bit obvious now, but they should be viewed in the context of their time frame. There was no body of attitude change research available at that time on which to draw. But the German propaganda machine did have a cold, calculating intuitive sense of the soft spots in human motivation; they knew how to make a message hit home with the American GIs.

Around November 1975, a more sophisticated persuasive appeal hit the homes of 760,000 American mothers. An undated letter signed by Frank Nicholas, President of Beech-Nut Baby Food Company, cautioned these mothers against the potential dangers to their babies of home-prepared foods. The letter concluded with the virtues of commercially prepared baby food, especially extolling Beech-Nut Baby Food as the "best possible food for babies." The letter was allegedly sent as a "public service cautioning mothers," according to the corporate director of Quality Assurance.

Before we examine the letter for the tactics and appeals employed, three points deserve mention: (1) In May 1976, *Consumers Reports* reported that homemade baby foods are, on the whole, more nutritious and wholesome than the commercially made kind. (2) A class-action suit was filed August 5, 1976 by four mothers against the Baker/Beech-Nut Cor-

---

Baker/Beech-Nut Corporation
2 CHURCH STREET • ANAJOHARIE, N.Y. 13317

FRANK C. NICHOLAS
PRESIDENT

Dear Mother:

Much publicity has appeared recently which urges mothers to make their own baby food at home. Some of this publicity is distributed by manufacturers of food grinders, blenders and other implements to sell grinders and blenders. Some is well-intentioned. Much is misinformed.

We at Beech-Nut feel obliged to advise you that some potential dangers for your child exist in the home preparation of baby food. Much of the publicity has been self-serving and has ignored this fact. Beech-Nut would never want to sell its product at the expense of the health and well-being of babies. That is why Beech-Nut, as a responsible corporate citizen, feels compelled to speak out in the interest of safety and good nutrition for your baby.

You, as a mother, should know that some cases of methemoglobinemia have been reported in medical literature from the feeding of home-prepared spinach puree, carrot soup and carrot juice. Beets may also be a problem.

Nitrates in these products can be converted to nitrites during transportation, from bacterial contamination or in baby's stomach which contains less acid than an adult's stomach. Nitrites combine with red blood cell pigments in a manner which prevents these pigments from performing their job of transporting oxygen to the body. With too much methemoglobin, baby's skin turns blue and asphyxiation could result.

Commercial blanching and processing eliminates most of the nitrates, eliminates bacteria and inactivates enzymes to prevent any remaining nitrates from converting to nitrites, thus eliminating the risk.

You, as a mother, should know that babies are more sensitive to bacteria than adults, and there is significant risk of bacterial contamination and resultant food poisoning in home-made baby food. Most

-over-

home-made baby foods are not sterile. Beech-Nut Baby Food is sterilized by heat and pressure cooking in hermetically sealed containers.

You, as a mother, should know that commercial baby food is adequate to the nutrition requirements of your baby. In contrast, do-it-yourself baby food loses nutrients four ways:

1. Through nutrient oxidation as a result of too much air inclusion, particularly when blenders are used.
2. Through pour-off of water-soluble nutrients.
3. Through use of raw foods of uncertain freshness.
4. Through freezing and thawing if food is made for subsequent meals.

The University of California, among others, has documented the greater loss of nutrients in home-prepared baby food compared to commercial products.

As a mother, you should know that Beech-Nut has dedicated over 40 years to making the purest, most nutritious baby foods using the best methods known to modern science and with the best medical advice available. Our standards in every case meet or exceed those established by federal and state regulatory agencies. Beech-Nut Baby Food contains no preservatives, artificial colors, artificial flavors or MSG. We assure you we will continue to make the best possible food for babies. We care.

Sincerely,

Frank C. Nicholas

Frank C. Nicholas
President

P.S. If you would like to know more or have any questions, please send me a note with your questions, or send your phone number and I or our technical people will be happy to call you at whatever time you indicate is convenient.

poration charging the company with "statutory and common law fraud." The suit argues that the letter was "a scare tactic with grossly misleading and false information about homemade baby food, designed to induce new mothers to buy Beech-Nut's products." (3) Christina Maslach, along with other social scientists, analyzed the letter for its persuasive tactics at the request of Public Advocates, Inc., a public interest law firm. The suit does not ask for monetary damages—instead it asks the court to force Beech-Nut to mount a corrective advertising campaign "to set the record straight."

We have here a strong fear appeal that (1) is from an apparently credible source, (2) describes a threat to the loved ones of the intended audience, and (3) deals with issues of relative unfamiliarity on which some expert knowledge is required. The literature on the effectiveness of fear appeals is far from simple, but the above characteristics are among the essential components of a forceful fear appeal. However, two more elements are necessary (according to the research by Howard Leventhal and his associates, 1970): (1) a recommendation for immediate action or counteraction, and (2) clear and simple directions for carrying out the recommendations.

If a mother did not want to take the risk of having her baby turn blue and become asphyxiated, she could stop serving home-made baby foods (or not begin to do so); start or keep serving commercially prepared baby foods; personally contact Mr. Nicholas or his "technical people" for more information; and buy Beech-Nut. Enclosed with the letter to concerned mothers was an offer of $15 worth of Beech-Nut Baby Foods for $10. A direct, economical solution to a scary problem, no?

Beech-Nut Budget Stretcher!!
Save $5!

Send your check or money order for $10 and we will send you $15 in coupons redeemable toward the purchase of Beech-Nut Baby Food. We will send you, within two weeks, a booklet containing fifteen $1 coupons good on any purchase of Beech-Nut Baby Food.

Offer to purchase booklet expires February 29, 1976. Please note additional terms on back.

While you analyze the specific tactics used in this appeal, you might want to check the May 1976 *Consumer Reports* article, which attempts to "set the record straight" by documenting as false many of the "scientific" claims made in the letter.

Beech-Nut is holding its ground by standing "fully behind the letter" (*San Francisco Bay Guardian*, August 6, 1976). Meanwhile, another baby food giant, Gerber's, was using a more subtle tactic to persuade parents not to do their own thing but to buy it Gerber's way. The tactic involves

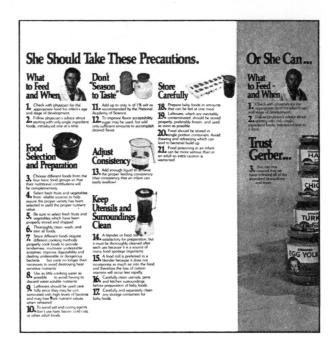

comparing the effort, time, thought, and risk involved in the twenty-one (advertising) steps required to make one's own baby food with the easy, three-step Gerber plan.

Whatever the overall effectiveness of such advertising campaigns in influencing consumer behavior, there were some unintended "boomerang" effects. "It never occurred to me to make my own baby food," said a young mother, "until Beech-Nut caused all this fuss. Now, from what I read, I'm uneasy about buying Jimmy's food in the jars."

WHO'S PREJUDICED? YOUR MOTHER!

Racial, ethnic, and religious prejudice may be viewed as a negative evaluation, and as a rejection of an individual solely because of his or her membership in a particular group. If those discriminated against (as well as those who are prejudiced) suffer because of this prejudice, then why do we not eliminate it? Dedicated social scientists and humanitarians have been concerned with this problem for a number of years. The United Nations and the United States have spent millions of dollars on *information* campaigns to correct stereotypes about minority groups, to present the facts, and to help people to get to know one another. They assumed that prejudice was based on ignorance and that every person's desire to know the truth would dispel false beliefs. From every indication we have, these campaigns have been very limited in their effectiveness.

© Los Angeles Times. Reprinted by permission.

A second approach used to combat prejudiced attitudes has assumed that *contact*, or physical proximity between members of the group in question, would make attitudes more favorable. For example, you take a class of white students on a tour of Harlem, or you mix races in a public housing project, a summer camp, an infantry outfit, or the classroom.

There is some equivocal evidence that as long as the contact continues, the prejudiced attitudes may weaken. However, once the person returns to a situation where the norms do not support tolerant attitudes, the new-found tolerance slips back into old prejudiced habits of thought, speech, and action. This raises the key issue not only of whether the techniques used produce a big immediate change, but also of whether the change generalizes to the social environment or group that supports the old behavior. Criminal recidivism and the return to drugs by "cured" drug addicts may be traced to "changed" individuals being sent back to an unchanged social setting in which their new attitudes and behavior are not socially supported. A newly emerging philosophy of change in therapeutic communities such as Synanon and San Francisco's Delancey Street Foundation (for former prisoners, prostitutes, and drug addicts) is to *not* send the members back if they want to stay on. You cannot go home to old stimuli and expect old responses not to be evoked. You cannot put cucumbers in a vinegar barrel and expect them not to emerge as pickles.

Judge for yourself whether information and contact alone are sufficient conditions for changing prejudice. Here is a case study of a college freshman trying to persuade a middle-aged housewife that she holds untenable attitudes toward Puerto Ricans who were then (1954) just beginning to move into "her" Southeast Bronx neighborhood. The woman has already had a great deal of contact with Puerto Ricans who live in her building, shop at the same stores, own some of these stores, and are friends of her daughters. The boy provides sensible, rational arguments in favor of a general attitude of tolerance and understanding of the problems of this new group of migrants to the American melting pot. In reading this account of the transcript,[1] note not only the student's efforts to change the woman's attitude, but also the techniques the woman uses to bolster her position. Also, try to see beyond her rational manifest concern to the nature and the variety of topics she raises, especially those that emerge when the student has trapped her in an inconsistency. There seems to be something lurking below the surface of her conscious rationality.

Interviewer (P. Zimbardo): You've been living in this neighborhood quite a number of years. Do you think there's been any change in the composition of the neighborhood?
Woman: There certainly has. I've been living in this house now for twenty-one years, and I daresay I'm ashamed to tell people that I live in the neighborhood I do.
Student: Why is that?
Woman: Because of what the Puerto Ricans have done to it.
Student: What do you mean, specifically?
Woman: Well, to start with, their filth. Second, the language they use, and third, because the teachers waste eight hours a day with them in school and find that they get nowhere the minute the children are released.
Student: You mean you never heard that language from anyone else but a Puerto Rican?
Woman: I certainly have, but not as much as I hear it from them.
Student: Maybe you listen to it from them more often than you listen to it from others.
Woman: I can't help it, because the streets are overcrowded with them.
Student: Well, why are they overcrowded with them?
Woman: It doesn't have to be overcrowded, they can live somewhere else, or gather somewhere else. But I find that this is the biggest dope center, because there's nothing done about it. We pay police the salaries that we do, we pay taxes, and yet what has been done?

---

[1] A transcript of a tape recording made by Zimbardo in a community center in New York City. The participants agreed to talk about conditions in their neighborhood and were aware they were being recorded. Comments by other participants were deleted from this presentation for purposes of space.

Student: What do you know about dope centers? You say this in the *biggest* dope center. Do you know of other dope centers. . . ?

Woman: I think they're the filthiest race, they're devoid of brains, and it's a disgrace with what goes on.

Student: Why do you say they're the filthiest race?

Woman: They are, because I've worked with colored people, and I find that they're 50 percent more immaculate than the Puerto Ricans.

Student: Well why are they dirty? Isn't there a reason why they're dirty?

Woman: They don't know any better, unfortunately.

Student: So then how can you condemn them because they don't know better? If you find a person that's ignorant, are you gonna condemn him?

Woman: You can condemn people for being poor, but you can't condemn them for being filthy. [She means the opposite, or does she?] Soap and water doesn't cost much. If a person is ignorant, he knows nothing about cleanliness. And if he's devoid of brains, he certainly doesn't know.

Student: All right, look, you say they're filthy and all that. But look at the sanitation problems in Puerto Rico.

Woman: I've never been to Puerto Rico, so I can't speak about Puerto Rico. I live in the Bronx and I can only tell you what happens here.

Student (overlaps): In New York here or even in the United States we have the highest standard of living. They don't have that in other places; if a person just comes over from a low standard of living into a high standard of living . . . .

Woman (interrupts): Why is it that most of the Puerto Ricans own the most beautiful cars, and yet 90 percent of them are on relief [social welfare]?

Student: A lot of people own cars and don't have a lot of money.

Woman: Not a lot. Puerto Ricans more than any other race.

Student: Why Puerto Ricans more than any other race?

Woman: 'Cause I happen to know someone that works on the Home Relief Bureau [Welfare Service]; and more Puerto Ricans than any other race. . . . But they know how to make babies every nine months.

Student: So are you going to condemn them for having *kids?*

Woman: Why do they have so many of them? *You could condemn them for having kids.* They should go out and look for jobs! The hospitals are flooded with them today. Do they know about going to pediatricians? No! Do they know how to raise children? No! What do they bring them up on? When the child's seven months old, it learns to drink beer from a can!

Student (interrupts): My God, the people . . . the people just came over here, how long have they been in the United States? What chance have they had?

Woman: They've been here much too long to suit me. [Discussion of Puerto Rican girls going behind the school yard at night with boys.]

Student: So you blame them for being *obvious* instead of hiding it . . . right? Instead of being sneaks about it?

Woman: Yes, because their parents don't know enough to take care of them.

Student: How do you know their parents don't know?

Woman: Because if you go to dance halls, who do you find there? More Puerto Ricans.

Student: You find anybody at dance halls. You mean before the Puerto Ricans came there were no dance halls?

Woman: Refined, but not like now. I lived in a building that was the most upstanding house on the block. Today it's disgraceful, because it's surrounded with Puerto Ricans.

Student: Surrounded with . . . Why? Do you think just because a person's Puerto Rican, right away he's filthy and he's dirty and he's dumb? You think just because a person's a Puerto Rican or something like that, that you call him dumb and ignorant because he's born Puerto Rican? A few years ago there was prejudice against the Jewish people. They weren't allowed in certain jobs, they're not allowed in colleges, they're not allowed in, uh . . . .

Woman (not listening): Then they shouldn't come here. They should stay in Puerto Rico.

Student: Is it so easy to find apartments now that you can go out and get all the apartments you want? So then why are you condemning?

Woman: It isn't easy, because I'm a little fussy. I want to stay away from them. I want to go to a neighborhood that *restricts them.*

Student: But you still didn't answer a question I asked before. Just because the . . . they're Puerto Ricans or something like that, they're . . . that they're filthy, they're dirty. How many years ago was it before the Jewish people were, uh, discriminated against?

Woman: Not that I know of.

Student: Not that you know of! How . . . the Jewish people . . . A Jewish person couldn't get into law school or anything like that then, you couldn't get into the Bell Telephone Company, you couldn't get into . . . to millions of jobs.

Woman: That's only hearsay. But can you prove it?

Student: It isn't, yes, I can prove it. I have relatives that tried out for the Bell Telephone Company and they couldn't get in because they were Jewish. I had a . . . one of my relatives graduated from law school. He was one of the first people who graduated like that.

Daughter: So tell us why has the Bronx come down so much?

Student: Because it's overpopulated?

Daughter: With dirty Spics!

Student: So what reason do you have to call them dirty Spics?

Daughter: What reason!

Woman: One, because they don't know how to bring up children. Second, because their morale [morals?] is so low. Third, because they're known to consume more alcohol than any other race in this world. And fourth, they're the biggest marijuana smokers.

Student: Who drinks more beer than Irish people?

Woman: Who wanted to shoot the President, if not the Puerto Ricans [reference to assassination attempt on President Truman by Puerto Rican Nationalists]?

Student: What about John Wilkes Booth, who tried to shoot Abraham Lincoln, what was he?

Woman: You're going back so many years! You pick up the paper and read about prostitutes. Who's involved? Puerto Ricans.

The South Bronx has become one of the nation's worst ghettos.

Interviewer: We seem to be going off on a tangent, so let's wind up the discussion with your views on how the problem could be solved.
Woman: It could be solved by dropping a token in the subway and sending them all back where they came from!

The student clearly had good intentions and worked hard to dissuade the woman from her anti-Puerto Rican position. He gave some sound arguments, refuted some of the opposing arguments, gave personal examples of prejudice toward him, and made a sincere appeal to view prejudice as ignorance that can be overcome by simply getting to know your disliked neighbors regardless of their race, religion, or ethnic background. And to what effect? The woman exhibited a "boomerang" effect, reacting with more overt hostility and prejudice than she showed initially.

Good intentions unsupported by sound psychological knowledge may get the student into heaven, but they will never change this woman's attitude. Where he failed was in not assessing the function her attitude serves in her total psychological makeup, and by accepting her rationalizations as rational statements. The major consequence of his puncturing one of her arguments, or directly confronting her with contrary evidence, was for her to become both emotionally upset (at points, both she and daughter were near hysteria) and more openly hostile over the course of the interview. Her tactical weapon was a non sequitur flank attack. She changed topics and regained her composure, while her adversary was shifting gears in order to make sense of and reply to a non sequitur that she had tossed off. Then she would counter-attack again.

The high-F momma Our prejudiced woman is extremely concerned with order in her environment: she engages in pseudoscientific thinking (using apparently logical forms of rhetoric); she denies causal explanations of events, preferring to see states and attributes as given; she is "anti-intra-ceptive" in that she refuses to acknowledge any contrary information about herself or her views; and finally, she relies heavily on appeals to authority and "hard statistical facts" (which, incidentally, the student never challenges). Of major significance, moreover, is the inference we may draw that a central preoccupation of this woman is sex. Her comments abound with sexual references. Think of the underlying construct that might integrate the topics the woman raises: cleanliness and filth, morals, prostitution, making babies, dance halls, and so on. It is instructive to compare the similarities between this woman's traits and those characterized as typical of high F-scale authoritarian women studied by Frenkel-Brunswick et al. (1958, p. 645). Sample F-scale items are given at the start of Chapter 2.

Undoing the unconscious Not all attitudes are based on rational beliefs. We sometimes take strong aversions to people before we know anything about them. Or, as another example, many people smoke knowing it could kill them in the long run, and not particularly liking it in the short. Daniel Katz (1960) argues convincingly that given attitudes may serve any of four different functions for the person who holds them. The origin of and arousal conditions for each function also differ, as outlined in Table 6.1. The column that lists "change conditions" details how each of the separate functions of an attitude requires its own unique set of change techniques.

In relating this functional approach (or Irving Sarnoff's (1960) psychoanalytic approach) to our case of the prejudiced mother, it is reasonable to diagnose her prejudiced attitudes as serving an ego-defensive function. They protect her from becoming aware of repressed conflicts that, if aroused, would create intense anxiety with which she could not cope. Her attitude, then, is a symptom of an underlying conflict, which may be based on repressed hostility developed many years ago toward her father, or on repressed expression of her sexuality, or some similar causal agent.

If this analysis were accurate (and one would need more information to establish such a claim), then the inescapable conclusion is that the technique used to change her attitude must be tailored to the particular motivational basis upon which her attitude was formed. Trying to persuade her rationally only knocks out her props, attacks her symptoms, makes her more anxious as these defenses are weakened, and leaves nothing to replace them or to protect her against threatening thoughts about herself.

To change her attitudes, threats to her repressed impulses must be removed, conditions must be created to allow for emotional catharsis (support for a talking-out of her problems), and self-insight should be developed through therapeutic techniques.

The intelligent reader will immediately see both the theoretical and practical limits to such a technique. Even if it were shown to be effective,

TABLE 6.1

Determinants of Attitude Formation, Arousal, and Change in Relation to Type of Function (From Katz 1960, p. 192)

Function	Origin and dynamics	Arousal conditions	Change conditions
Adjustment	Utility of attitudinal object in need satisfaction. Maximizing external rewards and minimizing punishments	1. Activation of needs 2. Salience of cues associated with need satisfaction	1. Need deprivation 2. Creation of new needs and new levels of aspiration 3. Shifting rewards and punishments 4. Emphasis on new and better paths for need satisfaction
Ego defense	Protecting against internal conflicts and external dangers	1. Posing of threats 2. Appeals to hatred and repressed impulses 3. Rise in frustrations 4. Use of authoritarian suggestion	1. Removal of threats 2. Catharsis 3. Development of self-insight
Value expression	Maintaining self-identity, enhancing favorable self-image; self-expression and self-determination	1. Salience of cues associated with values 2. Appeals to individual to reassert self-image 3. Ambiguities which threaten self-concept	1. Some degree of dissatisfaction with self 2. Greater appropriateness of new attitude for the self 3. Control of all environmental supports to undermine old values
Knowledge	Need for understanding, for meaningful cognitive organization, for consistency and clarity	1. Reinstatement of cues associated with old problem or of old problem itself	1. Ambiguity created by new information or change in environment 2. More meaningful information about problems

it would require an individualized approach, much time, and considerable skill on the part of the therapist. How can it even make a dent in the statistically enormous problem facing us in the United States?

WHAT'S A LITTLE CONFESSION BETWEEN FRIENDS?

"Please your majesty," said the knave, "I didn't write it and they can't prove I did; there's no name signed at the end." "If you didn't sign it," said the King, "that only makes the matter worse. You must *have meant some mischief, or else you'd have signed your name like an honest man." Lewis Carroll,* Alice's Adventures in Wonderland.

In New York City, after intensive interrogation by the police, George Whitmore, Jr., gave a sixty-one-page typewritten confession to the murder of two socialites. He was subsequently proved innocent. How can a man be made to incriminate himself like this when he knows he may forfeit his life as a result? If this occurs frequently, we must surely be dealing with a powerful set of attitude and behavior change techniques. As a matter of fact, about 80 percent of all arraigned suspects confess, after some period of police interrogation, to having committed a crime. Not all confessions are the direct result of interrogation tactics; "plea bargaining" often involves confession to a lesser offense in the hopes of getting a lesser sentence. While we do not feel that the police are justified in using unethical techniques, we do feel that they are worth your close examination.

Police interrogation has developed not by the amassing of systematic research evidence but by trial and error over a long period of time. The result has been a highly sophisticated array of techniques. They can be assigned to one or more of the following categories:

1 *Demand characteristics of the interrogation environment.* The environment is manipulated to create a given set or a particular frame of mind in the suspect.

2 *Perceptual and judgmental distortion.* The suspect's perception of the crime is manipulated.

3 *Distortion of the social-psychological situation.* The relationship between the interrogator and suspect is manipulated, and the social characteristics of the suspect are distorted to disadvantage.

4 *Utilization of personality and clinical psychology phenomena.* The interrogator plays upon the suspect's personal motives and needs, and tries to establish a therapeutic relationship.

5 *Semantic verbal distortion.* Words charged with emotion or prejudice are used.

The velvet glove approach   Psychology has replaced the physical abuses of the third degree, not only because the courts have made physically coerced confessions invalid, but also because the third degree is not as effective. "When you break a man by torture, he will always hate you. If you break him by your intelligence, he will always fear and respect you." (Kidd 1940, p. 49).[2] This quotation comes from one of the many police manuals that have been developed to transmit the most successful of the empirically developed interrogation techniques. The general approach of the manuals is expressed in the following excerpts:

> If one . . . has a layman's knowledge of practical psychology, and uses the salesman's approach, he can be successful in reaching into a man's brain and pulling out the facts he wants. (Mulbar 1951, p. 5)

> For the last decade, candidates for a detective's post undergo an intensive six-week course that stresses the interrogation of prisoners. Most detectives, and especially the detective commanders, have a built-in psychology based on instinct and experience in which a man's weak points are exploited. They can get prisoners to talk as a result of this. (Michael Murphy, former New York Police Commissioner, quoted in *The New York Times*, November 7, 1963.)

Specific directions are given for fully controlling the interrogation and the suspect. The interrogator should be alone with the suspect, and "the full weight of his personality must be brought to bear on the emotional situation." He or she should sit or stand physically close to the subject, with no furniture intervening. He or she must possess no distracting mannerisms, and must never lose his composure. The interrogator can establish authority by small gestures like prohibiting smoking, telling the suspect where to sit, or offering to get him or her a drink of water.

The interrogation should take place in an environment unfamiliar to the suspect. All psychological support from a familiar environment is thereby destroyed. The room should not be jail-like, but it should be quite sparsely furnished, quiet, and free of all internal and external distractions. There should not even be a telephone or ashtrays.

Confessions are often obtained by either minimizing the seriousness of the offense and allowing the suspect a face-saving out, or by using the opposite tactic of misrepresenting and exaggerating the seriousness of the crime.

Four general categories of influence techniques employed by the seasoned interrogator are extenuation, misrepresentation, the illusion of empathy, and the rhetoric of revelation.

---

[2] The techniques and quotations in this section come from Inbau and Reid (1953), Inbau and Reid (1962), Kidd (1940), Mulbar (1951), and O'Hara (1956).

Extenuation. The investigator says that he or she doesn't think the suspect's indiscretion is too serious, since there have been thousands of others in the same situation. Or the interrogator may shift the blame to circumstances (such as the environment, or a subject's weaknesses). In either case, the prisoner may confess, feeling less guilty than before.

Misrepresentation. The interrogator might obtain a confession by misrepresenting facts, especially if the suspect is already emotionally confused. For example, the interrogator may falsely claim to possess certain incriminating evidence, thus making the suspect feel that "the game is up" and he or she may as well confess. The interrogator may use a "bluff on a split pair" to pretend, quite elaborately, that the suspect's partner has just confessed. Or the interrogator may put the accused in a fixed "reverse" lineup in which he or she is accused by paid police confederates of a more serious crime than the one for which he or she was arraigned, and the suspect is grateful to be able to confess to only the lesser crime.

Illusion of empathy. There are several devices for making the prisoner want to confide in the interrogator. For instance, the interrogator may flatter a suspect who feels socially insecure, or may project an image of dignity and conservatism to prisoners who can be expected to admire these traits. The interrogator can pat the suspect on the shoulder, or offer to get a Coke. If two interrogators are working in tandem, they can use the "Mutt and Jeff" technique, in which one is very tough while the other "protects" the suspect. If the tough interrogator subsequently leaves the room, the suspect may make a confession to the friendly interrogator.

The rhetoric of revelation. The investigator's "speech should be suited to the situation, compelling for the educated subject and calculated to strike a responsive note in the subject of little letters" (O'Hara 1956). Sensitivity to language and the art of semantic distortion are essential to the successful interrogator. For noncriminal, juvenile suspects the effects of the crime on "mother"—the magic word—are played up. Uneducated people are flattered with titles like "Sir," "Mr.," or "Miss," while big shots are to be deflated by first-naming them. To avoid arousing further guilt in married women accused of extramarital sex or solicitation, "Mrs." is to be avoided because of its wifely connotations. Never ask *whether* the suspect committed the crime, but *why*. Finally, the detective is warned not to ask questions that can be answered "No."

SELLING FREEDOM: AGREEING TO DISAGREE

The approaches we have outlined so far have been based on experience, trial and error, clinical intuition, psychoanalytic theory, ingenuity,

Washington Star Syndicate, Inc.

many implicit assumptions, and a smattering of low-level psychological principles. Although some of them have been successful, their success depended more on the particular person who was employing the techniques, or "practicing his or her art," than on a sound social science base. When there is such a base, however, the control of behavior is predicated upon an understanding of the causal relations and, because it is explicitly spelled out, can be implemented by anyone. The approach adopted by Jacobo Varela (1971) tries to achieve this goal through the practical, systematic application of principles derived from psychological theories, and especially from the results of social psychological experiments.

This approach begins by rejecting two of the criticisms often leveled at the possible utility of laboratory-experimental findings: (1) that you cannot extrapolate from the laboratory to the real world when laboratory subjects are a captive audience in a novel environment that is under a high degree of control by the experimenter, and (2) that the time interval used in laboratory studies is rarely more than one hour, while in real life there is no such time constraint.

Instead of insisting on bringing more of real life into the laboratory, this approach says that since laboratory studies are shown to be effective in changing attitudes, then bring the laboratory into real life. If an hour is enough to persuade an intelligent, often critical undergraduate subject, it should be enough to change the behavior of the average businessperson or others—if a planned, concentrated, and powerful manipulation is used and tailored to the target audience.

Varela combines several basic techniques suggested from attitude change research into a systematic persuasion program. This planned program is then brought to bear on particular individuals identified as decision-makers or as holding attitudes or acting in ways that call for change. They might be people who control resources and do not want to buy your product, or who will not give you or certain minorities jobs or improved work/living conditions. They might be people who engage in antisocial behavior that may also be injurious to their health (such as crime, violence, and drug addiction). Or they can be individuals who need help to break phobias (of flying, for example), to control compulsions, or to handle personal family conflicts.

The basic approach is to tailor an individualized program of change to each specific person. This consists of first diagnosing exactly what are the person's relevant attitudes, beliefs, and current behaviors. Then a systematic attempt is made to confront each of these components of the person's overall attitude on the issue.

Attitude change by successive approximations　To change a strongly held set of attitudes and beliefs, Varela proposes a strategy of successive approximations. In this strategy, the most weakly held attitude elements are changed first. Then, one by one, each of the more staunchly endorsed elements are subjected to change tactics. To begin with, it is determined how strongly the person feels about various aspects of the issue. This is done by devising a series of statements that range from those that would be accepted by the person to those that would be rejected. These statements may come from one's knowledge of what the person has said previously or from an analysis of possible statements the person would be likely to endorse.

Next, each of these statements is subtly presented to the person during a conversation in order to discover how strongly he or she feels about each one. On the basis of that evaluative information, a scale of statements graded by intensity of affect is constructed. The scale items range from those the person accepts most strongly, to accepts, rejects, and rejects most strongly. Those that are accepted constitute the *latitude of acceptance*, while the rejected statements comprise the *latitude of rejection* (concepts developed by Hovland and Sherif 1961).

Armed with this knowledge of where the person stands on the issue and how much feeling and psychological energy are invested in various aspects of the general issue, a person other than the one who collected the initial latitude information proceeds with Part 2 of the change program.

The unique feature of this phase is to create *reactance* in the target person.

According to Jack Brehm's theory of reactance, "the perception that a communication is attempting to influence will tend to be seen as a threat to one's freedom to decide for oneself" (1966, p. 94). This is a reverse use of manipulative intent, and is also the "Marc Antony effect." Reactance can be used in an ingenious way to get the person to disagree with statements that he or she would ordinarily agree with, and to agree with statements that were previously disagreed with. The attitude change agent merely implies that there is some limit on the freedom of the person to decide for himself or herself. Reactance is generated by asserting what the person already agrees with in terms such as, "There is no question but . . . ," "You would have to say that . . . ," "It is always the case that . . . ," and so on. The induced reactance leads the person to mildly disagree with these unqualified assertions, and thus weakens support for his or her original position. Then the change agent proceeds in the same way to strongly disagree with statements in the person's latitude of rejection ("There's no way anyone could support the view that . . ."). The target person continues to disagree with the change agent's persuasive assertion, in order to maintain his or her perceived freedom of opinion, and in so doing agrees with the attitude item that had previously been most strongly rejected.

When this is done, the entire attitude structure has shifted its direction and resistance to change has been substantially weakened. The change agent ultimately reinforces each of the person's disagreements and is seen as "coming around" to agree with him or her. It is almost as if the person being changed perceives the change agent as the one he or she has influenced. Where the goal is to have the target person be more optimistic and positive about the topic (or problem), the latitude of acceptance is expanded. Where the goal is to develop a more negative attitude toward the topic (such as taking drugs), the method used is to expand the latitude of rejection.

Let's look at this approach in actual practice. The salesperson's goal here is to get a retail store owner to stop buying from a competitor and thus to be open to new accounts from—guess who.

The customer has often bought from Company *A*, which is a very reputable firm that has high-quality goods at reasonable prices with excellent payment terms. However, it makes few model changes and does not give exclusive lines. This last point is a source of irritation to many retailers, who do not wish to see the same goods that they are selling available at the lowest-quality stores in lower-class sections of town.

The customer's initial attitudes toward the rival company are systematically manipulated by a combination of the reactance approach and the reinforcement approach. An example of how this technique can be employed follows:

(−3) Company A Gives Exclusive Lines

Salesperson: [Saying he liked a style in the customer's store and wonders whether Company *A* made it] Yes? Well, you are lucky to have that made *exclusively* for you!

Retailer: No, they don't give exclusives.

(−2) Company A Makes Frequent Style Changes

Salesperson [In an apparent defense of Company *A*] You're right, that's too bad, but at least they make frequent style changes.

Retailer: Sorry, I must disagree, they rarely do.

(−1) Company A Is Very Regular in Deliveries

Salesperson: Even if it is true that they don't (and I do believe you), you must admit that they make up for it by being regular and prompt in their deliveries.

Retailer: Here you're just wrong, they aren't so prompt, and their deliveries are often irregular.

(+1) Company A Offers Good Promotional Assistance

Salesperson: That's surprising to hear, but judging from what I know of other companies, Company *A* is certainly good in things like promotional assistance.

Retailer: [Now disagreeing mildly with a statement he previously would have agreed with] Well, sometimes they do, but you're not right if you mean they always do.

(+2) Company A Offers Very Favorable Terms

Salesperson: Of course, *you* know better than I do about that, but I've heard that there's *no question* about the very favorable terms Company *A* offers.

Retailer: I don't know where you get your information but there *is* some question about that issue; their terms are favorable to them, but not necessarily for the small shopowner.

(+3) Company A Is a Very Responsible Firm
[This is the "most accepted" statement that is to be modified.]

Salesperson: You may be right, I never thought of it like that, but I am sure that you would *have to say* that Company *A* is a very responsible firm.
Retailer: [As actually happened in one case] Not at all! They *used* to be a very responsible firm, but they aren't any longer!

In this way, the customer is not only guided to buy now, and to reject old loyalties to the opposition, but the general approach used is likely to engender a long-term commitment on the part of the client, because he or she has not been forced to buy anything. Rather, the salespeople have been attentive, approving, reinforcing, concerned with his opinions, altruistic in saying nice things about their rivals—and they have allowed most of the work of persuasion to be done by the retailer.

From Research to Reality

Applied science is a conjuror, whose bottomless hat yields impartially the softest of angora rabbits and the most petrifying of Medusas. Aldous Huxley, *Tomorrow and Tomorrow and Tomorrow,* 1956

Varela is a social science engineer applying principles derived from research to problems of an economic and social nature. His background as an engineer provided the applied orientation. His lack of formal psychological training kept him from developing the pessimism that prevents many social psychologists from believing that their research can have an impact on real-world issues. Varela's text, *Psychological Solutions to Social Problems* (1971), is aptly subtitled: *An Introduction to Social Technology.* The utility of this technology enables him to "visualize a world in the not-too-distant future in which social problems will be solved more with ingenuity than by using force, threat, or archaic or despotic violence" (p. 286).

In the approach described, the full impact of the persuasion program was brought to bear on each retailer because the returns for each successful persuasion were substantial. This indulgence of resources is obviously not possible where the goal is to change attitudes and behaviors of many people in the community. Then it becomes important to include in every practical persuasion program some attempt to assess which subset of variables makes a difference in achieving the desired outcomes. This is beautifully illustrated in a field experiment to determine if sustained education campaigns can help adults reduce risk of heart attack and stroke. Let us turn our attention to that model union of sound research applied to a problem of personal and community relevance.

GETTING TO THE HEART OF THE MATTER

The traditional medical model proposes that practitioners wait for people to get sick or injured before enacting treatment. In contrast, the public health model calls for action to prevent or minimize possible anticipated pathology. Communications researchers John Farquhar and Nathan Maccoby (1976) are heading an interdisciplinary program at Stanford University in which the public health model is at the core of an ongoing attitude and behavior change study designed to prevent heart disease.

Three communities (each with populations of 12,000 to 15,000) were designated as the focus of a field study to test the effectiveness of communications designed to alter coronary risk factors. Random samples of about 500 people, aged thirty-five to fifty-nine, were interviewed and medically examined before the study began and again at the end of each year of the three-year project. In addition, separate groups were studied of subjects who were not given the initial testing. This control was used in order to rule out changes due solely to being sensitized by the pre-measures to the issue of coronary risk. Such sensitization, rather than persuasive techniques, might lead them to change their behavior.

The treatment (outlined in Table 6.2) consisted of a multimedia campaign in one town (Gilroy, California) that was *supplemented* by intensive behavior modification training in the second town (Watsonville, California). The control community (Tracy, California) received no special input related to heart-disease risks, other than that which occurred naturally in the media. The citizens of this town provided the "untreated" base level against which the effectiveness of media alone and media plus personalized instruction behavior modification could be assessed.

The media campaign A variety of media channels in Spanish and English were used to carry messages about coronary risk factors and about what the individual could do to increase resistance to heart disease. Local TV, radio, newspapers, and direct mail carried specially prepared stories, spot announcements, ads, and health heart tests on a random interval schedule throughout the period of study.

Behavior modification Strategies developed on the basis of social learning theory, as outlined in Chapter 3, were applied in small groups of fifteen people (or individually at home if group attendance was not possible). Modeling and reinforcement for desired, specific acts related to dieting, smoking, and exercise were prominent in a five-part process: (1) analysis of existing behavior and desired behavioral objectives, (2) modeling of new

TABLE 6.2
Survey and Campaign Sequence in Each of Three Communities
(From Farquhar et al. 1976)

Community	1972 →	1973	→	1974	→
Watsonville (W)	Baseline survey (0)	Media campaign Intensive instruction for 2/3 of high risk participants	Second survey (1)	Media campaign Intensive instruction for 2/3 of high risk participants	Third survey (2)
Gilroy (G)	Baseline survey (0)	Media campaign	Second survey (1)	Media campaign	Third survey (2)
Tracy (T)	Baseline survey (0)		Second survey (1)		Third survey (2)

acts by instructor or model, (3) guided practice by the learner of the new acts, (4) reinforcement for putting acts into practice, and (5) maintenance of new behaviors without artificial (extrinsic) intervention. Reinforcement came from instructor and spouse encouragement, group support, weigh-ins, progress report feedback, and the anticipation of the gratification of doing well on the physical examinations. This regimen was given to a randomly selected group of subjects in the top 25 percent high-risk category. Risk-level scores were based on blood pressure, cholesterol level, smoking rate, age, weight, and hereditary factors.

Solid, successful outcomes   The three-year results are just in and are most encouraging, as can be seen in the graphs in Fig. 6.1. Attitudes and behavior were changed more in the media-programmed town than in the control town. High-risk participants given the addition of intensive behavior modification training changed much more than those exposed to only persuasive communications.

By the second year of the study, cigarette smoking had declined by 44 percent among Watsonville's intensive treatment group. The media-only town showed a small, but statistically significant, decrease compared to the unchanged smoking habits in the control community. Egg consumption declined in this same pattern across the three samples. While cholesterol levels dropped considerably in Watsonville and somewhat in Gilroy, they

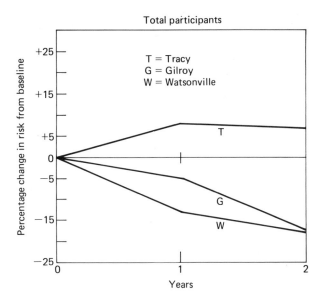

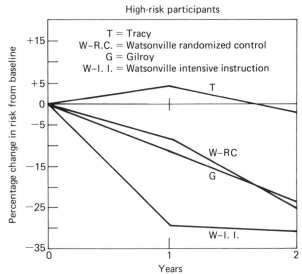

Fig. 6.1 Percentage change from baseline (0) in risk of coronary heart disease after one or two years of health education in various study groups from three communities (from Farquhar et al. 1977).

rose in the control community during this same time. The one clear-cut failure thus far is for any change strategy to reduce weight, even though obesity is a major heart risk factor.

Mass media were effective in the teaching of basic information about appropriate skills. But the impressive changes created by the intensive program of behavior modification far surpass those generated by persuasive communications alone. Follow-up study is planned to assess the durability of these initial changes. The ultimate dependent variable is, of course, measured in terms of life and death. Three-quarters of the annual deaths in the United States before age sixty-five and an estimated 750,000 nonfatal illnesses annually are attributable to coronary heart disease. The costs in terms of health care, lost productivity, and human suffering are enormous. It appears from the results of this pioneering research that public education can effectively encourage the population to modify behavior patterns that influence the risk of heart disease. The researchers are on target when they conclude that, "If these results can be replicated on a national scale, significant human and economic benefits can be expected" (Farquhar et al. 1977, p. 31).

Don't Say "It's Only a Paper Moon"

Where it is a duty to worship the sun, it is pretty sure to be a crime to examine the laws of heat. John Morley, *Voltaire*, 1872

Conversion is a change process in which a person gives up one ordered view of the world and one philosophical perspective for another. Children are not converted to their parents' religion, they simply *become* Christians, Jews, or whatever. It is when they give up the one for another that a world view is being *changed,* rather than merely being formed.

For years Catholic Masses have included a prayer for the conversion of Russia. While such a communication is yet to achieve its persuasive intent, other religious groups have been able to effect mass conversions with more direct strategies. We return here to our initial discussion of the impact of the philosophy and influence strategies practiced by followers of Reverend Moon's Unification church.

One systematic, sociological investigation of the conditions under which these conversions occur highlighted seven essential features (see Lofland and Stark 1954, p. 874):

1 The person experiences enduring, acutely felt tensions.

2 These tensions are seen within a religious problem-solving perspective;

3 This perspective leads the person to define himself or herself as a religious seeker.

4 The person encounters the agent of the particular movement at a turning point in his or her life.

5 An affective bond is formed (or pre-exists) with one or more prior converts.

6 Extra-cult attachments are absent or neutralized.

7 If the person is to become a deployable agent, he or she is exposed to intensive interaction. (A "deployable agent" works outside the confines of the movement's place of business—in the community as a recruiter.)

This type of analysis, however, does not give us any leads as to the content or process of that "intensive interaction"—the influence tactics and

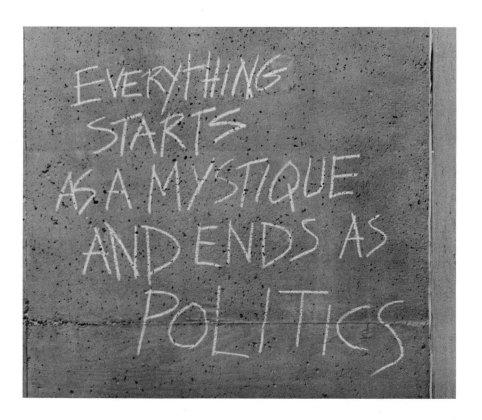

strategies. To do so, we offer excerpts from a first-person account of one of our students who spent a weekend at the conversion camp of the Moonies in Boonville, California. From his account and a remarkably similar newspaper report by a young woman (Julie Smith, *San Francisco Chronicle*, December 11, 1975), we are alerted to what may be the variables and processes operating. You may be surprised at how mundane these tactics of conversion are. Mundane, yes, but as Hannah Arendt (1963) warned, never underestimate the subtle power of banality.

PRINCIPLES OF PERSUASIVE CONVERSION

Initial feelings of alienation and isolation are brushed aside by the displays of group solidarity, consensus, and support. The individual is submerged in the group and encouraged toward deindividuated actions and feelings (see Zimbardo 1970). The individual is made to feel the group's power, which he or she can share in. Potent social reinforcers are dispensed freely—smiles, approval, acceptance, praise, physical contact, and apparent love. Nonacceptable responses elicit an immediate uniform reaction from all members of the group; they are all saddened, never angered, by deviant acts or thoughts. The consequence is the arousal of guilt for upsetting them

PROJECT VOLUNTEER
WEEKEND SEMINAR   sponsored by C.C.P

Weekend of _____

Name _____   Todays Date _____
Address _____ City ____   Fee #18 _____
Phone _____   Deposit _____

REQUIREMENTS:

1. Have an open *heart* and mind.
2. Attend *all* activities of the two day seminar.
3. Cooperate with staff members and all other participants.

Signed _____   Invited by _____

by your disagreement. The intensity of the emotional and physical experience is exhilarating and alters one's time perspective so as to expand the present and diminish past concerns and future apprehensions. With that change in one's temporal orientation, out goes reflection, past commitments to the world you left behind, and anxiety about what is to come. Instead, there is the mindless joy in the impulsive pleasures of the here-and-now, of living for the moment.

Then there are informational inputs from skilled lecturers that are to be listened to uncritically. An "open mind" means a nonevaluative vulnerable mind set of acceptance. A childlike atmosphere filled with simple demands that are easy to satisfy recreates the passivity, dependence, and obedience of childhood (and invokes our elementary-school conditioning). Minimal obedience is all that is required at first. Dissonance follows once the foot is in the door, and then attitudes fall in line to justify compliant actions.

Attractive, similar peers model sincerity, happiness, vitality, and the unconditional acceptance of the cult's ideas and of each other as followers. Specialized rhetoric and semantic distortion help confuse reality-testing and make reattributions easier. Agreement is required not with "new" ideas or principles, but with familiar words and comfortable, nonobjectionable phrases. Then, of course, there is the guest-host role relationship in which the guest performs at the pleasure of the host and feels gratitude for any special consideration shown.

These are but some of the host of elements of the influence process that is brought to bear upon each potential convert. They form an amalgamation of virtually all the basic techniques and principles derived from the major theories of attitude and behavior change. How are they put into practice? Alex's personal account of his weekend with the Moonies offers some clues for our inquiry into the pragmatics of conversion.

BEING A PERSONAL ACCOUNT OF MY NEAR CONVERSION TO THE MOON CULT

The next day Larry picked me up. His friendly smile helped me to forget some of my fears. When he asked me why I wanted to go to the farm I told nim I was always interested in sources of positive energy. I was a little suspicious about his friendliness and figured that he would put less pressure on me if I played along. He nodded and smiled as I talked about what I felt about man's future and what must be done. He agreed very strongly with what I said and told me everyone in "the family," as he called the rest of the church, was interested in the same thing. He frequently looked me right in the eyes and smiled as he talked. It seemed like he was sincere and I began to feel confident that I wouldn't be held against my will.

We stopped at the family's house in Berkeley to join more brothers and sisters and their recruits and board the "Spirit Van" and the "Elephant Express," two brightly colored buses, so we could be in a group for the one-hundred mile trip to the farm. The first thing we did on the bus was a "choo-choo." All the brothers and sisters joined hands and chanted with increasing intensity, "choo-choo-choo, Choo-Choo-Choo, CHOO-CHOO-CHOO! YEA! YEA! POWW!!!" The act made us a group, as though in some strange way we had all experienced something important together. The power of the choo-choo frightened me, but it made me feel more comfortable and there was something very relaxing about building up the energy and releasing it. Larry played the guitar and we all began singing: *If I had a Hammer, You've Gotta Have Heart, Over the Rainbow.* Larry even talked me into singing a duet of *Amazing Grace.* We were strongly applauded and I, loving singing, was quite happy.... [After a late arrival, everyone slept in sleeping bags in a converted chicken house—sexes separated.]

After about six hours of sleep I was awakened by a guitar, violin, and two brothers filling the Chicken Palace with, "The red, red robin came bop-bop-bopping along...." Everyone rocketed out of their sleeping bags and into their clothes, shaking hands and asking, "How are you, brother?" "Great! Just Great!" was everyone's response. It was great to see everybody so happy. We all went out to the field and began singing; hand in hand or with arms around each other we formed a great circle. "Is everybody happy?" cried David, one of the leaders. "Yesss!!" screamed the crowd wildly. I believed it and let it flow into me. I felt that if I was in control of myself, there was no reason not to enjoy all this good energy. With all the love flowing around I just wanted to be part of it and help spread it. David led some exercises and everyone hopped around ecstatically blurting approval.

After the exercises, discussion groups of thirteen were formed. David said it was to enhance appreciation of the seminar but I couldn't help thinking it was designed to increase the pressure to adopt the family's ideas.... [After the discussion and a group walk in the hills, food was passed out—usually rice, broccoli, and salad.] We did another choo-choo and began passing out the food. Each time a family member got anything he would break it in half and give both pieces away. I recalled the disgusting food fights in the dorm. Kristina (the discussion leader) then asked us, one by one, to discuss our life's goals and direction. All the family members talked about how they hadn't known what they wanted, how to change the world, or how to be happy until they joined the family. They now had to grow spiritually in this little piece of heaven. I always wanted to take time out from my worldly pursuits to examine what I really wanted to do in life and whether or not I was heading in the right direction. If only I could believe they weren't being brainwashed I'd stay. When it was my turn to talk I told

Black Star/Mark Rattner.

The Reverend Sun Myung Moon.

of my desire to help the world after I got myself ready. This time I wasn't just playing along. . . .

[Later at Kristina's lecture she told the group about "sharing."] "We must share our experiences if we want to know the truth. We must try to experience something greater than ourselves; consciousness is multidimensional and we are all one." The crowd was getting excited. "It's always great when we lose the distance we feel between ourselves and others. . . ." She said we must live only in the present if we want to know truth. The audience applauded wildly, stood, yelled with delight, and looked around to see that all their brothers and sisters understood. I loved what she said. I even loved her. I knew she was talking about things in my life. I wanted to change and felt guilty about knowing I would return to Stanford.

After the lecture and lunch we had another choo-choo. They were really fun now and they were bringing our group closer together. . . .

It was then time for dodgeball. Annie, a bouncy red-headed sister and two-year family member, grabbed my hand and dragged me, running with the others like children after the ice-cream man to the field. I used to think people got fanatical at basketball games but not like that. We formed two teams and each team got in a large, tight, arm-in-arm circle. We were the Righteous Rockets and were to chant "Blast with love!" throughout the game. We were told that chanting was the most important part. The fiercest players were chosen to be on the front line and the game began. The other team was chanting "Roar with love!" I couldn't understand what was making everyone so fanatical and wild-eyed. I still tried to get involved because I didn't want to stick out. . . . [He attacks "the enemy" effectively.] When they gave me slaps on the back, I chanted louder and tried harder. It was great! I chanted for the rest of the games, one and a half hours. It began to ring in my ears. It was release, it was energy, it was power! We were all leaping up and down and throwing our fists with the chant. I lost myself and became part of the group. After the games we all joined hands in a large circle and chanted, "A victory for one is a victory for all! Victory! Victory! Victory! choo-choo-choo, Choo-Choo-Choo, CHOO-CHOO-CHOO! YEA! YEA! POWW!!!"

Exhausted, I joined my discussion group and walked to a far corner of the field. We all lay back in a circle with our legs in the center and rested. I felt very peaceful. I didn't know what to make of the dodgeball game. It seemed a little like a Nazi rally but it wasn't harming anyone and it was fun. I felt very safe, among sincere, loving friends, and in a beautiful place. [A lecture follows by a distinguished professional.]

We then met in groups and Kristina asked if we had any questions. I told them of my disagreement with Dr. D., and their faces immediately dropped. They said that nature acts in specific, egoless ways and we must follow its example. I replied that I thought it was just a semantic problem. They seemed disappointed and very concerned. "You have to suspend your views like we all did," said Annie. "They were formed in the evil of the outer world. Hear all the lectures and then weigh them. You have to learn more before you can make those decisions." They looked so concerned that I knew I wouldn't get anywhere. I told them I saw their point and would keep an open mind. They all lit up with love again and I was again accepted. . . .

Charming women can true converts make, we love the precepts for the teacher's sake. George Farquhar, *The Constant Couple,* 1699

[Later on there was yet another lecture]

He said that we must separate from society because we need practice to learn how to be good. "There is a gap between belief and action!" he cried, "If you're not part of the solution, you're part of the problem!" I knew I wasn't doing much for the world by going to college. I felt guilty about returning to my ego-centered activities at Stanford but I didn't know whether his solution was what he claimed. . . .

On the way to dinner I saw Larry and Kristina. "Who founded your move-ment?" I asked. They said it was Oni. "What about Sun Moon?" I asked. They denied any connections whatsoever with him. I told them I heard that he bought them their land but they said it was donated by local farmers. Then I knew they were lying. I felt lucky to have known the truth about them before I went. I was frightened about those who didn't have that knowledge. I was going to leave.

After dinner Kristina and I walked hand in hand to the Chicken Palace. She said we were going to the initiation of the new members. Everyone in-side was cheering and screaming, jumping up and down with linked arms, higher and higher, praising the Heavenly Father. I watched nervously as the tempo quickened and the noise became louder. Was I strong enough to keep from getting caught up in it all?

"And now brothers and sisters, the moment you've all been waiting for," shouted David. "The stupendous! The Magnificent! The one and only seven-day training session!" The Chicken Palace flew! The converts chanted, "Thank you Heavenly Father!" as they stomped. I felt a sense of loss, not for myself, but for all those who were *losing their individuality.* It was frightening. I gath-ered my things and silently walked out . . .

. . .

Our chronicler was able to resist, perhaps in part because the academic assignment to document his experiences enabled him to maintain a "will-ing suspension of disbelief." But his attitudes have not been unaffected, if you will recall his comments noted in Chapter 1.

The Moon cult is not interested in merely influencing attitudes without correlated behavior change. For every Alex who finds the power to resist their conversion attempt, other youngsters yield. Would you?

Stanford Daily, May 10, 1976

The fiancee of a resident here left to spend an Easter weekend at the Unification Church's New Ideal Ranch three weeks ago. She did not re-turn at the scheduled time and an attempt to remove the young woman from the ranch by a group of her friends has failed.

"I don't know how she fell for it," Kidd said. "We were in the Coffee House a month before all this happened when some Moonies came in and informed us that they intended to take over Stanford."

"They got her for sure," he added. "She's not even aware of what she's doing."

The Ethics of Intervention

Recently a father sought advice from a doctor who dispenses that service in a national magazine column. "I love my country and I want my boy to love it too," he wrote. "Is it O.K. for me to give him a little pep talk while he's asleep; no big deal, just some patriotic stuff?"

The request was not for technical advice as to whether this influence attempt would work, but rather for the ethical advice of *should* it be attempted. The *goals* seem admirable enough—love of one's country and shared family values. It is the *means* that give us qualms. If it were shown that persuasion under sleep did work, why would the man want to use that approach rather than openly communicating his attitudes and values? We assume he is counting on the absence of resistance to the persuasion to reduce any hassle with his son and to make the child believe the source of the belief was self-initiated and not externally induced.

This example raises ethical considerations about interventions because it highlights a specific manipulative technique that exploits the vulnerability of a sleeping child. But suppose patriotic Dad changed his subliminal strategy and brought it to the surface. He could easily arrange the physical and social home environment so that "Buy America" was an inescapable message. Through his control of what was read, heard, and viewed, by modeling patriotism, having an American flag here, playing a little Kate Smith's "God Bless America" there, and so forth, he might get the point across. A persuasive environment could be created that would have a high probability of turning junior into a chip off the old block. Would *you* judge that to be unethical? Would it be easy to make that judgment if the father's intentions were not explicit or unintentional, nor his plan of attack so formalized?

Ethical issues are an inescapable part of social life. They arise whenever one person has an impact on the life of another. And we cannot avoid having an "impact" on others or being "impacted" upon if we are to live as social beings. Ethical concerns go to an appraisal of the nature of that impact.

Why would *brainwashing* be unethical, while *modeling* the same desired outcome would not? The term *brainwashing* itself contains part of the answer in that the subject is assumed to be passive, without choice or freedom of will to escape his or her brain being laundered. By contrast, we assume one has an option to imitate or ignore the model (under most circumstances).

The second part of the answer lies in the presumed persuasive power of a unitary entity, agency, or procedure. We are most disturbed by influence attempts in which a little input seems to have a big, quick, reliable output in most people. Where a number of factors operate over a long period of time and affect some people but not others, their "impact" is evaluated more in terms of dispositional properties of the target individuals (their personality traits) than in the power of the technique. This is so even when the impact on particular individuals may be substantial.

"COERCION," ETHICS, AND THE LAW

We judge an influence attempt to be "coercive," and thereby unethical, when some or all of the following conditions are present: (1) no informed consent, (2) physical confinement or psychological constraint, (3) inaccessibility to usual sources of information and social supports, (4) intensive direct contact with agents of control, (5) threat of dire consequences for failure to change, (6) use of special "nonordinary" techniques that overwhelm reason, and (7) vulnerability of "victim" due to tender age, educational level, mental condition, or other personal characteristics.

The evaluation of coercion is not merely an academic or ethical issue. It has legal consequences, as we saw in the determination of the guilt or innocence of Patty Hearst. The jury finally judged her to be guilty of acting on her own volition when she participated in the bank robbery. The jurors reported after the trial that they could not believe she continued to be coerced even when her captors were not physically present, despite Patty's testimony that she "felt their presence" and "unspoken commands." The "coercion" state of mind at the robbery was judged in terms of her reaction to the conditions she experienced *after* the robbery—conditions that did not fit the criteria of coercion outlined above. "It is possible," said one juror, "for a person to be coerced, but I don't believe it is possible for someone to be coerced all the time." (*San Francisco Chronicle*, March 22, 1976).

The legal status of coercion has been an issue of concern for the Supreme Court in deciding on the admissibility of evidence secured through the kinds of police interrogation tactics described earlier. "Third-degree" physical coercion, bribes, and threats are considered inherently coercive, and thus are not sanctioned. Psychological coercion is harder to legislate. In fact, the Court sidesteps the tricky problem by relying on obvious, nonsocial psychological variables in rendering its decision, such as prolonged duration without breaks, interrogations in relays, young age, the "weaker tender sex," limited mental capacity, and so forth.

By what criteria could the conversion process of the Moonies be judged to be coercive?

ETHICS IN RESEARCH AND THERAPY

The specialized perspective of the scientist inevitably creates ethical dilemmas, if only because scientific knowledge and techniques that can be used for human betterment can usually be turned to manipulative and exploitative purposes as well. American Psychological Association, *Ethical Principles*, 1973

Any research that has an outcome that speaks to issues of importance to the human condition should be conducted with explicitly formulated ethical principles. The rights of the subject must be protected; the researcher must be accountable; and the benefits to the subjects, society, and knowledge must outweigh the costs and liabilities.

The cost/benefit analysis puts the ethical determination on a *relative* rather than absolute basis. The investigator (and supervising committee of the school, research center, and profession) must estimate and balance three subjective parameters of *cost* and also of *benefit:* (1) their magnitude, (2) the probability of the anticipated consequences, and (3) the number of people expected to benefit or suffer. But these are all subjective judgments open to personal interpretations, affected by the state of available information, the moral values of individual researchers, and the operating policies of sponsoring agencies.

Is it possible to study the attitude change process experimentally if the researcher must inform all subjects in advance that their attitudes are about to be assaulted by persuasive communications? If one finds that a treatment has a beneficial effect, is the researcher ethically bound to offer it to the control population from whom it was withheld? Bandura did so in his study on snake phobia (see Chapter 4); should the same be demanded of the researchers in the heart disease field study? Are they obligated ethically to provide the successful intensive behavior modification treatment to all their subjects in the other two communities who want it? Who should finance this expensive application of research findings? What about the egg farmers and cigarette companies—do they, too, judge the reduced egg and cigarette consumption to be a benefit of the research, or is it judged as a serious loss of revenue?

It is not only research that poses such problems; therapy as a form of attitude and behavior control also raises many ethical issues. Those concerns are most apparent when therapy is not sought by the patient but is required by the state or one's employer. Can there ever be meaningful therapy in a total institution from which the prisoner, patient, or soldier is not free to leave? Even where the means of persuasion are openly discussed between patient and client, what if the goals of the client conflict with those of society, or vice versa? Should therapists be changing the attitudes and behavior of individuals so they will fit in better with their environment or should they have a responsibility to change social conditions that elicit and maintain dysfunctional behavior? Should therapists be sustainers of the status quo or activists in challenging pathological aspects of society? Both means and ends must separately and collectively be subjected to the continuous scrutiny of an informed, concerned ethical appraisal.

The Politics of Intervention

Give us the child for eight years, and it will be a Bolshevist forever. Lenin, Speech to the Commissars of Education, Moscow, 1923

Give me a dozen healthy infants, well-formed, and my own specified world to bring them up in and I'll guarantee to take any one at random and train him to become any type of specialist I might select—doctor, lawyer, artist, merchant-chief, and, yes, even into beggar-man and thief, regardless of his talents, penchants, tendencies, abilities, vocations, and race of his ancestors. Watson 1926, p. 10

Every change in one part of a system creates a reaction in another sector. Even when you know how to produce a desired effect and the benefits far outweigh the risks, there is one more obstacle to overcome before principles of change become policy—*power*. When new ideas are transplanted into policy, they invariably are opposed because change is threatening. All the forces that benefited from maintaining the old ways are challenged by the new. Ingrained habits of thought and action must be altered, and life-styles may be affected. Economic security and self-esteem may be undermined. Inventions put people out of work, while investigations reveal inadequacies and ineffectiveness.

To be effective as an agent of social change, one must recognize two sources of power: one's own and that of all adversaries. Then the task becomes the difficult one of changing the balance of power in your favor. This is never easy and often impossible. People do not always like to do things "for their own good," especially not when they are told and shown that they should.

Resistance to innovation in a social, political, or economic system is the analogue of resistance to persuasion in the individual—multiplied by a "hard-head" factor of 10^{10}. For every dollar spent by the American Cancer Society and the National Institutes of Health to change smoking and alcohol consumption (which research shows adversely affect health), industry counters with more mass-media appeals to keep those behaviors going. For example, a recent issue of *Time* magazine that contained an excellent, in-

depth analysis of alcoholism also carried a dozen pages of splashy ads extolling the joys of a good drink. Proponents for the Nuclear Initiative in the 1976 California election believed there should be a moratorium on expansion of nuclear power plants until further study proved them safe and their waste products could be adequately disposed of. The concerted counter force in dollars and other resources exerted by the Pacific Gas and Electric Company as well as other segments of business and government doomed the measure at the polls.

When a national commission was being formed to investigate the link between TV-filmed violence and aggression, the TV industry was able to blackball some of the leading social scientists whose research supported the existence of that relationship—Albert Bandura among them. Since legislators who make the laws that influence our behavior are not themselves resistant to the influence of lobbying, their decisions are often the direct product of the power exerted on them. We need look no further than the annual budget for "defense" that the Pentagon sends to Congress to appreciate the power of political intervention.

. . .

In drawing our journey together to a close we must be cautious about urging you to go out and change the world. Idealists, freedom-fighters, self-actualizers, liberationists, and revolutionaries are, under other attributional perspectives, mad dissidents, troublemakers, opportunists, and usurpers. To all would-be agents of social control, we say, Do not demand that we give you our children to live in a world of *your* design even if you can *guarantee* they will emerge as saints not sinners, specialists and not nobodies. The world should be of *their* design, too, their world even if created by their follies, fantasies, and foibles. They must choose rationally to follow life's paths, not be chosen randomly to play out someone else's script. Most crucial is our realization that what you now ask to be *given*, you would *take* if and when you had enough power to do so. Our actions as agents of change must then be informed with knowledge, tempered with wisdom, and always infused with compassion.

the experiment as a source of information

In psychology, all research involves making observations of behavior. Some research, called field research, observes phenomena or the operation of variables as they exist naturally. That is, the researcher attempts to make systematic, relatively objective, and unbiased observations of things "as they are." The researcher does not interfere with their functioning nor try to change or control any of the variables. Indeed, the major problem may be that his or her attempts to observe behavior may actually change the behavior (the psychological equivalent of Heisenberg's indeterminacy principle in physics). The researcher's task is to establish whether, and to what degree, sets of variables are co-related. For example, one field researcher showed that college women at Bennington College in Vermont became increasingly liberal in their political and social attitudes from freshman to senior year. Another field study demonstrated that prejudice decreases with increased personal contact between black and white housewives in a housing project. Studies such as these are valuable in locating significant problem areas, describing and analyzing interesting behavioral phenomena, and suggesting variables that might play a vital role in the relationships obtained.

Attitude surveys and polls form one subclass of observational research. However, regardless of the care, effort, and skill that go into such studies, they are severely limited in the kind of information they can provide. In most cases, a correlational study cannot yield unequivocal conclusions about the nature of the *causal* relationship involved. Two events or behaviors may be highly correlated,[1] yet we might not be certain whether A caused B, or B caused A, or the relation was coincidental, or one indirectly caused the other through the operation of an intermediate (unknown variable), or whether a third variable caused the occurrence of both A and B, and so on. These arguments are not mere academic exercises. In fact, they form the basis of the reply of the statisticians working for cigarette companies to the statisticians of the American Cancer Society regarding the correlational evidence supporting the smoking-cancer link. (The reader is referred, specifically, to the skillful reply of E. Cuyler Hammond, Smoking and death rates—a riddle in cause and effect, *American Scientist*, **46**, No. 4, 1958, pp. 331–354.)

In contrast to this naturalistic field research stands the *experiment*. An experiment simply represents a special way of making observations, which, under appropriate conditions, allows for its conclusions to be statements of causality. It is only on the basis of such conclusions that a science of psychology can meaningfully approach its goals of prediction and control of behavior.

The experimenter systematically varies one set of conditions (stimulus events) while attempting to exercise control over all others to which the subjects might be responsive but that are irrelevant for testing the particular hypothesis (an idea about how two or more variables are related). As the experimenter manipulates or induces change in these independent variables, he or she observes a small subset of behavior thought to be related to the known changes in the stimulus events. The experimenter does not wait for the behavior to occur naturally, but creates the conditions which he or she believes will elicit its occurrence. In this sense, the experimenter creates an artificial environment or interferes with a natural process. This is done in order to (1) make the event occur under known conditions which can be independently replicated on subsequent occasions; (2) make it occur when the experimenter is prepared to make accurate observations (of the dependent variables); (3) make it possible to determine the direction and magnitude of the effect that the independent variable has upon the dependent one; and (4) eliminate the possibility that the relationship between

---

[1] When the variation in one set of data is related to the variation in a corresponding second set (for example, two test scores for each person), the conclusion can be expressed mathematically as the coefficient of correlation, or r. This value may range from -1.0 through 0 to $+1.0$. When $r = 0$, the two distributions of data bear no relation to each other. A positive value of r indicates that variation in each set of data is in a common direction; as A increases, so does B. A negative value of r indicates that A and B go in opposite directions. As r approaches either $+1.0$ or -1.0, it becomes more likely to predict one event knowing the other; that is, to explain the variation in one set of observations from knowledge of the variation in the other.

the independent and dependent variable is the result of something other than a direct causal link, for example, Y causes both A and B.

An experiment begins with three basic decisions. From among the infinite array of stimuli that a variety of subjects could perceive and respond to at many levels in numerous dimensions, the experimenter selects a specific stimulus, organism (or subject), and response mode. An experiment can be conceived graphically as a set of three overlapping circles representing the population of all (1) stimuli, (2) organisms, and (3) responses relevant to the general problem under investigation. What the researcher studies is the very small area or point of their intersection. For example, in a study of the effects of light intensity on reaction time, the stimulus variable might be two levels of illumination: the subjects, twenty college sophomores taking a particular course at a given college; and the response, lifting the right index finger off an electrically wired key.

The set of all stimuli are placed into categories according to theoretically meaningful definitions. For example, in the Yale attitude change approach the set of all possible communications are categorized according to whether they are two-sided or one-sided, fear-arousing or not, state their conclusions explicitly or implicitly, and so on. When stimuli are categorized in this way, the experimenter consciously decides to *ignore* certain properties of the stimuli and emphasize others. For example, the number of times a certain word appears or the length of the sentences or even the content may be irrelevant. This means that the experimenter will select from a large category of one-sided, fear-arousing communications that draw explicit conclusions. The particular one he or she chooses may use the pronoun, "you" more or less frequently than other communications, and may be about the nuclear initiative rather than birth control. The hope is that the *same* results will hold across all of these irrelevant characteristics (that is, that content, length, syntax, and so on, will not change the basic relationships being examined).

The identical points can be made about the experimenter's selection of types of organisms and responses. Those researchers who study rats or pigeons to find out about people assume that the many differences between people and rats do *not* affect the basic causal relationships established by the research. The fact that rats use their sense of smell more than humans should not matter when the researcher's interest is focused on the effects that reward schedules have on rate of responding.

Given that experimenters can select from a large number of specific instances in a broad category of stimuli (or organisms or responses), the decision as to which ones to use is often made on the grounds of convenience, ease and accuracy of measurement, and the extent to which control is possible. Two issues that naturally arise are: (1) Can the selected instance really be measured in such a way that the same outcome will result regardless of who does the measurement or when it is made? and (2) Does the selected instance accurately portray the process or conceptual variable of interest? The first issue is concerned with *reliability*, and the second with *validity*.

Reliability can be equated with consistency or stability. Will the selected response measure yield the same value on repeated occasions if everything else is the same? Can the same results be obtained under very similar circumstances of testing?

Validity is a more complex issue to demonstrate, and has several meanings, only a few of which will be mentioned. *Conceptual validity* implies that the treatments, observations, and measurements made by the experimenter are adequate concrete representations of the broader abstract class that the experimenter really wants to learn something about. He or she is interested in reaction time, not index finger elevation; or in attitudes, and not a check mark on a ten-point questionnaire scale. Ideally, what is desired is a specific set of operations that anchors the abstract concept to events in the real world, but is at the same time as pure an instance of the concept as possible. This notion of validity asks whether appropriate correspondence rules have been established (see Chapter 3).

Predictive validity describes the condition in which one may predict (from knowledge of a specific behavior) a second, operationally different but conceptually related behavior. For example, one can predict academic success in college on the basis of college board scores, or reaction times in highway driving on the basis of reaction times to lights in a laboratory.

The validity of a measure can also be thought of in another way. First, we assume that any variation in test scores has two components: true variance and error variance. As the obtained score is closer to the (hypothetical) true score, it becomes a more valid measure. As its variation is influenced not only by variation in the relevant response being studied, but also by extraneous sources of error, it loses its status as a valid representation of the underlying true response sytem. *Systematic errors* bias the score in a given direction, while *random errors* can cause the score to deviate from its true value in any direction.

These omnipresent sources of error are the barriers to be overcome in attempting to uncover orderly relationships in the "booming, buzzing world of confusion" around us. Systematic errors may arise when the experimenter unintentionally gives the subject cues as to when the stimulus will be presented, or when an experimenter who knows which subject received a given treatment (such as a drug) is also responsible for making subjective ratings of his or her behavior. Random errors result from environmental disturbances or methodological inadequacies. A transient or irregularly occuring event could alter the true response to the manipulated stimulus on any given occasion (as when an unexpected noise occurs during a conditioning procedure). Similarly, the true score could be elevated or depressed in unsystematic and unknown ways if the experimenter presents the stimulus differently to each subject within the same condition, or else has not established an explicit criterion for measuring the presence or quality of a response. Systematic errors may be minimized by use of controlled procedures, objective scoring methods, randomization, and control groups. Elimination of random errors depends largely upon standard methodology and use of an environment not subject to random changes in features that could affect the subject's response.

To recast the goal of research in light of this present discussion, we might say that an experiment is a set of objective procedures for isolating a signal from a background of noise. The true score, or signal, must be conceptually purified to distinguish it from similar signals. The treatment procedures are designed to amplify the signal, while the measurement procedures should be able to detect even a weak signal. This is possible only when adequate control can be exercised over competing signals and background noise, either by minimizing them or by being able to precisely evaluate their contribution to the observed value of the primary signal.

Drawing Inferences from Experiments

But what about the generalizability of the findings of an experiment? Few scientists are satisfied with conclusions limited to the details of the specific stimuli and operations used with a unique sample of subjects who gave a particular response. We want our conclusions to be at a higher level of abstraction. The extent to which one is willing to generalize from a single experiment to broad statements about stimuli, organisms, and responses is in part related to the state of knowledge in the specific area, the researcher's personal willingness to take risks, and his or her commitment to either a theoretical or a primarily empirical approach. However, we shall soon see that this process of inference is not as subjective as it might seem. In fact, there are several precise means for drawing inferences from the limited observations a researcher has actually made and applying them to larger, unobserved populations.

Before describing such procedures, we should mention the important function in experiments served by the technique of *random assignment* of subjects to treatment conditions. In order to be able to say treatment *A* had a greater effect on a given behavior than did treatment *B*, we must assume that the subjects were not different before exposure to the treatment variable. One way of achieving this goal is to select subjects in such a way that it is equally likely that a subject might be in the experimental treatment group or in the nontreatment control group. If assignment to a given condition is based solely on a chance procedure (such as a toss of a coin, or use of a table of random numbers[2]), it usually ensures that any of the multitude of organismic factors that might influence the results are *equally* distributed among the treatment cells *prior to* exposure to the independent variable. For example, random assignment would generally produce equal numbers of males and females in each condition. This process enables one to make statements of causality because other explanations for any differences in the behavior of the two groups can not be readily explained by such factors as sex of the subject.

There is always a risk involved in making inferences from a study, even if it is well-designed and carefully executed. However, the extent of this risk can be calculated by means of statistically objective procedures that evaluate the probability that a given conclusion from a particular set of observations may be false. Suppose we wished to evaluate whether participation in a group discussion changed attitudes toward drug addiction. We might measure the opinions of the participants both before and after the discussion. The opinion scale ratings of our sample of subjects would first be summarized in a convenient and efficient manner by certain *descriptive statistics*. "What is the typical or average score before the discussion and what after?" is a question answerable by computing means, medians, or modes. "How much do individual subjects deviate from this representative value?" can be answered by establishing the variability of response (the range, or the standard deviation).

However, in order to determine whether it was group discussion that changed attitudes in the direction advocated, it is necessary to compare the obtained descriptive statistics with the estimated change that might

---

[2] A process by which all subjects are first given a number and are then distributed into the various cells in the research design according to a pattern determined by the appearance of their number among a larger set of randomly generated numbers.

have occurred from the mere act of repeated measurement of opinions, in the absence of the discussion. Comparison of the obtained distribution of scores with different types of *theoretical* distributions allows one to estimate the probability that the data are not due to chance but to a statistically reliable relationship (*inferential statistics*). Different behavior (between groups of initially comparable subjects) in response to the treatment variable is more likely to be a "real" difference, as a direct function of three factors: number of observations, magnitude of the difference, and variability of the response. An obtained difference is more likely to be a significant one as the number (N) of observations increases, as the difference between groups in performance (measured by some descriptive statistic) is greater, and as the variation within each separate group decreases.

The concept of *significance* is defined in psychology as the minimum criterion for establishing that a given result is due to treatment effects rather than chance fluctuation (error variance) in the observations. A probability level, arbitrarily set at $p < .05$ (p is less than .05, or 5 percent), is this minimum standard. This means that the difference found would occur only five times in one hundred by chance alone. Therefore, we may infer that this occasion is one of the ninety-five times when the difference is not attributable to chance. Under certain circumstances. the researcher may demand a more stringent rejection probability, such as $p < .01$ or even $p < .001$ (that is, only one time in one thousand will the experimenter draw a false conclusion by accepting the obtained difference as a real one).

Although the risk involved in drawing an inference is reduced by couching the conclusion in probabilistic rather than absolute terms, there is still considerable risk involved in making inferences in either of two directions from the sample of behavior observed. One can make inferences upward to a more abstract, conceptual level of explanation, or downward to a more concrete, specific instance. In the former case, there may be an error in extrapolation in that the particular results do not reveal the presumed general relationship or theoretical process. In the latter, there is the problem of assuming that a general relationship can predict a specific person's behavior.

For each of these cases there are two types of errors possible. If the significance of an obtained difference is $p < .05$, then the experimenter will be wrong five times in a hundred in concluding that he or she has found a real effect. This is because chance alone can generate differences of that magnitude, and a particular experiment may represent one of those five possible chance occurrences. Here we have a type 1 (or alpha) error: inferring that a relationship exists when it does not. Looking at our probability and decision-making process differently, suppose the significance of a difference is rejected because it is at the .06 level of probability (beyond the conventional limit of scientific acceptability). Then ninety-four times out of a hundred the investigator will conclude that no relationship exists when, to the contrary, it does. This is a type 2 (or beta) error.

How does the psychologist decide whether to be more risky (type 1 error) or more conservative (type 2 error)? Clearly, his or her strategy should be determined by the action implications of each type of conclusion, by the relative costs or dangers of each type of error, and finally by the stimulation or inhibition of creative thinking each may cause. For example, in making upward inferences to generate conceptual, theoretical statements about physical or psychological reality, progress may be more impaired by a type 2 error (which could serve to close off an area of investigation prematurely) than by a type 1 error (which ought to be readily discovered by others in independent replications). However, if replication studies are rare, then a type 1 error may be perpetuated, resulting in much wasted effort testing derivatives of the original, unsubstantiated hypothesis.

The Laboratory Versus the Real World

What faces the experimentalist is the dilemma of gaining control while losing power. The full range and intensity of psychological variables cannot be achieved in the laboratory setting. This is because there is only a relatively brief exposure to the stimulus in an experiment. The subject's task is often of limited relevance to other life experiences and has minimal implications for his or her future functioning. In addition, the nature and intensity of the experimental manipulations are limited by legal, ethical, and moral considerations. But while the power of variables is often best demonstrated under uncontrolled natural circumstances, studying phenomena at this level risks a loss of understanding of the processes involved, lack of specification of causality, and inability to analyze the complex network of factors into relevant component variables. On the other hand, the gains achieved by the superior control of an experiment may be offset by its trivial content. As a result of purifying, standardizing, controlling, and selecting certain stimulus and response dimensions, the experimenter may have created a very distant watered-down version of the phenomena or problems he or she set out to study. Under such conditions the results of the investigation may have no practical significance, since it is not possible to extrapolate from them to action-oriented problems.

It is possible to get around some of these limitations in any particular experiment by *combining* research strategies and by conducting several different experiments on the same topic. For example, suppose an experimenter is worried that the use of monetary rewards to vary "justification" in a forced-compliance dissonance experiment may not be the same as varying "justification" by giving subjects social reasons for complying. He or she can assess this possibility by including *conceptual replications* of "justification" in the experiment or by conducting several different experiments that *systematically replicate* the conceptual variables being studied.

EXPERIMENTAL VALIDITY

It is possible to summarize the issues being raised here by noting that the conclusions we draw from experiments can suffer in two different ways. We can erroneously conclude that a causal relationship exists between the specific manipulations and the specific measures being used, when in fact the observed relationship is due to some other factor, an artifact, or confounding variable. In this case we would be drawing an incorrect conclusion about the *internal validity* of the experiment. In addition, it is also possible to conclude erroneously that the specific causal relationship applies across *all other* instances of the conceptual variables not assessed in the study; that is, it generalizes to other people, settings, measures, and conceptually equivalent manipulations. In this second case the *external validity* of the experiment is at issue. One way to avoid drawing both kinds of invalid conclusions is to outline the more common sources of invalidity that crop up in experimental research. Once we have listed them, we can then examine different ways of designing experiments and note whether or not they overcome each type of fault.

Sources of internal invalidity Let us first consider what some of the sources of *internal invalidity* might be.[3]

1 *Internal artifacts.* It is possible that an uncontrolled event that the experimenter did not want to occur caused the effect the experimenter observed. If this happened, a conclusion that the experimental operations were causing the effect would be incorrect.

2 *Subject changes.* Rather than stimulus events (the independent variable) occurring outside of the subject, it is possible that they occurred inside of him or her. For example, the subject may have been sick, or worried about a personal problem.

---

[3] The remaining parts of this postscript are largely derived from a book by Campbell and Stanley (1963).

3 *Testing sensitization.* Taking an initial test (premeasure) may affect how the subject reacts to a second test (postmeasure).

4 *Problems with equipment.* The equipment used in the experiment may change as a function of use or time.

5 *Subject selection biases.* If subjects are not assigned to experimental groups at *random* then there is always a possibility that differences between experimental groups are caused not by differences in the independent variable, but rather by preexisting differences between the subjects in the various groups.

6 *Attrition.* If, after subjects have been randomly assigned to conditions, an uncontrollable factor eliminates some of the subjects from the final analysis of the results, valid conclusions about the effect of the independent variable on the dependent variable cannot be drawn. One uncontrolled factor might be the subject's choice not to continue in the experiment. Another might be some feature inherent in the experiment itself.

Sources of external invalidity Before the sources of *external validity*, or generalizability, can be understood, the concept of *interaction* must be discussed. Let us suppose that we are concerned with the effects that the amount of vicarious reinforcement has on imitation. To study this, we expose young children to a film of an adult male model who beats up a bobo doll by kicking it, sitting on it, hitting it with a hammer, and so on. After engaging in these actions, the model receives none, one, two, four, or ten candy bars. The children are then given the opportunity to "play" with the bobo doll, and the researcher records the frequency with which they engage in the same types of "aggressive" activities as the model. Suppose the average number of imitated responses increased as the size of the reward given to the model increased. The researcher concludes that an increase in the amount of vicarious reinforcement causes people to imitate more.

Note that the above conclusion is not qualified. It implies that the same *relationship* between amount of vicarious reward and amount of imitation will hold across all types of models, all types of subjects, all types of rewards, all types of responses, all settings and all media used to present the model's actions. The conclusion did not say that the relationship applied only to children in a particular age group from a given school, who observed a particular male model in a film do certain specific things to a bobo doll and receive candy bars afterwards. What if the relationship is different when a female model hits the bobo doll? Let us suppose the amount of imitation actually decreases with increasing rewards to female models. If the relationship between an independent variable (amount of vicarious reinforcement) and a dependent variable (amount of imitation) changes as a function of some other variable (in this example, sex of model), it is said that the two variables *interact* to determine the outcome.

Interactions can be of many types. The amount of imitation could increase for *both* models, but at different rates. Alternatively, the relation might be reversed (increasing for one, decreasing for another). It might even be that the relationship holds in one case but fails to emerge (amount of vicarious reinforcement has no effect at all) in the second case. In short, the presence of an interaction limits the range of situations, settings, subjects, and so forth to which the result or relationship of interest can be generalized. In the study of persuasion and attitude change it is rare to find variables that are not limited or qualified by their interaction with other variables. Interaction is the rule, main effects the exception.

We can now examine some of the more common factors which may limit the generality of experimental results.

1 *Reactive effects of measurement.* When subjects are given a test, say a self-rating attitude scale, it may be that taking the test itself influences how the subject will behave. In the attitude measurement example, the test may become the stimulus condition that elicits the attitude; either the subject did not have the attitude before, or changes his or her true response after realizing the intent of the test or experiment. Thus, any findings would be limited to subjects who had taken the test.

2 *Interaction of selection bias and experimental variable.* The effect of an experimental variable may show up only on certain kinds of subjects. For example, if only subjects with extreme attitudes were studied, it is possible that variables that normally change the attitudes of more moderate subjects would not have an effect on these extreme ones.

3 *Reactive effects of experiment.* Specific differences between the conditions existing in the experimental setting and the conditions existing outside of it may be crucial in determining whether or not the results of the experiment can be applied. For example, experimental subjects might always be highly motivated to attend to the communication, a condition that would not occur naturally. It is obviously very important, in a practical approach, that this condition be noted in the experiments from which the change program is devised.

4 *Multiple treatment effects.* Sometimes each subject is measured with and without the experimental variable present. It is thus possible for sequential effects to occur; that is, the first manipulation affects how the second manipulation will influence the subject's behavior. The results would only apply to subjects who had been exposed to more than one treatment and possibly only one order of treatment.

EXPERIMENTAL DESIGNS

Now that we have presented a few of the more common sources of internal and external invalidity, let us see how well these sources of error can be eliminated by various experimental designs.

Table A.1 presents, in summary form, a set of five highly sophisticated experimental designs. The symbol O in the table refers to observation or measurement, while the symbol M is used to refer to an experimental manipulation that is presented in that condition. In each of these experiments there are at least two groups of subjects. Some of the subjects experience the manipulation; others do not. Those subjects who experience the manipulation and those who do not are always determined randomly. This random assignment of subjects to conditions is indicated by an R in front of each group. So, for example, the simplest design presented in Table A.1 is a two-group design in which the subjects are randomly assigned to one or the other group. Only subjects in group 1 experience the manipulation, after which both groups are observed.

Group 1   R   M   O
Group 2   R   O

Also in the table is a list of the various sources of invalidity previously described. For each design, if a "yes" appears in the column for the particular source of invalidity, it means that the design is not able to remove that particular kind of error. A "no" means that it does not have that problem.

The "best" design to use to minimize sources of artifact (error variance) is the Separate Sample Pretest-Posttest design. Here the experimenter randomly assigns subjects to a number of conditions. The experimenter initially measures the pre-treatment responses of only half of all the subjects. The remaining half are measured some time later. However, those subjects who are measured later are also divided in half so that one group experiences the manipulation and the other does not. Furthermore, the reader should note a very distinctive feature of this design. It is possible to demonstrate that the conceptual status of the independent variable is not limited to a single set of specific operations. By using two different sets of operations (M_1 and M_2), both derived from the same conceptual independent variable, general conclusions can be drawn from concrete observations to abstract variables.

In summary, some subjects are measured early, some later. Of those who are measured later, some get a manipulation, others do not. Of those subjects who experience a manipulation some experience one form of it, while others experience a different one. Furthermore, different measurement techniques are used, and for each measurement technique some subjects experience, and others do not, each of the manipulations.

From this description the reader can see that, in any design, randomization is very important. It is also important that the *observations* made of the subjects do not interfere with the behavioral effects of the experimental *manipulations*.

TABLE A.1
Some Experimental Designs which Minimize Sources of Invalidity

Experimental designs	Internal sources						External sources			
	1 External artifacts	2 Subject changes	3 Testing sensitization	4 Problems with equipment	5 Subject selection biases	6 Attrition	1 Reactive measurements	2 Interaction of selection biases and experimental variable	3 Reactive effects of experiment	4 Multiple treatment effects
1. *Pretest-posttest design* Group 1 R O O 2 R O M O	No	No	No	No	No	No	Yes	Maybe	Maybe	No
2. *Solomon four-group design* Group 1 R O M O 2 R O O 3 R M O 4 R O	No	No	No	No	No	No	No	Maybe	Maybe	No
3. *Posttest-only design* Group 1 R M O 2 R O	No	No	No	No	No	No	No	Maybe	Maybe	No

4. *Time series with control*

Group: Time →
1 R OOOOOOO
2 R OOOMOOO

No	No	No	No	No	Yes	No	Maybe	No

5. *Separate sample pretest-posttest design*

Group
1 {R O M₁ O
2 {R O   O

R*

3 {R O   O
4 {R O   O

R*

5 {R O M₂ O
6 {R O   O

R*

7 {R O   O
8 {R O   O

No	No	No	No	No	No	No	No	No

* Here one randomizes both by assignment of individuals to groups and by whether or not comparison groups experience the manipulation.

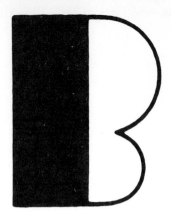

techniques of attitude measurement

Throughout this text, we have talked about the concept of *attitude*—how people define it, and how they think it relates (or does not relate) to behavior. However, we have not discussed how people *measure* this concept. If you stop to think about it, you will realize that measuring an attitude is not an easy task. How do you measure something that is inside a person's mind? As you might guess, the only solution to that problem is to get the person to make the internal attitude external, so that you can then assess it. Put another way, you must get the person to translate an internal *attitude* into an external *behavior*. This behavior might involve completing a paper-and-pencil test or questionnaire, and in the first section of this Postscript we present four of the most widely used tests. However, this behavior might also involve a wide range of diverse responses, which we enumerate and discuss in the second section.

Attitude Scales

Several different paper-and-pencil tests have been developed to measure attitudes. Of these tests, four have been fairly highly refined and have been used most extensively. These major techniques are: Thurstone's method of equal-appearing intervals, Likert's method of summated ratings, Guttman's scalogram, and Osgood's semantic differential. A brief review of each of these methods will hopefully provide the reader with a clearer understanding of how the social psychologist obtains the data from which he or she so elegantly extrapolates.

Each of the techniques to be discussed makes different assumptions about the nature of the test items that are used and the kind of information they provide about a person's attitudes. However, there are certain basic assumptions that are common to all of these methods. First of all, it is assumed that subjective attitudes can be measured by a quantitative technique, so that each person's opinion can be represented by some numerical score. Secondly, all of these methods assume that a particular test item has the same meaning for all respondents, and thus a given response will be scored identically for everyone making it. Such assumptions may not always be justified, but as yet no measurement technique has been developed that does not include them.

THURSTONE'S METHOD OF EQUAL-APPEARING INTERVALS

The first major technique of attitude measurement was developed by Thurstone, in 1929, in his study of attitudes toward religion. The scale he constructed introduced precise measurement to an area of research where it had never been used before. Thurstone assumed that one could obtain statements of opinion about a particular issue and could order them according to a dimension of expressed favorableness-unfavorableness toward the issue. Furthermore, the ordering of these statements could be such that there appeared to be an equal distance between adjacent statements on the continuum. Because of the latter assumption, one can make judgments about the degree of discrepancy among different people's attitudes. Thurstone also assumed that the statements are uncorrelated and that each statement has a position that is independent of the others. That is, acceptance of one statement does not necessarily imply the acceptance of any others.

A Thurstone scale is made up of about twenty independent statements of opinion about a particular issue. Each statement has a numerical scale value determined by its average judged position on the continuum. People's *attitudes* on the issue are measured by asking them to check those statements with which they agree. Each person's *score* is the mean scale value of those items which he or she checked. An example of a shortened version of such a scale follows.

Trait: Attitude toward open housing		
Scale value		Statement
Least favorable	1.5	A. A person should refuse to rent to anyone he or she doesn't like.
	3.0	B. Federal laws enforcing open housing should apply only to public housing, not to private neighborhoods.
	4.5	C. Local governments should publicly urge people to engage in fair housing practices.
	6.0	D. Only in extreme cases of discrimination in housing should there be some sort of legal intervention.
Most favorable	7.5	E. A person must rent to the first eligible applicant, regardless of race, color, or creed.

The hallmark of a Thurstone scale is that the intervals between the statements are approximately equal. This property of the scale is achieved by the method in which it is constructed. The first step is to collect a large number of opinion statements about some particular issue. Any statements that are confusing, ambiguous, double-barreled, or likely to be approved by individuals with opposed attitudes are immediately discarded. Each of the remaining statements is then sorted into one of eleven categories by a group of judges, according to the degree of favorableness or unfavorableness toward the issue expressed by the statement, *regardless* of the judges' own attitudes. These categories thus make up a scale that ranges from very favorable, through neutral, to extremely unfavorable opinions about the issue. By tabulating the ratings of all the judges, it is possible to calculate both the numerical scale position of each statement (its average scale value), as well as the extent to which the judges agreed in its placement (its spread of ratings). The statements that are selected for use on the final scale are those that have high interjudge agreement and fall at relatively equally spaced intervals along the continuum. A person's attitude on the particular issue is then derived from his or her responses to this final set of scale items.

LIKERT'S METHOD OF SUMMATED RATINGS

One of the practical drawbacks of the Thurstone scale is that its construction is extremely laborious and time-consuming. To cope with this problem,

Likert developed a different technique, which could produce an equally reliable attitude scale with relative ease. The Likert scale is made up of a series of opinion statements about some issue. However, in contrast to the Thurstone scale, a person's attitude is measured by asking him or her to indicate the *extent* of agreement or disagreement with each item. This is done by having the person rate each item on a five-point scale of response (strongly agree, agree, undecided, disagree, strongly disagree). A person's attitude score is the sum of his or her individual ratings. An example of a single scale item is the following:

A. "The Women's Liberation movement is a good thing"

Rating value	
1	a) Strongly agree
2	b) Agree
3	c) Undecided
4	d) Disagree
5	e) Strongly disagree

Likert assumes that each statement that is used in the scale is a linear function of the same attitude dimension. This assumption is the basis for the operation of adding up a person's individual scores (or summating the ratings, to put it more formally) to obtain the final score. A further implication is that the items in a scale must be highly correlated with a common attribute and thus with each other, as opposed to Thurstone's distinct and independent items. It is important to note that at no point does Likert assume equal intervals between scale values. For example, it is quite possible that the difference between "agree" and "strongly agree" is much larger than the difference between "agree" and "undecided." This means that a Likert scale can provide information on the *ordering* of people's attitudes on a continuum, but it is unable to indicate how close or how far apart different attitudes might be.

Likert's method of scale construction is similar to Thurstone's in the initial collecting and editing of a variety of opinion statements. The remaining statements are then rated by a sample group of subjects on the five-point response scale in terms of their *own* opinions about the statements. This is in contrast to the Thurstone technique, where the ratings are made by trained judges and based not on personal opinions but on some relatively objective evaluation of where the statements fall on a continuum. The Likert scale is composed of those items that best differentiate between sample subjects with the highest and lowest total scores.

GUTTMAN'S SCALOGRAM

A third scaling technique is based on the assumption that a single, unidimensional trait can be measured by a set of statements that are ordered along a continuum of "difficulty of acceptance." That is, the statements range from those that are easy for most people to accept to those that few persons would endorse. Such scale items are *cumulative*, since the acceptance of one item implies that the person accepts all those of lesser magnitude (those less difficult to accept). To the extent that this is true, one can predict a person's attitude toward other statements on the basis of knowing the most difficult item he or she will accept. An example of such a scale might be the following:

Trait: Attitude toward open housing	
Acceptability	Statement
Least difficult to accept	A. Generally speaking, people should be able to live anywhere they want.
	B. Real estate agencies should not discriminate against minority groups.
	C. The city should actively support the idea of open housing.
	D. There should be a local review board that would pass on cases of extreme discrimination in housing.
Most difficult to accept	E. There should be federal laws to enforce open housing.

In order to obtain a scale that represents a single dimension, Guttman presents sample subjects with an initial set of items and records the extent to which they respond to the items with specified answer patterns. These patterns, which are referred to as *scale types*, follow a certain step-like order. The subject may accept none of the items in the set (score 0), accept item A only (score 1), accept items A and B only (score 2), accept items A, B, and C only (score 3), and so on. If the subject gives a nonscale response pattern (for example, accepts item C only and not those of lesser magnitude), it is assumed that he or she has made one or more response errors. By analyzing the number of response errors made, Guttman is able to determine the degree to which the initial set of items reflects a unidimensional attribute (that is, the extent to which they are "scalable"). The final scale is obtained by eliminating poor items and retesting sample subjects until a scalable set of items has been developed.

A person's attitude is then measured by having him or her check all the statements on the scale that are acceptable. The final score is that of the appropriate scale type or (if the person has given a nonscale response pattern) that of the scale type closest to his or her response. As the latter scoring procedure implies, it is almost impossible to develop a perfect unidimensional scale. This may be because people are actually responding not on the single dimension hypothesized, but rather on a different one, or on multiple dimensions.

OSGOOD'S SEMANTIC DIFFERENTIAL

The three methods just described attempt to measure attitudes by having people indicate the extent of their agreement with various opinion statements. In contrast to this approach, Osgood has studied attitudes by focusing on the *meaning* that people give to a word or concept. Underlying this technique is the basic assumption of a hypothetical semantic space of an unknown number of dimensions, in which the meaning of any word or concept can be represented as a particular point. Osgood's procedure is to have people judge a particular concept on a set of semantic scales. These scales are defined by verbal opposites with a midpoint of neutrality, and are usually composed of seven discriminable steps. For example, a particular person's meaning of the concept of Nuclear Power is measured by his or her ratings of it on a set of semantic scales:

good	——	——	——	——	——	——	——	bad
strong	——	——	——	——	——	——	——	weak
fast	——	——	——	——	——	——	——	slow
active	——	——	——	——	——	——	——	passive

and so on.

An analysis of the ratings collected by this method may reveal the particular dimensions that people use to qualify their experience, the types of concepts that are regarded as similar or different in meaning, and the intensity of the meaning given to a particular concept. Osgood's own research has indicated that there are three dominant, independent dimensions that people use in judging concepts. He refers to these dimensions as the evaluative factor (such as good-bad), the potency factor (such as strong-weak), and the activity factor (such as active-passive). Although this method can provide a lot of information about a concept, it is not exactly clear how the concept's *meaning* for a person is related to opinion statements he or she would make about it.

Attitude Measurement: To Each One's Own

In making comparisons across studies, we note one glaring fact—the lack of common methods for measuring attitudes, and a similar confusion regarding the definition of attitudes. To illustrate the chaos that can result from failure to adopt common standards, we need only outline the variety of measures used to define attitude change. There are two parts to this problem; first, the subject's response task may be markedly different from one study to another, and second, even when they are identical, the experiments may use different techniques of translating these common responses into quantitatively derived dependent variables. An example of the latter problem can be seen when two studies ask the subject to give his or her opinion by checking one point along a pro-con, like-dislike scale. Attitude change may then be described in terms of any one of the following measures: (1) percentage of subjects showing any positive change at all; (2) percentage of subjects showing "large," "moderate," "small," or "no" change (categories arbitrarily defined); (3) net percentage change (positive minus negative changes); (4) any of the above for an arbitrarily determined combination of opinion items; (5) the absolute mean scale distance changed; (6) distance changed relative to amount of change possible; and (7) scale distance change weighted (corrected) for the subjective distance between scale points (that is, two units movement across neutral is "worth more" than two units within one side of the scale).

The *a priori* rating scales that have been used have varied in the number of scale points (from four to one hundred), in the presence and number of verbal labels at various points, and in their arrangement (horizontal or vertical).

Attitudes have been measured by scale ratings of verbal statements (agree-disagree, true-false, like-dislike, and so on), of objects (good-bad, desirable-undesirable), of other people (like-dislike), and of self (degree of esteem, confidence). They have been measured by ratings of acceptance and rejection of individual opinion statements (latitudes of acceptance-rejection) and by choices, ranking of alternatives, perceived instrumental value of items or actions, ratings of mood, ratings of intention, willingness to endorse an action or product, and likelihood of future behavior.

Behavioral, or nonquestionnaire (non-paper-and-pencil), measures of attitude have also included an impressively divergent array. Verbal reports (about smoking, serving certain foods, dental hygiene practices) have been used, as well as observations of actual compliance with recommendations (taking an X-ray, getting tetanus shots, eating, agreeing with group norm, and so on). Time measures (decision time, time spent listening to supportive information, and so on), physiological measures (galvanic skin response to indicate reactions of a prejudiced person to stimuli associated with minority group), and learning measures (recall of stimuli) have all been conceived of as indicators of attitude. There are many others that rely on unobtrusive observational methods (for example, a count of empty beer and whiskey bottles in the garbage cans, as indicative of attitudes toward liquor in a given neighborhood; druggists' records of which doctors prescribe new drugs; the seating pattern of black and white students in classrooms and cafeterias).

Two additional comments about attitude measurement deserve to be made. First, while attitudes are sometimes defined as being composed of at least two components, cognitive and affective, what is traditionally done in attitude change studies is to present a set of belief or cognitive statements in a communication, and to then measure only changes in affect. Even more curious is the paradox of two seemingly interdependent areas of investigation—psychological scaling (psychometrics) and attitude change—existing independently and even in ignorance of each other. Few of the hundreds of studies performed on attitude change make use of the scaling techniques developed by Thurstone, Likert, Guttman, Osgood, and others. On the other hand, it is equally rare for those interested in measurement and scaling procedures to be concerned with the use of their techniques as part of an empirical study of communication and attitude change (Osgood's use of the semantic differential is a notable exception).

The lack of a common definition of attitude, or of what constitutes a valid and reliable measurement of it, is similarly reflected in the failure to use comparable attitude topics, communications with similar structure, or even standardized manipulations of the independent variables.

Having seen the great variety of measures (operational definitions) employed for attitudes, we should not be surprised that results in this area often conflict. The experimenters who use the various measures of attitude often make their decisions on the basis of ease of measurement, or intuition. There is often no theoretical reason why the measurements used *should* be measuring the same thing. It is merely assumed that they do. Since the results from various experiments sometimes conflict, we are left with the conclusion that the measures probably do not measure the same thing.

on becoming a social change agent

"But what can *I* do to change anything?" asks the concerned citizen who perceives that social forces are determining an undesirable destiny. Start by trying to change the attitudes and behavior of one other person, and then another, and another. As more people who share your beliefs and values also become active agents of persuasion, the potential for basic political and social reform increases.

Central to any program of change is a statement of the goals or specific behavioral objectives, a catalogue of potentially useful techniques to implement these goals, and a means of evaluating the success of the techniques and the entire action program. We will provide one possible set of goals along with relevant questions that must be answered about resources, priorities, and related matters. A sample of techniques follows, gleaned from the available, though often inadequate, attitude-change literature and from our observation, experience, and intuition, as well as from pragmatically oriented, "naive" psychological sources such as salespeople, police interrogators, and others (discussed in Chapters 2 and 6).

Specifying Your Goals

Before embarking on your change program, the goals or consequences that you wish your program to have must be considered. In trying to decide on the goals, serious thought should be given to the following issues.

221

1 *Begin by being specific.* Even if your final goal is to change the structure of the entire established system, start out with more specific goals. The more specific your initial goals, the easier it will be to devise a technique for changing attitudes or behavior. (For example, it is not enough to want to stop environmental pollution. You must specify those sources of pollution that should be stopped first.) You must then decide who or what organization requires changing, what kind of change (behavior or attitude) is required, and how that change can be most effectively produced.

2 *Almost any general goal one has can be broken down into many specific subgoals.* Reaching each subgoal will make it more likely that the final goal will be attained. By dividing things into small, *highly specific,* and attainable subgoals one can shape each unit of change, reinforce the people or organization who changed, and move on to the next *very specific* subgoal, until, by successive approximations and reinforcement, the final goal has been attained.

3 *When each subgoal is specified, try to estimate both the long-term ideological goals and the short-term tactical consequences of reaching and not reaching that goal.* It is essential, in specifying a goal, to keep in mind what might happen if you fail to reach that goal. What will it mean to you? More importantly, what will the people or organization whom you are trying to influence learn about you? Always weigh the positive and negative consequences of attempting to produce a specific change, with regard to both your successes and your failures. It is almost always true that it is better to have many very small successes and no failures, than one big success and a big failure.

4 *Review the questions outlined in Chapter 1.* These are meant to direct your attention to a sample of the types of question one should ask oneself before starting out.

5 *Compare your goals with the resources at your disposal.* Try to specify tactical goals that match the resources you have. If you cannot, then make one of your first approximations or subgoals the stockpiling of appropriate resources (money, mass support, support of influential people or groups, and so forth).

6 *Your final consideration ought to be evaluation of the success of each change attempt.* This is so important to any influence program that we are presenting this in its own section (see the next to last section of this Postscript).

A Sample of Influence Techniques and Approaches

There are many ways to organize this set of persuasive techniques. Our functional organization follows four major steps that an individual must face in an interpersonal influence attempt:

1 Preparing for the initial contact
2 Gaining access to and establishing the contact
3 Maintaining, intensifying, directing the interpersonal relationship
4 Obtaining the commitment and terminating the contact

You should be forewarned that there are probably no simple generalizations as to the effect of any given variable or technique on changing attitudes. Rather, the rule is that any laws of attitude change involve complex sets of interactions among a host of variables. The power of any given technique will vary with many factors associated with the source (credibility, attractiveness, power, delivery, and style), with the organization of the message, with the nature of the arguments and appeals used, and with the characteristics of the receivers (intelligence, information level, involvement, self-esteem, sex), as well as with many situational elements. Therefore, these suggested techniques should be viewed as simplistic approximations of the complex reality we are trying to understand and manipulate. Individually, they will work for some of the people some of the time. It is up to you to help develop a more adequate technology of attitude change by being aware of the many subtleties and complexities involved and carefully evaluating your hits and misses.

PREPARING FOR THE INITIAL CONTACT

1 *Be informed.*   Get as much accurate, up-to-date, reliable evidence as you can. Commit important facts, arguments, statistics and quotations to memory so that they are "natural" to your delivery. You should see yourself as more expert on the particular issue of concern than the people you will try to persuade. Your perceived competence is your single most important source trait.

2 *Learn as much as you can about those you will engage.*   Be familiar with their neighborhood, local issues, basic values, language style (use of diction, clichés, idioms), sources of local pride and discontent, the nature of popular influence media, and their attitudes on the issue in question. You can obtain this information from local businesspeople (barbers, cab drivers, grocery-store employees, bartenders), from salespeople, from signatures on newspaper petitions, and from distinguishing characteristics of the neigh-

borhood or the individual home. You can also encourage the people to verbalize their opinions by having them call in to the campus radio station, respond to telephone surveys, or come to "open campus" meetings.

3 *Actively role-play the anticipated situation with a friend.* Imagine, and then work through as realistically as possible, the persuasion situation in which you will operate. If possible, tape-record or videotape such dress rehearsals, and then critically analyze your performance. Switch roles and try to be the target person in the situation where he or she is experiencing the pressure to comply with a request for some commitment.

4 *Do a critical self-appraisal.* Before you actually start out, analyze your own personal strengths and weaknesses and your appearance, and verbalize any source of fear, anxiety, or anticipated embarrassment with one or more others with whom you feel comfortable.

5 *Be confident that you will be effective more often than not.* You must expect some setbacks, but you must be dedicated to winning, to making the "sale." If you do not handle the situation carefully, you may produce the undesirable effect of increasing the person's resistance to any further influence attempts by others; or you may generate a "boomerang" effect, causing the person to become even more extremely "con" on this position.

6 *Be sensitive to the varied reasons underlying the attitude(s) in question.* Attitudes are formed and maintained because of needs for information (cognitive clarity and consistency), for social acceptance by other people, or for ego protection from unacceptable impulses and ideas. Attitudes of high ego-involvement probably have all three of these motivational bases. New informational input helps in the first instance; providing new sources of reinforcement is necessary for the second; while substituting other attitudes and actions that will satisfy the same underlying ego needs must be used for the third. Information *per se* is probably the *least* effective way of changing attitudes and behavior. It must be part of a general approach, which sees the individual as more than a rational information processor—as sometimes irrational, inconsistent, responsive to social reward, and concerned about how he or she appears to both self and others.

7 *Be aware that, even as a stranger, you can exert considerable influence.* You can serve as a model for some behavior by publicly engaging in it, and you can provide a new source of social contact, recognition, and reward for many people.

GAINING ACCESS TO AND ESTABLISHING THE CONTACT

1 Before you can persuade, you must get the person to acknowledge your presence, to attend to you, and to follow your presentation. People are wary of an assault on their privacy and their life space, either by a stranger thrusting a leaflet into their hand or by an unknown person on their doorstep.

A. In distributing materials in the street, make eye contact while the person is a short distance away, smile, and then present the leaflet at the level of his or her hand (as in a handshake), saying "thank you" just before they accept it. Then say, "I hope you will look it over as soon as you have time," since the person will feel awkward at either accepting it and not stopping to read it, or by being made to stop ongoing activity unexpectedly.

B. You might want to consider an initial phone call or letter to people you will contact at home. However, the nature of your visit should be described in generalities that will neither threaten nor offer reasons for preparing counterarguments (for example, "to find out your views on several important issues facing our country, such as ecology, education, and the economy").

2 If you are making a home contact, be aware of the particular situation you have encountered. Be sure that the person is willing to give you the required time to present your case. You might be interrupting dinner, a phone call, a family quarrel, a visit with guests, or some bad news. You do not want the dominant motivation of the homeowner to be to get rid of you as soon as possible.

3 Where possible, it is advisable to select a contact situation where you and the target person are either equals (you are a "guest" in the home only as long as the host allows it), or you have some power advantage. This occurs where you are buying merchandise, paying for a service, or where the person is dependent on you for your services.

4 Those people known or expected to be against your position should be contacted not in their familiar surroundings but ideally on your ground. This both becomes the first act of yielding (as the police manuals tell us), and allows you greater confidence and situational control. You can then arrange a modeling situation in which a prestigious model engages in the desired goal behavior before the target person.

5 Although strangers can influence everyday behavior, persuasion is enhanced when the target perceives some basic similarity with the source. This "strategy of identification" (practiced by all good entertainers and politicians) involves finding some commonality between you. Physical similarity is the most obvious: age, sex, race, ethnic features, dress (length and style of hair), voice, dialect, regionalisms and appropriate slang, jargon, or group-identifying phrases (such as "What can you expect from the

Goyim?", "If the market bottoms out at 550, then what do you think will happen?").

Arrange canvassing to optimize this perceived similarity by selecting neighborhoods and locations that are approximately matched to the available canvassers. The canvasser should try to uncover as many points of similarity as possible because similarity breeds familiarity, which promotes liking and enhances credibility and greater acceptance of the message.

6 Similarity may be created and combined with an "overhead communication" approach, as in the following example: A young coed enters a laundromat with a basket of laundry, puts it in the machine, asks another customer for change of a quarter to make a phone call to her mother, pretends to call Mom, describes the chores she is and will be doing ("She's a good daughter"), then may proceed to talk to her mother briefly about the attitude topic and agree with her mother's course of action. She talks loudly enough to let the target audience hear, but goes about her business when she is finished, unless one of them initiates the conversation.

7 Students are not seen as credible sources on most issues that concern them directly; to be effective, it is important to increase source credibility. This may be accomplished in a number of ways:

A. Impress the audience with your expertise, concern, and dedication, being forceful but not overbearing.

B. Argue on some points that are against your own best interests; indicate the sacrifices you have made and would be willing to make.

C. Have a respected person introduce you, or make the contact for you.

D. Begin by agreeing with what the audience wants to hear, using a "pro-them" approach (the Mark Antony effect).

E. Minimize your manipulative intent until you ask for the commitment.

8 The potential for persuasion in general is greater if the message is delivered in a situation where there is positive affect serving as a minimal distractor, and if small compliances (like agreeing to talk to you for ten minutes) precede the escalation to more extreme ones (the "foot-in-the-door technique").

9 Avoid group situations where the majority are known or expected to be against you, since they will provide support for each other and make salient a group norm that you will attack.

MAINTAINING, INTENSIFYING, AND DIRECTING THE INTERPERSONAL RELATIONSHIP

Once you have managed to get the person to listen to you, you must hold this attention while trying to get your message (and yourself) accepted.

1 You have the power to reinforce many behaviors of the target person—a power you should use judiciously but with conscious awareness of what and how you are reinforcing.

A. Attentive listening to what the other person has to say about anything of personal interest is absolutely necessary. This not only "opens up" the person for a dialogue, and helps in establishing his or her primary values, beliefs, and the organization of his or her thinking, but it establishes you as someone open to what others have to say. (The opportunity to tell a college student where to get off may be very rewarding for many people.)

B. Use eye contact with the person as a reward when the target person says something with which you agree. Always maintain as close physical proximity as seems acceptable.

C. Individuate the person by using names (with Mr., Mrs., Ms., or titles, when there is an age or status discrepancy). Make the person feel you are reacting to his or her uniqueness and individuality (which you should be) and are not reacting in a programmed way to your stereotyped conception of a housewife, blue-collar worker, and so on. Similarly, help the other person to individuate you, to break through the categorization and pigeon-holing process that makes you just an anonymous canvasser. At some point, describe something personal or unique about your feelings, background, or interests (which you expect will be acceptable). However, once this is accomplished, don't allow yourself to be the exception to the stereotype—say "most other students are like me in how we feel about X."

D. Reinforce specific behaviors explicitly and immediately, by nodding, saying "Good," "That's an interesting point," and so on. Reinforce more general classes of behavior by smiling, by making it obvious you enjoy the interaction, and by being impressed by the person's openness, sensitivity, intelligence, or articulateness. As a college student with much "book learning" you can still learn a lot from people who have gone to "the school of hard knocks," and who have "real-life learning," and "street savvy" to offer you. Let them know that's how you feel when talking to someone who has not had the benefit of a college education.

E. The person must perceive that you personally care about and are enthusiastic about the topic of discussion; moreover, you should be perceived as really caring about the compliant act of the person—at a personal level and not merely as part of your role.

F. Your reinforcement rate should increase over the course of the inter-action, so that at the end of the time the person is sorry to see you leave.

2   Be aware of the sources of resentment against you for what you repre-sent by your physical appearance, group membership (as a student), and so on; work to differentiate those feelings and reactions from the goal of your influence attempt.

3   Plan the organization of your presentation well enough so that it seems natural and unplanned, and be *flexible* enough to modify it as necessary.

A. Do not put your best arguments in the middle of your presentation where they are least well remembered. Put your strongest arguments first if you want to motivate or interest uninvolved people; use a climax order with people whose interest is already high.

B. Draw your conclusions explicitly. Implicit conclusion drawing should be left for only very intelligent audiences.

C. Repeat the main points in your argument, and the major points of agreement between you and the target person.

4   In tailoring your approach to the target person:

A. Do not put him or her on the defensive, or even encourage or force a public defense of (and thus commitment to) a "con-you" position. Op-posing beliefs are to be seen as providing the opportunity for open dis-cussion, as a starting point to find areas of common agreement. If the person is "pro-you," then *do* get a public commitment early, and try to make it more stable and more extreme by applying reinforcements appropriately.

B. Get the person to role-play your position or one which he or she does not agree with (if the situation allows it).

C. Have the person restate your ideas and conclusions, in his or her own words (encourage active participation, especially if participation is "pro-you").

D. A person who appears to be very authoritarian in manner and thinking will probably be more impressed by status sources and appeals to power, control, decisiveness, and one-sided generalizations than by in-formational appeals, expert testimony, unbiased presentation of both sides of the issue and so on. Any approach must be responsive to the dominant personality and social characteristics of the person to whom you are talking.

E. Play the devil's advocate for a "pro-you" person in order to get that person to defend his or her position, to articulate it clearly, to practice handling counterarguments, and to be reinforced for doing so by your "coming around" to agree with the position.

F. For the "con-you" person, the "reactance technique" (see Chapter 6) may be effective. You limit the person's sense of psychological freedom by stating a very extreme position, one with which he or she could not entirely agree, prefacing it with, "*no one* could disagree with the statement that . . . ," or "you *must* acknowledge that . . . ," or "*everybody* is convinced that . . . ." It is expected that the response will be, "*I* don't agree," and then you reinforce this overt statement of disagreement with positions on the "other side" of the issue. For such a person, the goal of the interaction may be to instill doubt in his or her former set of beliefs, or force a wedge between some apparently inseparable cognitive links. In this way, the person might become more receptive to subsequent persuasion by the mass media or through exposure to new events.

G. Although a more personal relationship can be established in a two-person interaction, there is much to be gained from teamwork. Working in pairs provides each student with social support, lowers apprehension about initiating each new contact, and allows one of you to be "off the firing line" and appraising the situation, to come in when help is needed, to refocus the direction, or to respond to some specific trait detected in the target person. The third party also permits a better evaluation of the dynamics of the interaction after it is terminated. Teamwork can be used to tactical advantage, as the police recommend with the "Mutt and Jeff" technique (see Chapter 6), modified as the "militant and the moderate." In addition, a consistent, agreeing minority of two individuals who are perceived as strangers (or at least not in collusion) has been shown to be effective in modifying the attitudes of a majority. This may be even more so when the minority disagree on other issues, but totally agree on this one.

GETTING THE COMMITMENT AND TERMINATING THE CONTACT

You must now get what you came for; don't insist that the person accept and believe what you've said before he or she makes the behavioral commitment. Get the behavioral commitment anyway, and attitude change will follow. The ideal conclusion of the contact would also leave the person feeling that the time spent was worthwhile and that his or her self-esteem is higher than it was before you arrived.

1 Do not overstay your welcome, or be forced to stay longer than is worthwhile according to your time schedule. Timing is essential both in knowing when to ask for the commitment, and in knowing when to quit with an intractable person. For a person who needs more time to think, encourage it, but get a commitment to allow you to come back.

2   You might provide several behavioral alternatives for the person, arranged in degrees of difficulty. *After* getting commitment on the easy alternatives, push for the more difficult ones.

3   Be clear as to what actions are requested, or what has been agreed on or concluded. If fear appeals have been used, then solutions must be offered that are clear, explicit, and involve a concrete course of action to alleviate the danger.

4   A "bandwagon" effect may be used to indicate prestigious others who have joined in the action.

5   When you believe the target person is about to make the commitment (or after a verbal agreement is made), then stress the fact that the decision is his or her own; it involves free choice and no pressure. At the same time, minimize extrinsic sources of justification for the discrepant compliance. By creating dissonance (see Chapter 3) at this point, you impel the individual to make his or her behavior internally consistent by generating intrinsic justifications for that behavior. But afterwards, reinforce the person's behavior with thanks and appreciation.

6   Emotionally inoculate the person from counterattacks by noting that there will be people who will disagree with his or her action by saying "A, B, and C." How will the person respond to such critics?

7   Broaden the contact in three ways. First, get the name of one or more neighbors who would agree with the person's position. You will talk to them, too, and use the person's name if that is okay. Secondly, see if the person will go out and proselytize friends and relatives to further support the action taken. This extends your influence and is the *best* commitment from the person. Finally, honestly react to something about the person that is irrelevant to the main social/political issue at hand: the house, decor, hair, clothes, an avocation mentioned, or a favor that you can do related to something mentioned.

8   Finally, indicate that there is a possibility for future contact (for "surveillance" of the commitment), and that you would like to talk again about other things. Perhaps you could call again or be called (leave your name and number).

9   Thank the person for his or her time and the interesting dialogue. For those who made the commitment, emphasize how much better things

would be if there were more such people. For the recalcitrant person, say you'll think about all of the things he or she has said if the person will do the same about what you said.

10 Before going to the next interaction, stop and think about what you have learned about yourself and about human nature, where you were effective, and where you went wrong. Think about (or complete) an evaluation of this interaction.

Evaluation of the Change Program

One of the most important aspects of any activity whose goal is to produce a change in the behavior or attitudes of people is evaluation of the effectiveness of that activity in producing the hoped-for change. Evaluation is important for a number of reasons. First, many of the techniques you have just read about have not been tested in field settings, and therefore some of them may not work. Second, some techniques may be more effective than others, and without an evaluation of the relative effectiveness of each of the techniques you will not know whether you are using the most effective technique possible. Third, shaping (see the section on specifying goals) can only work if you know when each subgoal has been reached; the next goal in the series should not be attempted until each previous subgoal has been achieved. Fourth, information you obtain about the effectiveness of various techniques can be used by others who have the same goals as you do. Avoiding the repetition of mistakes will greatly increase the long-term effectiveness of any organized change program.

To aid you in devising a method of evaluation, a sample of the types of objective data you might want to gather daily is outlined below.

A Format for Evaluating Your Persuasion Attempt

1   The change agent (you)

A.   Physical characteristics

　　1. Sex

　　2. Age

　　3. Dress

　　4. Race/ethnic background

　　5. Unusual physical characteristics

　　6. Others thought to be relevant

B. Psychological characteristics
1. Educational level
2. Socioeconomic background
3. Interpersonal contact made alone or with _____ others (how many?)
4. Familiarity with change techniques employed
5. Dominant personality features (forceful, serious, shy, sincere, and so on)
6. Other

2 The target person (or group)
A. Physical characteristics (same as above)
B. Psychological characteristics
1. Same as above plus those below.
2. History of attitude or behavior to be changed
    a) Does the person initially agree or disagree with you?
    b) Has the person acted either in favor of or in opposition to this goal in the past?
    c) Have others tried to change the person (failed or succeeded)?
    d) If yes to former question, what techniques were employed?
3. Influence of target person
    a) Does person have control of many resources other than his or her vote or attitude? (Assess spread of potential influence.)
    b) Will person have time to work for/with you to change others?

3 Situation in which contact is made
A. Place (home of target person or other)
B. Time of day: Activity that target person was engaged in immediately before contact
C. Duration of contact
D. Your role
E. Target person's role
F. Other relevent events that occurred during contact

4 What was your goal for this contact (be specific!)?
5 What techniques were employed to reach that goal?
6 To what degree was your goal achieved?
7 On what *objective, behavioral* data do you base this answer?

8   What other evidence might you have gathered? (Describe)

9   What factors do you feel produced the final result for this contact (with regard to you, the target person, the situation, the technique, the goal)?

10 Any other general comments that might affect future attempts.

Concluding Statement

Any individual who plans to go out into the "real world" to try to influence others, change attitudes, and modify behavior must be aware of the personal as well as the social consequences of such a decision:

> The psychologist can hardly do anything without realizing that for him the acquisition of knowledge opens up the most terrifying prospects of controlling what people do and how they think and how they behave and how they feel. *J. Robert Oppenheimer*

Here are five samples of do-it-yourself home and field research based upon the theories, models, and research presented in the text. We hope you will do some or all of them in order to get a better perspective of how it feels to be directly involved in data gathering ventures.

student projects

Know Your Ads, Know Yourself

The Yale attitude change approach, social comparison theory, and parts of social learning theory suggest that the kinds of persuasive appeals and communicators (models) to which the public are exposed will affect both their attitudes and behavior. New *standards* for dress and action can be created. For example, attitudes toward various behaviors by different people (for example, housework by men, executive-level decision making by women, resolution of interpersonal conflict by violence versus negotiation) might be affected by the kinds of advertisements displayed on television or in magazines. It would not be surprising to find that young girls expect to spend their time doing housework while young boys expect to work in offices and provide money for the family if advertisements for detergents, vacuum cleaners, diapers, floor wax, food preparation, toilet tissue, and other things associated with housework are always presented with women playing the major roles, while commercials about automobiles, computers, air travel, and technical books have males playing the major roles. In short, the content of television and magazine advertising is certainly a major source of social influence.

In this project, your goal is to "survey" the kinds of appeals and the standards being set by television or magazine advertising. Focusing on television, this can be accomplished by randomly sampling (see Postscript A) several different time periods on several days to observe characteristics of TV advertisements. You can develop a chart like the one in Table D.1. Note the time, duration, and nature of the program preceding (and/or following) the ad; the product or service being sold; characteristics of the major actors; intended audience; and kind of appeal (emotional, logical-scientific, "guilt" by association, celebrity endorsement, bandwagon, social rewards, plainfolks, nostalgia, sex, and so on).

After collecting your data, you can summarize them in different ways. You could examine the frequency with which certain model characteristics are associated (such as male, female) with products or services of a given type (such as housework, business). Alternatively, or in addition, you might note whether different types of appeals are used (logical-scientific, social rewards) for different intended audiences (adults, teenagers). Do some kinds of appeals always last longer than others? Are different types of appeals ever present in the same ad and, if so, which ones? The answers to these and other questions could provide major insights into the way we are all being targeted for persuasion.

On Being Deviant for a Day

To determine your place in the social matrices in which you live, study, work, and play, make a major change in an attribute of yours and see if others notice it.

Change your usual clothing in a dramatic way by wearing a dress or a suit if you typically wear jeans (or vice versa). You might change your hair style, shave your moustache or beard, or wear something unusual for you—a weird hat, beads, or lipstick for example. Or you might change a behavioral attribute, such as being assertive if you're shy, shutting up if you're usually talkative, being critical if you're accepting, and so forth. Do this for one full day and proceed with your typical rounds.

Things to note: Which people seem to notice the change, and which of them also comment on it? What is the quality of their reaction? To what do they attribute the change? (You should not "explain" it to them). How do you react to their reaction? Do you avoid or feel especially awkward in certain situations with certain people? What do you infer about yourself and others from that feeling? What do you infer about the force of social norms of appropriate behavior?

Finally, do you notice any change in your adaptation to your new role as deviant over the course of the day?

TABLE D.1
Example of a Chart to Use When Collecting Data about TV Advertisements

Time of day	Nature of program	Type of appeal— first/second/ third	Characteristics of major actor— sex/role/age/other	Audience intended	Duration

Does Dissonance Inevitably Follow Decisions?

Dissonance is assumed to follow decision making. The magnitude of dissonance will in part be a function of all the reasons that exist at the time of decision for *not* making it. Dissonance reduction should then be observable in post-decision changes in the number and quality of those factors that supported the decision and those that opposed it. Following the decision, the object of the decision will be enhanced as the ratio of initially negative to initially positive reasons increases.

More simply put, if there are four good reasons to get engaged to a certain person, there will be more dissonance after you make the decision to become engaged when there are three reasons *not* to do so than when there is only one against it. You should reduce this greater dissonance by liking (loving) your fiancé more, and/or seeing more good qualities and fewer bad ones in your beloved. Comparable changes in attitudes should occur for other important decisions.

For your Student Project, select some important decision that friends are about to make—choosing a major, graduate or professional school, job, or roomate; buying a car; becoming engaged; and so on.

Ask them to list all the positive and negative things they can about that major, school, job, person, and so on *before* the decision is made. Also ask them to estimate how much they like, value, or respect the object of the decision. Use a seven-point scale labeled:

1   Extremely positive
2   Very positive
3   Strongly positive
4   Moderately positive
5   Weakly positive
6   Neutral
7   Slightly negative

The scale is weighted toward the positive end because people wouldn't be considering the decision if it were more negative than "slightly so."

Shortly *after* the decision has been made, repeat your assessment of the positive and negative cognitive components that entered the decision as well as the overall evaluation of the object of choice. The question to be answered by the data is whether people are more positive toward the chosen alternative and/or less positive toward the unchosen one after the choice than they were before it.

You can study different people about to make the same type of decision, or several people across many decision opportunities. You can also focus on differences between qualitatively different types of decisions. Among the latter are: risk–no risk, competitive–noncompetitive, social–nonsocial, short duration–long duration, acquisition–getting rid of, and so forth.

Do Clothes Make the Attribution?

To what extent are the impressions people form of you based upon their inferences of your social status as determined by your attire? The following project may offer an answer to the question of whether or not the clothes make the person.

1 Decide on what attire represents high and low status in the area where you will perform the study. (How will you do this?)

2 Obtain a high degree of consensus on the validity of this status distinction by asking a series of people (judges) to evaluate the criterion items.

3 Get a partner who will assist you by recording the data while you act as subject.

4 Dressed in a given status attire, visit a bank, clothing store, and a university office.

5 Prepare rehearse, and deliver a standard request for information and/or advice in each site.

6 Now dress in the other status attire and repeat the procedure in three equivalent sites.

7 Reverse roles with your partner and have him or her visit the same sites you did dressed in the status attire opposite to that which you wore in each.

8 You then act as experimenter, inconspicuously recording (with a stop watch):
   a) Time to initiate service, inquire to help, and so forth
   b) Time from first eye contact to first word or movement in model's direction
   c) Total duration of the contact
   d) The first comment made by the personnel

    e) The nature of the service received

    f) The last comment made by the personnel

Also note reactions (or their absence) of other people in the setting to you and your partner. Try to establish equivalent conditions across your replication sites and record just what was going on before, during, and after the dressed-up or dressed-down model appeared.

In your analysis, how do you tell whether you or your clothes made a difference in how service personnel reacted? You can also study sex, race, and physical stigma effects in this same way.

Self-Knowledge, a Key to Success

One of the first steps in any behavior modification program (whether about smoking, overeating, assertiveness, ineffective study habits, or anything else) is to determine how to measure the problem behavior and to take a *baseline*. This is a necessary first step in discovering (1) what conditions are associated with the act and (2) whether later influence techniques are effective in modifying the base rate. Informal (rather than formal) evaluation of the success of change attempts leads more often to inaccurate conclusions than to reliable ones.

You can apply some of these principles to your own behavior by selecting some class or category of your own actions that you would like to change, and then recording the frequency of its occurrence. For example, someone may have pointed out that you say "uhm" or "you know" very often, or that you dominate conversations by interrupting others. You may want to change the frequency of some appetitive behavior (such as smoking, drinking, or eating sweets). On the other hand, you might wish to reduce or eliminate fingernail biting, knuckle cracking, or some other gesture. Maybe you cannot look people in the eye, or you have trouble greeting them. Concentrating on your studies might be a problem.

Begin by specifying the kind of behavior in some detail. You must decide what kinds of actions will and will not be counted. Is putting your finger in your mouth but not actually chewing on the nail an instance of fingernail biting? If you look at someone's face but not into their eyes does that qualify as "eye contact"? Is gum to be considered a sweet? Once you have established the boundaries of your response class you need to develop an efficient method of recording the number of times you engage in the activity per week, per day, or per hour. One simple suggestion for a baseline count of the behavior is to fill one pocket with a fixed number of pennies and simply transfer a penny to another pocket each time that you engage in the crucial response. At the end of the day or hour you can simply count up how many pennies you have transferred. Another, more thorough, method is to keep a chart on an index card, and record the time, location, and correlated information every time the action occurs.

After collecting the data for a week or two you should draw a graph that plots the number of times you engaged in the activity each day. Careful examination of the graph may suggest some insights, not only about how often you perform the crucial action, but also when you are more or less likely to do it (time of day), and under what circumstances (people, activities, and physical environment associated with it). Once you have established this baseline, you may wish to institute some program of behavioral change and then repeat this baseline procedure later on to see if any change has actually occurred.

references

*Abelson, H. I., and Karlins, M. 1970. *Persuasion: How Opinions and Attitudes Are Changed.* 2d rev. ed. New York: Springer.

Abelson, R. P., and Zimbardo, P. G. 1970. *Canvassing for Peace: A Manual for Volunteers.* Ann Arbor, Mich.: Society for the Psychological Study of Social Issues.

*Adorno, T. W.; Frenkel-Brunswik, E.; Levinson, D. J.; and Sanford, R. N. 1950. *The Authoritarian Personality.* New York: Harper & Row. Copyright 1950 by the American Jewish Committee. By permission of Harper & Row, Publishers.

Allen, V. L. 1965. Situational factors in conformity. In *Advances in Experimental Social Psychology,* ed. L. Berkowitz, Vol. 2. New York: Academic.

Appelbaum, R. P. 1970. *Theories of Social Change.* Chicago: Markham.

*Arendt, H. 1963. *Eichmann in Jerusalem: A Report on the Banality of Evil.* New York: Viking.

Aronson, E. 1969. The theory of cognitive dissonance: A current perspective. In *Advances in Experimental Social Psychology,* ed. L. Berkowitz, Vol. 4. New York: Academic.

*Asch, S. E. 1956. Studies of independence and conformity: 1. A minority of one against a unanimous majority. *Psychological Monographs* 70 (9, Whole No. 416).

*Audi, R. 1972. On the conception and measurement of attitudes in contemporary Anglo-American psychology. *Journal for the Theory of Social Behavior* 2: 179–203.

*Bandura, A. 1977. *Social Learning Theory.* Englewood Cliffs, N.J.: Prentice-Hall.

*Bandura, A.; Blanchard, E. D.; and Ritter, B. J. 1969. Relative efficacy of desensitization and modeling therapeutic approaches for inducing behavioral, affective, and attitudinal changes. *Journal of Personality and Social Psychology* 13: 173–199.

*Batson, D. 1976. Moon madness: Greed or creed.? *American Psychological Association Monitor* 7 (no. 6): 1, 32.

*Bem, D. J. 1970. *Beliefs, Attitudes, and Human Affairs.* Belmont, Calif.: Brooks/Cole.

* Specific references cited in the text are marked with an asterisk.

*Bem, D. J. 1972. Self-perception theory. In *Advances in Experimental Social Psychology*, ed. L. Berkowitz, Vol. 6. New York: Academic.

*Berdie, R. 1947. Playing the dozens. *Journal of Abnormal and Social Psychology* 42: 120–121.

Bickman, L., and Henchy, T., eds. 1972. *Beyond the Laboratory: Field Research in Social Psychology*. New York: McGraw-Hill.

Biderman, A. D.; Oldham, S. S.; Ward, S. K.; and Eby, M. A. 1972. *An Inventory of Surveys of the Public on Crime, Justice and Related Topics*. Washington, D.C.: U.S. Department of Justice.

Boies, K. 1972. Role playing as a behavior change technique: Review of the empirical literature. *Psychotherapy: Theory, Research and Practice* 2: 185–192.

*Brehm, J. W. 1966. *A Theory of Psychological Reactance*. New York: Academic.

*Brehm, J. W., and Cohen, A. R., eds. 1962. *Explorations in Cognitive Dissonance*. New York: Wiley.

Bugental, D. B.; Henker, B.; and Whalen, C. K. 1976. Attributional antecedents of verbal and vocal assertiveness. *Journal of Personality and Social Psychology* 34: 405–411.

Butler, M. 1972. Social policy research and the realities of the system: Violence done to T.V. research. Unpublished report, Institute for Communication Research at Stanford University.

Byrne, D. Attitudes and Attraction. 1969. In *Advances in Experimental Social Psychology*, ed. L. Berkowitz, Vol. 4. New York: Academic.

Campbell, D. T. 1969. Reforms as experiments. *American Psychologist* 24: 409–429.

*Campbell, D. T., and Stanley, J. C. 1963. *Experimental and Quasi-experimental Designs for Research*. Chicago: Rand McNally.

Caplan, N., and Nelson, S. D. 1973. On being useful: The nature and consequences of psychological research on social problems. *American Psychologist* 28: 199–211.

Carlsmith, J. M.; Ellsworth P. C.; and Aronson, E. 1976. *Methods of Research in Social Psychology*. Reading, Mass.: Addison-Wesley.

Cartwright, D., and Zander, A., eds. 1968. *Group Dynamics: Research and Theory*. 3d ed. New York: Harper & Row.

*Christie, R., and Geis, F. L., eds. 1970. *Studies in Machiavellianism*. New York: Academic.

Cialdini, R. B., and Mirel, H. L. 1976. Sense of personal control and attributions about yielding and resisting persuasion targets. *Journal of Personality and Social Psychology* 33: 395–402.

Cohen, A. R. 1959. Communication discrepancy and attitude change: A dissonance theory approach. *Journal of Personality* 27: 386–396.

*Crawford, T. J. 1973a. Beliefs about birth control: A consistency theory analysis. *Representative Research in Social Psychology* 4: 54–65.

*Crawford, T. J. 1973*b*. Police overperception of ghetto hostility. *Journal of Police Science and Administration* 1: 168–174.

Cummings, W. H., and Venkatesan, M. 1974. *Cognitive dissonance and consumer behavior: A critical review.* Working paper series No. 74-1, University of Iowa Bureau of Business and Economic Research.

*Davenport, W. 1965. Sexual patterns and their regulation in a society of the Southwest Pacific. In *Sex and Behavior*, ed. F. Beach. New York: Wiley.

Davey, A. G. 1972. Education of indoctrination. *Journal of Moral Education* 2, 5–15.

Dawes, R. M. 1972. *Fundamentals of Attitude Measurement.* New York: Wiley.

Deutsch, M., and Hornstein, H. A., eds. 1975. *Applying Social Psychology: Implications for Research, Practice, and Training.* Hillsdale, N.J.: Lawrence Erlbaum Associates.

*Dostoevsky, F. 1945. *The gambler.* In *The Short Novels of Dostoevsky*, trans. C. Garnett. New York: Dial Press.

Duval, S., and Wicklund, R. A. 1972. *A Theory of Objective Self-Awareness* New York: Academic.

*Ebbesen, E. B., and Konečni, V. J. 1975. Analysis of legal decision-making: Bail-setting and sentencing. Paper presented at American Psychological Association Convention, September.

Elms, A. C., ed. 1969. *Role Playing, Reward, and Attitude Change.* New York: Van Nostrand Reinhold.

Elms, A. C. 1976. *Personality in Politics.* New York: Harcourt Brace Jovanovich.

Ethical Aspects of Experimentation with Human Subjects. 1969. *Daedalus.* Spring issue.

Etzioni, A. 1972. Human beings are not very easy to change after all. *Saturday Review,* 55: 45–47.

*Farquhar, J. W., et al. 1977. Community education for cardiovascular health. Submitted to *New England Journal of Medicine.*

Feather, N. T. 1967. A structural balance approach to the analysis of communication effects. In *Advances in Experimental Social Psychology*, ed. L. Berkowitz, Vol. 3. New York: Academic.

*Festinger, L. 1950. Informal social communication. *Psychological Review* 57: 271–282.

*Festinger, L. 1954. A theory of social comparison processes. *Human Relations* 7: 117–140.

*Festinger, L. 1957. *A Theory of Cognitive Dissonance.* Evanston, Illinois: Row, Peterson.

Fishbein, M., and Ajzen, I. 1975. *Belief, Attitude, Intention and Behavior.* Reading, Mass.: Addison-Wesley.

*Frank, J. D. 1961. *Persuasion and healing.* Baltimore: Johns Hopkins.

Freedman, J. L., and Sears, D. O. 1965. Selective exposure. In *Advances in Experimental Social Psychology*, ed. L. Berkowitz, Vol. 2. New York: Academic.

*Frenkel-Brunswick, E.; Levinson, D. J.; and Sanford, R. N. The anti-democratic personality. In *Readings in Social Psychology*, eds. E. E. Maccoby, T. M. Newcomb, and E. L. Hartley, pp. 636–646. New York: Holt.

Gerard, H. B.; Conolley, E. S.; and Wilhelmy, R. A. 1974. Compliance, justification, and cognitive change. In *Advances in Experimental Social Psychology*, ed. L. Berkowitz, Vol. 7. New York: Academic.

Greenwald, A. G. 1970. When does role playing produce attitude change? Toward an answer. *Journal of Personality and Social Psychology* 16: 214–219.

*Hammond, E. C. 1958. Smoking and death rates—a riddle in cause and effect. *American Scientist* 46: 331–354.

Hansen, R. D., and Lowe, C. A. 1976. Distinctiveness and consequences: The influence of behavioral information on actors' and observers' attributions. *Journal of Personality and Social Psychology* 34: 425–433.

*Hart, R. P.; Friedrich, G. W.; and Brooks, W. D. 1975. *Public Communication.* New York: Harper & Row. Copyright © 1975 by Roderick P. Hart, Gustav W. Friedrich, and William D. Brooks. By permission of Harper & Row, Publishers, Inc.

Hass, R. G., and Mann, R. W. 1976. Anticipatory belief change: Persuasion or impression management? *Journal of Personality and Social Psychology* 34: 105–111.

*Heider, F. 1958. *The Psychology of Interpersonal Relations.* New York: Wiley.

*Hermann, P. J. 1965. *Better Settlements through Leverage.* Rochester, N.Y.: Lawyers Cooperative.

Himmelfarb, S., and Eagly, A. H., eds. 1974. *Readings in Attitude Change.* New York: Wiley.

Himmelweit, H. T. 1975. Studies of societal influences: problems and implications. In *Applying Social Psychology*, eds. M. Deutsch and H. A. Hornstein. Hillsdale, N.J.: Lawrence Erlbaum Associates.

*Hitler, A. 1933. *Mein Kamf.* Trans. by E. T. S. Dugdale. Cambridge, Massachusetts: Riverside.

Hollander, E. P., and Julian, J. W. 1970. Studies in leader legitimacy, influence, and innovation. In *Advances in Experimental Social Psychology*, ed. L. Berkowitz, Vol. 5. New York: Academic.

Hornstein, H. A.; Bunker, B. B.; Burke, W. W.; Gindes, M.; and Lewicki, R. J., eds. 1971. *Social Intervention: A Behavioral Science Approach.* New York: The Free Press.

*Hovland, C. I. 1959. Reconciling conflicting results derived from experimental and survey studies of attitude change. *American Psychologist* 14: 8–17.

*Hovland, C. I.; Janis, I. L.; and Kelley, H. H. 1953. *Communication and Persuasion*. New Haven: Yale.

*Hovland, C. I.; Lumsdaine, A. A.; and Sheffield, F. D. 1949. *Experiments on Mass Communication*. Vol. III of *Studies in Social Psychology in World War II*. Princeton, N.J.: Princeton.

*Hovland, C. I., and Weiss, W. 1951. The influence of source credibility on communication effectiveness. *Public Opinion Quarterly* 15: 635–650.

Hunt, W., ed. 1971. *Human Behavior and Its Control*. Cambridge, Mass.: Schenkman.

*Hunter, E. 1951. *Brainwashing in Red China*. New York: Vanguard.

*Inbau, F. E., and Reid, J. E. 1953. *Lie Detection and Criminal Interrogation*. Baltimore: Williams and Wilkins.

*Inbau, F. E. and Reid, J. E. 1962. *Criminal Interrogation and Confessions*. Baltimore: Williams and Wilkins.

*Insko, C. I. 1967. *Theories of Attitude Change*. New York: Appleton-Century-Crofts.

*James, W. 1936. *The Varieties of Religious Experience*. New York: Modern Library.

Janis, I. L. 1967. Effects of fear arousal on attitude change: Recent developments in theory and experimental research. In *Advances in Experimental Social Psychology*, ed. L. Berkowitz, Vol. 3. New York: Academic.

*Janis, I. L., and King, B. T. 1954. The influence of role-playing on opinion change. *Journal of Abnormal and Social Psychology* 49: 211–218.

*Jansen, M. J., and Stolurow, L. M. 1962. An experimental study of role playing. *Psychological Monographs* 76, No. 31.

Jones, E. E., and Davis, K. E. 1965. From acts to dispositions: The attribution process in person perception. In *Advances in Experimental Social Psychology*, ed. L. Berkowitz, Vol. 2. New York: Academic.

*Katz, D. 1960. The functional approach to the study of attitudes. *Public Opinion Quarterly* 24: 163–204.

*Katz, E. and Lazarsfeld, P. F. 1955. *Personal Influence*. Glencoe, Ill.: The Free Press.

Kautilya's Arthaśāstra. 1961. 7th ed. Trans. by R. Shamasastry. Mysore, India: Mysore Printing and Publishing House.

*Kelley, H. H. 1967. Attribution theory in social psychology. In *Nebraska Symposium on Motivation, 1967*, ed. D. Levine, Vol. 51. Lincoln: University of Nebraska Press.

*Kelley, H. H. (1972a). Attribution in social interaction. In *Attribution: Perceiving the Causes of Behavior*, eds. E. E. Jones, D. E. Kanouse, H. H. Kelley, R. E. Nisbett, S. Valins, and B. Weiner. Morristown, N.J.: General Learning Press.

*Kelley, H. H. (1972*b*). Causal schemata and the attribution process. In *Attribution: Perceiving the Causes of Behavior,* eds. E. E. Jones, D. E. Kanouse, H. H. Kelley, R. E. Nisbett, S. Valins, and B. Weiner. Morristown, N.J.: General Learning Press.

Kelman, H. C. 1964. Compliance, identification, and internalization, three processes of attitude change. *Journal of Conflict Resolution* 2: 51–66.

Kelman, H. C. 1967. Human use of human subjects: The problem of deception in social psychological experiments. *Psychological Bulletin* 67: 1–11.

*Kidd, W. R. 1940. Police interrogation. *The Police Journal.* New York.

*Kiesler, C. A.; Collins, B. E.; and Miller, N. 1969. *Attitude Change: A Critical Analysis of Theoretical Approaches.* New York: Wiley.

*Kiesler, C. A., and Kiesler, S. B. 1969. *Conformity.* Reading, Mass.: Addison-Wesley.

*King, B. T. and Janis, I. L. 1956. Comparison of the effectiveness of improvised versus non-improvised role playing in producing opinion changes. *Human Relations* 9: 177–186.

*Kutschinsky, B. 1971. The effect of pornography: A pilot experiment on perception, behavior, and attitudes. Technical report of the Commission on Obscenity and Pornography, Vol. 8. Washington, D.C.: U.S. Government Printing Office.

*Leventhal, H. 1970. Findings and theory in the study of fear communications. In *Advances in Experimental Social Psychology,* Vol. 5, ed. L. Berkowitz. New York: Academic.

*Lewin, K. Forces behind food habits and methods of change. *Bulletin of the National Research Council,* 1943, 108, 35–65.

*Lewin, K. 1947. Group decision and social change. In *Readings in Social Psychology,* eds. T. Newcomb and E. Hartley. New York: Holt.

*Linebarger, P. M. A. 1954. *Psychological Warfare.* Washington, D.C.: Combat Forces Press.

*Lofland, J., and Stark, R. 1954. Becoming a world-saver: A theory of conversion to a deviant perspective. *American Sociological Review* 32: 862–875.

*Maccoby, N., and Farquhar, J. W. 1975. Communication for health: Unselling heart disease. *Journal of Communication* 25: 114–126.

*Machiavelli, N. 1950. *Discourses.* 2 vols. New York: Humanities. (Originally published 1531).

Mahoney, M. 1972. Research issues in self-management. *Behavior Therapy* 3: 45–63.

Mahoney, M. J., and Thoresen, C. E. 1974. *Self-Control: Power to the Person.* Monterey, Ca.: Brooks/Cole.

*Mann, J.; Sidman, J.; and Starr, S. 1971. Effects of erotic films on sexual behavior of married couples. Technical report of the Commission on Obscenity and Pornography, Vol. 8. Washington, D.C.: U.S. Government Printing Office.

*Marshall, G. 1976. The affective consequences of "inadequately explained" physiological arousal. Unpublished doctoral dissertation, Stanford University.

*Maslach, C. 1977. Negative emotional biasing of unexplained arousal. In *Emotions and Emotion-Cognition Interactions in Psychopathology,* ed. C. E. Izard. New York: Plenum Press.

McGuire, W. J. 1964. Inducing resistance to persuasion: Some contemporary approaches. In *Advances in Experimental Social Psychology,* ed. L. Berkowitz, Vol. 1. New York: Academic.

*McGuire, W. J. 1969. The nature of attitudes and attitude change. In *Handbook of Social Psychology,* eds. G. Lindzey and E. Aronson, Vol. III, 136–314. Reading, Mass.: Addison-Wesley.

*Milgram, S. 1974. *Obedience to Authority.* New York: Harper & Row.

Moscovici, S., and Faucheux, C. 1972. Social influence, conformity bias, and the study of active minorities. In *Advances in experimental social psychology,* ed. L. Berkowitz, Vol. 6. New York: Academic.

*Mulbar, H. 1951. *Interrogation.* Springfield, Ill.: Thomas.

*Newcomb, T.; Koenig, K.; Flacks, R.; and Warwick, D. 1967. *Persistence and Change: Bennington College and Its Students after 25 years.* New York: Wiley.

Nisbett, R. E., and Borgida, E. 1975. Attribution and the psychology of prediction. *Journal of Personality and Social Psychology* 32: 932–943.

*Nizer, L. 1961. *My Life in Court.* New York: Pyramid.

Nuttin, J. M., Jr. 1975. *The Illusion of Attitude Change: Towards a Response Contagion Theory of Persuasion.* New York: Academic Press.

*O'Hara, C. E. 1956. *Fundamentals of Criminal Investigation.* Springfield, Ill.: Thomas.

*Orne, M. T., and Evans, F. J. 1965. Social control in the psychological experiment: Antisocial behavior and hypnosis. *Journal of Personality and Social Psychology* 1: 189–200.

Patrick, E., and Dulack, T. 1976. *Let Our Children Go?* New York: E. P. Dutton.

*Paul, G. 1966. *Insight versus Desensitization in Psychotherapy.* Stanford: Stanford University Press.

*Penick, S. B.; Filion, R.; Fox, S.; and Stunkard, A. 1971. Behavior modification in the treatment of obesity. *Psychosomatic Medicine* 33: 49–55.

*Prescott, J. W. 1975. Body pleasure and the origins of violence. *The Futurist,* 64–74.

*Qualter, T. H. 1962. *Propaganda and Psychological Warfare.* New York: Random House.

Robinson, J. P., and Shaver, P. R., eds. 1973. *Measures of Social Psychological Attitudes.* Ann Arbor, Mich.: Institute for Social Research, 1973.

Rokeach, M. 1966–1967. Attitude change and behavior change. *Public Opinion Quarterly* 30: 529–550.

Rokeach, M. 1969. *Beliefs, Attitudes, and Values.* San Francisco: Jossey-Bass.

*Rokeach, M. 1971. Long-range experimental modification of values, attitudes, and behavior. *American Psychologist* 26: 453–459.

*Rosenberg, M. J., and Hovland, C. I. 1960. Cognitive, affective, and behavioral components of attitudes. In *Attitude Organization and Change,* eds. C. I. Hovland and M. J. Rosenberg. New Haven: Yale University Press.

Ross, N. 1976. When what is said is important: A comparison of expert and attractive sources. *Journal of Experimental Social Psychology* 12: 294–300.

*Rotter, J. B. 1966. Generalized expectancies for internal versus external control of reinforcement. *Psychological Monographs* 80 (No. 1) (Whole No. 609). Copyright 1966 by the American Psychological Association. Reprinted by permission.

Rudd, J. B. 1971. Teaching for changed attitudes and values. Washington, D.C. Home Economics Education Association.

Runkel, P. J., and McGrath, J. E. 1972. *Research on Human Behavior.* New York: Holt.

*Sarnoff, I. 1960. Psychoanalytic theory and social attitudes. *Public Opinion Quarterly,* 24: 251–279.

Sartre, J. P. 1964. *St. Genet.* London: W. H. Allen. Translated from the French by Bernard Frechtman.

Sayre, J. 1972. Teaching moral values through behavior modification. Danville, Illinois: The Interstate.

*Schachter, S. 1951. Deviation, rejection, and communication. *Journal of Abnormal and Social Psychology* 46: 190–207.

*Schachter, S., and Singer, J. E. 1962. Cognitive, social and physiological determinants of emotional state. *Psychological Review* 69: 379–399. Copyright 1962 by the American Psychological Association. Reprinted by permission.

*Schein, E. H.; Schneier, I.; and Barker, C. H. 1961. *Coercive Persuasion.* New York: Norton.

Schopler, J. 1965. Social power. In *Advances in Experimental Social Psychology,* ed. L. Berkowitz, Vol. 2. New York: Academic.

Schwitzgebel, R. K., and Kolb, D. A. 1974. *Changing Human Behavior: Principles of Planned Intervention.* New York: McGraw-Hill.

Schwitzgebel, R. L., and Schwitzgebel, R. K., eds. 1973. *Psychotechnology: Electronic Control of Mind and Behavior.* New York: Holt.

Shaver, K. G. 1975. *An Introduction to Attribution Processes.* Cambridge, Mass.: Winthrop.

Shaw, M. E. 1976. *Group Dynamics: The Psychology of Small Group Behavior.* 2d ed. New York: McGraw-Hill.

*Sherif, M. 1936. *The Psychology of Social Norms.* New York: Harper & Row.

*Sherif, M., and Hovland, C. I. 1961. *Social judgment: Assimilation and Contrast Effects in Communication and Attitude Change.* Vol. 4, *Yale Studies in Attitude and Communication.* New Haven: Yale University Press.

Sindell, J., and Sindell, D. 1963. *Let's Talk Settlement.* Tucson, Ariz.: Lawyers and Judges Publishing.

*Skinner, B. F. 1975. The steep and thorny way to a science of behavior. *American Psychologist* 30: 42–49.

*Smith, E. E. 1961a. Methods for changing consumer attitudes: A report of three experiments. Project Report, Quartermaster Food and Container Institute for the Armed Forces (PRA Report 61-2).

*Smith, E. E. 1961b. The power of dissonance techniques to change attitudes. *Public Opinion Quarterly,* 25: 626–639.

Smith, L. 1974. Indoctrination and intent. *Journal of Moral Education* 3: 229–233.

*Snyder, M., and Ebbesen, E. B. 1972. Dissonance awareness: A test of dissonance theory versus self-perception theory: *Journal of Experimental Social Psychology* 8: 502–517.

Steiner, I. D. 1970. Perceived freedom. In *Advances in Experimental Social Psychology,* ed. L. Berkowitz, Vol. 5. New York: Academic.

*Stouffer, S. A.; Suchman, E. A.; DeVinney, L. C.; Star, S. A.; and Williams, R. M., Jr. 1949. *The American Soldier: Adjustments during Army Life.* Vol. I of *Studies in Social Psychology in World War II.* Princeton, N.J.: Princeton University Press.

*Szasz, T. 1976. Patty Hearst's conversion: Some call it brainwashing. *The New Republic* 174: 10–12.

Tannenbaum, P. 1967. The congruity principle revisited: Studies in the reduction, induction, and generalization of persuasion. In *Advances in Experimental Social Psychology,* ed. L. Berkowitz, Vol. 3. New York: Academic.

Tate, E. 1972. *An Annotated Bibliography of Studies on Counterattitudinal Advocacy.* University of Saskatchewan Press.

Taylor, J. G. 1971. *The Shape of Minds to Come.* Baltimore: Penguin.

Triandis, H. C. 1971. *Attitude and Attitude Change.* New York: Wiley.

Tversky, A., and Kahneman, D. 1974. Judgment under uncertainty: Heuristics and biases. *Science* 185: 1124–1131.

U.S.A. vs. *Patricia Campbell Hearst.* 1976. Transcripts of the trial.

Van Fleet, J. K. 1970. *Power with People.* West Nyack, N.Y.: Parker.

*Varela, J. A. 1971. *Psychological Solutions to Social Problems: An Introduction to Social Technology.* New York: Academic.

Walters, R. H., and Parke, R. D. 1964. Social motivation, dependency, and susceptibility to social influences. In *Advances in Experimental Social Psychology,* ed. L. Berkowitz, Vol. 1. New York: Academic.

Watson, J. B. 1926. What the nursery has to say about instincts. In C. Murchison (Ed.). *Psychologies of 1925*. Worcester, Mass.: Clark University Press, pp. 1–34.

Webb, E. J.; Campbell, D. T.; Schwartz, R. D.; and Sechrest, L. 1966. *Unobtrusive measures: Nonreactive research in the social sciences*. Chicago: Rand McNally.

Wicklund, R. A. 1974. *Freedom and Reactance*. Potomac, Md.: Lawrence Erlbaum Associates.

Wixon, D. R., and Laird, J. D. 1976. Awareness and attitude change in the forced-compliance paradigm: The importance of when. *Journal of Personality and Social Psychology* 34: 376–384.

*Wolfgang, M., and Ferracuti, F. 1967. *The Subculture of Violence: Towards an Integrated Theory in Criminology*. London: Tavistock.

*Zimbardo, P. G. 1970. The human choice: Individuation, reason, and order versus deindividuation, impulse, and chaos. In *Nebraska symposium on motivation, 1969*, eds. W. Arnold and D. Levine, Vol. 17. Lincoln: University of Nebraska Press.

Zimbardo, P. G. 1971. Coercion and compliance: The psychology of police confessions. In *The Triple Revolution Emerging: Social Problems in Depth*, eds. R. Perrucci and M. Pilisuk. Boston: Little, Brown.

Zimbardo, P. G. 1972. The tactics and ethics of persuasion. In *Attitudes, Conflict and Social Change*, eds. E. McGinnies and B. King. New York: Academic.

*Zimbardo, P. G.; Weisenberg, M.; Firestone, I.; and Levy, B. 1965. Communicator effectiveness in producing public confromity and private attitude change. *Journal of Personality* 33: 233–256.

index